Praise for *Together Beyond Words*

"This book and the incredible story it brings to us is so much more than a simple telling; it's an offering of light and hope. Nitsan Joy Gordon's work is visionary, wise and important. It's a call for all of us to do the deep healing that must precede a lasting peace. She asks us to live beyond our stories into the heart of love. This is a message for the world."

PAULA D'ARCY
Writer, retreat leader, conference and seminar speaker.

"In this powerful book, Nitsan Gordon takes us with her on her amazing journey toward bringing healing and peace to the chronic pain and conflict that plague relations among Jews, Arabs, and Palestinians in Israel. Having co-led several Together Beyond Words workshops with her, I can testify to the power of having traditional enemies express their most painful truths and feel witnessed by one another — particularly for Palestinians to feel heard by Jews and watch Jews work on the legacy burdens that drive their racist and oppressive behaviors. Through dance, movement, and psychodramatic techniques, Nitsan creates exceptionally safe spaces for these encounters that are building an important grassroots movement for cross-conflict connection and change. Reading this beautifully written, engaging book, is moving, enlightening, and left me with even more admiration for Nitsan's courage and persistence."

RICHARD SCHWARTZ
Ph.D., developer of the Internal Family Systems model (IFS).

"I love this book. It tells the story of a girl, and all the life experiences that led her to become a brave and powerful woman; A woman who was touched by injustice, pain, and bigotry. A woman who could have led a privileged life, a woman who could have not listened to the calling. But a woman who most certainly did. Read this delightful book. Let yourself be inspired. There is so much we can do with this one precious life. Nitsan is a testament to that."

ANN BRADNEY
CPRA, founder and director of the Radical Aliveness
Institute. Faculty member at Esalen educational institute.

"This inspiring book not only tells the story of one woman's brave journey from a border kibbutz to a lifelong dedication to peace building; more than that, it gives us a heartening example of what can happen when two visionary change makers – Esalen Institute and Together Beyond Words – combine their creativity in the service of our highest human values."

NANCY LUNNEY WHEELER
M.A., pioneering leader in education for personal and social
transformation. Senior advisor at Esalen educational institute.

"The importance of this book, in my humble opinion, lies in the ability of the author/healer and her colleagues to reach across the boundaries of religious beliefs, ethnicity, skin color and nationality to the essence of our existence as human beings that yearn to live in harmony and peace with one another.."

DR MARIAM MAR'I
Director of the Akko Arab Women's Pedagogical Center.

"All over the world, nations and communities and cultures are experiencing the pain and destruction that happens when one group demonizes another, when people lose the ability to see the human in each other. But all over the world, people are also transforming trauma and pain into healing and peace. It takes hard work--brave and patient work--to do this, and the Israeli Peace Activist, Nitsan Joy Gordon, has been doing this kind of work for many years. Her new book, Together Beyond Words: Women on a Quest for Peace in the Middle East, is a roadmap for all of us who want to be part of the solution."

ELIZABETH LESSER
Cofounder of Omega Institute, New York Times bestselling
author of Broken Open, Cassandra Speaks, and other books.

Together
Beyond Words

Nitsan Joy Gordon

Together
Beyond Words

Women on a Quest for Peace
in the Middle East

éditions

Cover illustration: © 2022 Hülya Özdemir

Photos Credit p151-158: Gal Mosenzon / Magical Children of Light (GM) - Aviv Perez (AP) Joshua Yelin / Pashi (PS) - Gilad Reshef (GR) Assaf Pocker (ASA). All rights reserved. 2022

If you wish to be regularly informed of our publications, all you have to do is subscribe to our newsletter by e-mail, from our website: leseditionsdunona.com where you will find all our publications.

ISBN: 978-2-493605-04-7

© Les Éditions du Ā, Fontainebleau, France 2023

To my beloved children, Shir and Ben,
my wonderful grandchildren, Danielle,
Shalomi, Maayan and Noor
and to all children.

May our work and the work
of peacebuilders in every country,
make the world you inherit
more just and peaceful.

CONTENTS

Foreword: Marianne Williamson   13

Introduction: One Holy Spot on Earth   15

Part 1 – Evolving: Everybody Hurts Sometimes   21

    1.   Golda Meir and My Grandmother's Tears   23
    2.   Nights in White Satin   29
    3.   Good and Bad   33
    4.   Lost in Translation   37
    5.   Rescuing Beetles in the Deep South   41
    6.   Standing Up in the Ghetto   45
    7.   The Failure Club   51
    8.   Back in Israel – Who Am I?   55
    9.   Tummy to Tummy   59
    10.   Sisterhood   65
    11.   The Purple Hairpin   69
    12.   Searching for Sheik Zaabalawi   73

Part 2 – Creating: Together Beyond Words   83

    13.   Ladies and Jelly Beans   85
    14.   Dance Therapy with Vietnam Veterans   97
    15.   Prejudice Unveiled   105
    16.   Choices   113
    17.   Dance, Dialogue and Hope   117
    18.   Mervat's Scream   121
    19.   When We Listen   129
    20.   For Crying (and Laughing) Out Loud   139
    21.   When Touch Can Heal   147
    22.   Birthing Together Beyond Words   163
    23.   Our First Meeting   169
    24.   The Second Intifada… and We Continue to Meet   179

Part 3 – Transforming: Emotional Pain into Understanding and Empathy

Stories from Our Workshops   187

25. Esalen   189
26. Gather the Women   195
27. Armed with Love   201
28. The Way Back Home   209
29. Finding Our Voices   213
30. Sharing Our Fears   219
31. The Whistle   221
32. "We are not Occupied"   225
33. The Self that Heals   231
34. A Museum of Humanity's Suffering and Healing   237
35. Acknowledging the Pain of Others   247
36. Intertwined   251
37. Feeling What is Yours to Feel   257
38. The Courage to Be a Woman with a Voice   261
39. A Moment in Each Other's Shoes   265
40. A Place to Belong   273
41. Bringing a Bit of Light…   277
42. Then Oren Approached   281

Epilogue   288

Afterword: Healing, Transforming, Peacebuilding and Never Stopping,
by **Leymah R. Gbowee**, Nobel Peace Laureate   291

Appendix I: The Together Beyond Words Approach   294
Appendix II: The Creation of a Nonverbal Prejudice Scale 302
Appendix III: Increasing Emotional Intelligence   304
Appendix IV: Other Approaches that we apply in our work   306
Appendix V: Peacebuilding Organizations   310
Bibliography   313
Acknowledgements   317

We cannot have a healed society, we cannot have change, we cannot have justice, if we do not reclaim and repair the human spirit, if we don't do the inner work that has been underemphasized, that we have not trained ourselves to do, the work that is upon us now.

Angel Kyodo Williams

Foreword

By Marianne Williamson

American bestselling author, political activist,
and spiritual thought leader.[1]

No one can authentically encounter the Israeli-Palestinian conflict without agony. The hatred, fear and suffering in this drama are so real and seemingly intractable, it's like a horror story that never ends. Nothing seems less helpful than those who would presume that there are easy answers.

"Beyond all ideas of right and wrong, there is a field. I'll meet you there," wrote the poet Rumi. The problem is not that people don't believe this field exists; the problem is how hard it can be to get there. In Israel and Palestine – and elsewhere in the world – there is so much pain, and there are so many layers of often unprocessed trauma that stand in our way as we seek to reach it. How blessed are those who do the work of trying to pave the way.

God knows, some brilliant minds have tried. But perhaps that is the point: the mind alone can't do it. As Einstein reminded us that the problems of the world will not be solved with the level of thinking at which they were created, our species stands perched in a mysterious limbo: will we perpetuate the madness of humanity's collision course with itself, or will we consider the possibility that there might be another away? There is a new kind of peacebuilding rising among us, going way beyond the purview of diplomat or soldier. For peace is not the absence of war; war is the absence of peace. True, fundamental peace is not an artificial comfort; it is a return to our essential nature. It is raw. It is emotional. It is real. At times it is harrowing. It stems from facing the internal wars that are

---

1. https://marianne.com

reflected in our external violence. Peacemakers aren't softies. They're the bravest of the brave.

It's difficult to read this book by Nitsan Joy Gordon without awe at her emotionally bravery, and the bravery of the women who have joined with her – both Arab and Jew – to pave a path to peace for themselves and others. That path is not a path of avoiding their pain, but of allowing themselves to feel their pain; not a path of explaining themselves, but of listening to others; not a path of always saying yes, but of sometimes saying no. The courage to remain awake, not only to one's own pain but to the pain of the other, is the work of the modern peacemaker. The women in this book are extraordinary examples of what that looks like and where it can lead.

In *A Course in Miracles,* it is said that the "holiest spot on earth is where an ancient hatred has become a present love." Whenever I have read that line, and I have read it often, I have thought of Israel and Palestine. The Holy Land, the place where several major religions find their portal to God, is a place on the planet where the peace of God seems sometimes hardest to attain. Whether looked at from a political or a spiritual perspective, this cannot be an accident. There – in that holy yet tortured place – lay both the problem and the Answer, humanity's greatest division and greatest opportunity for peace. It is a land of an ancient hatred longing for a present love.

Reading this book, you feel such a present love is possible, even if only expressed in fleeting moments of resolution. Nitsan was only five years old when her father first told her to seek resolution. It wasn't to be just with her little brother, as she might have thought then; the search for resolution was to be her life's calling. In order to claim that calling, however, she would have to enter the darkest regions of her own pain, acknowledge the pain of others and invite them to dwell in those regions with her. Her work, and the work of the other women whose stories are told in this book, is truly the Great Work.

And they do it so well. What a blessing on Israel and Palestine, and a gift to the entire world.

October 2022.

Introduction

One Holy Spot on Earth

*The holiest spot on earth is where an ancient
hatred has become a present love.*
A Course in Miracle

Pain that is not transformed is transmitted.
Richard Rohr

Leaning back on the smooth cream-colored bathroom door, I look down at my blue sandals, the same ones all the other five- and six-year-olds at the kibbutz have. They are not so new anymore; we received them a while ago, right before Passover and the dust and wear have turned them from shiny to drab.

Looking up I see my blond three-year-old brother, Mor, who is sitting on top of the toilet cover staring at me with tears running down his face. His feet are so far from the floor that I'm not sure how he made it up there. The door to the bathroom is not locked, but I know we cannot go out yet because when our father put us inside the bathroom in the middle of our fight he said, "You can only come out after you resolve this."

I peek again at my brother and he stares back. I am not sure what to do now. I don't know what "resolve" means and have no idea if we have done it yet or not. *Is just being quiet enough? Do I need to say something to Mor? How do Abba and Ima and other people resolve? Will we be stuck here forever?*

The bright red train we were fighting over is on the floor where Mor threw it and I make no move to pick it up.

"Can we go out now?" Mor asks in a tearful voice, blue eyes watery.

"No, we have to resolve," I tell him.

A little while later, I hold out my hand. Mor slides off the toilet and puts his little one in mine. We open the door and walk out hand in hand towards my father, who is sitting and reading on the green couch in the tiny living room of our kibbutz apartment.

"We resolve," I say to him.

He hugs us both and says, "Good, now you can play together."

And this is how at the age of five I learned that conflicts are resolved by spending time together in the bathroom.

Later I was able to expand the possible scenes of conflict resolution from the bathroom to the living room, porch, kitchen and even to large workshop spaces, but the concept of spending time together with someone from the other side of the conflict remained a key component in the conflict resolution process.

And I care deeply about conflict resolution. *Why?* There is not one answer but rather many stories I share in the first part of this book as I explore what led me to devote my life's work to "Resolve." The second part of the book includes the stories of *How?* How do we Resolve? The different tools I learned that comprise our own approach to spending time together in ways that resolve conflicts. And the final part are the stories of *What.* What actually happens in our workshops and meetings that leads to resolution between Arab Palestinians and Jews?

The conflict I chose to "Resolve" is the most talked and written about conflict in the world. There are many reasons for the world's obsession with a country no larger than New Jersey with a population the size of Togo. I will mention only one. Israel is a spiritual center of five world religions – Jewish, Druze, Muslim, Christian and Bahai, so naturally what happens here is important to people of these faiths from all over the world.

Our conflict, also known as the Israeli-Palestinian Conflict, has lasted for anywhere between 100 to 140 years, depending on whom you ask and when you begin counting, with over 236,000 casualties, and unfortunately, there does not seem to be an end in sight.

In the early nineties, when my children were quite young and we spent time in fortified shelters hiding from Katyusha rockets fired at us from Lebanon by the Hezbollah, I began searching for something I could do that would contribute to the resolution of this conflict.

I had a BA in Psychology and a Masters in Dance/Movement Therapy and knew that one reason for this protracted conflict and our inability to find a solution is the trauma, the painful emotions driving our decisions and behavior. Trauma is so prevalent and chronic in this area that David Eshel calls Israel, the West Bank, and Gaza "a perfect laboratory for studying Post-Traumatic Stress Disorder (PTSD) and other anxiety-related ailments."[2]

I also knew that, in the absence of emotional healing, early trauma can have a lifelong impact in the form of rigid, irrational behavior, and that our emotions bias our decision-making[3]. So I concluded that when people don't engage in healing their traumas, their painful emotions frequently lead them to behave rigidly and irrationally, hurting themselves and others. As Richard Rohr puts it: *Pain that is not transformed is transmitted*[4].

When I realized how our past influences our present and future in Israel, I felt a calling to do more for coexistence and peace, using my skills as a dance/movement therapist and a group facilitator.

For years, I had stood at intersections with Women in Black, holding signs calling on the government to bring our soldiers home from Lebanon, and participated in demonstrations for peace before the Oslo Accords, but it did not seem like enough. Consequently, in 1994 I approached Dr Mariam Mari-Ryan, a Muslim woman and the director of the Akko Arab Women's Pedagogical Center, where I was working, to speak about further possibilities.

We both understood that the destructive behavior, prejudices, and violence around and sometimes inside us are driven by fear, anger, grief, and despair related to our painful histories and to the ceaseless conflict. We believed that women – in particular, early childhood educators – could have a unique role in transforming these destructive behaviors. So, we developed a pilot project whose goal was to empower and train early childhood educators in what we called peace building. Our first program received financial support from the Abraham Fund[5].

Then, on November 4, 1995, before we began, Prime Minister Yitzhak Rabin was murdered by Yigal Amir, a Jew, and the whole country shook. The peace process was stalled, many hopes were shattered and we decided to move ahead.

In February 1996 we began our program with a 56-hour workshop using the multidisciplinary approach, I had developed. The workshop was

2. https://defense-update.com/20070601_ptsd.html

3. De Martino, B., Kumaran, D., Seymour, B., & Dolan, R. J. (2006, August 4). Frames, biases, and rational decision-making in the human brain. Science, 313(5787), 684-687.

4. https://myemail.constantcontact.com/Richard-Rohr-s-Daily-Meditation----August-17-- 2013.html?-soid=1103098668616&aid=VsvGk1wUnuI

5. https://abrahaminitiatives.org/

co-led by two Arab Palestinian facilitators, a Jewish facilitator, and myself. Our goal was to create a place, a safe haven of sorts, where the 24 Arab Palestinian and Jewish early childhood educators who participated would be able to share their feelings and learn to transform their pain rather than transmitting it. We hoped that through this process of meeting, growing to know and care about one another, and learning peacebuilding skills, they would be moved to do more for coexistence and peace.

Gathering the women for the first group was not easy. I literally had to climb fences in order to reach them. Working together as Arab and Jewish co-facilitators was also an adjustment that involved inner healing work for each of us.

In addition, we learned that most of the issues we were dealing with were not only personal but related to oppression that has lasted for years. This includes the oppression of women and the feminine qualities in women and men and the prejudice and oppression of minorities, in so many different ways, including language. We also learned to hold complexity: that every story has at least two sides and that we need to create a space where people with opposing narratives would feel comfortable in sharing their pain.

Despite the hardships, something about our approach worked really well, and by the second year there was no need to climb fences to reach the teachers. They themselves contacted us because they heard we were doing something unique and wanted to try it out.

Seven years and several groups later, in 2003, we became a nonprofit organization dedicated to empowering women and providing them with peacebuilding skills.

We named our approach "Beyond Words" to signify that the painful emotions shared in our workshops are often beyond words, that our healing approach is also frequently nonverbal, and that to resolve the conflict something is needed that is more than speeches, conversations, shouting matches, debates, and even dialogue. Something that brings to the forefront the power of emotions to destroy and to connect and the need to transform pain so it is not transmitted. Later we added the word "Together" to emphasize the particular power of a beyond words healing process when it happens in conjunction and in the same space with the "other", with our former "enemy". Hence the name *Together Beyond Words* (TBW).

Since our first group, we have worked with hundreds of people, creating places where Arab Palestinians and Jews, both women and, beginning in 2014, men, can express their painful emotions rather than acting them out; where empathy and understanding for "the other" are enhanced; where women can reclaim their power in the public sphere; and where women and men can become allies in working for a more compassionate and peaceful community.

What actually happens in our workshops is described in stories that constitute the third part of this book. But it can be summarized in the words of Amichai, a Jewish man in his late twenties, who participated in the TBW 2018 Peace Leadership Training with Ann Bradney and wrote afterwards:

> Together we cried and screamed the pain that had been frozen in the body for too many years, we experienced fear and terror, anger and hatred, immense love, passion and yearning, and such deep human connection. And we were able to see beyond all the stories, to truly see ourselves and one another. We saw that within us there exists everything, all of it, all the voices and the parts, the feelings and the needs.
>
> I saw within myself all the narratives and points of view at the same time. I saw the voices of extreme rightists, and extreme leftists, Arabs and Jews, women and men, courage and fear, compassion and hatred. And mostly, I saw how much love I have in my heart, how much love there is in everyone's heart. I will not be the same again after this experience.

I've learned a lot about what it means to "resolve" since that day spent standing in the bathroom with my three-year-old brother. I don't know when the bombing, the prejudice, the violence will stop; none of us do. But I do know something about conflict resolution, about the deep healing work that is necessary to create a sound basis for a lasting peace, and it includes creating places to feel and heal that are available to everyone.

I hope and pray this book will encourage you, the reader, to create your own **safe havens** for emotional healing and for the healing of those around you so we can all live in a more compassionate and peaceful world.

May it be so...

Part 1

Evolving: Everybody Hurts Sometimes

We were born with so many abilities: the ability to enjoy life and connect with others, the ability to have all our feelings. We were born with intelligence and curiosity. We came here as beautiful, alive creatures with a great desire to experience this miraculous life. We came here ready for a life full of sights, smells, flavors, sounds, touch and connection. We came open and interested; we came because we wanted to come. We came with the ability to overcome challenges. We came with the ability to heal from hurts[6].

And all of us were hurt, in small and large ways, when we were young.

---

6. Words said during one of our workshops by Liry Meshi Yohel, one of the facilitators.

Chapter 1

Golda Meir and My Grandmother's Tears
The Early Twentieth Century

> *The past is never where you think you left it.*
> Katherine Anne Porter

Once upon a time...

Truly it is difficult to know where to begin this story, my story. Should I start with how my grandmother Rachel lived in a small town in Ukraine and, at seven, wanting to surprise her mother, took the basket of laundry downhill to wash in the river? How, on the way back up the hill, the dripping wet laundry in its basket became so heavy that it fell from her small hands into a puddle and she had to drag the muddy clothes back home, truly "surprising" her mother?

Or maybe the story of how her mother hid her in a chicken coop when she was twelve so she would not be raped during the 1919 Petliura Pogroms?

But then again, it may be better to begin with my grandmother Chaya.

For many years Chaya's father, Isaac, had a dream. His dream was to emigrate to the Holy Land where he would buy an orchard that would sustain the family. In his dream the orchard had oranges, lemons, grapefruits and other citrus fruits that grew in the Holy Land.

In the Diaspora, the family lived in scarcity, saving every penny so they could embark on this journey. Isaac even bought a lottery ticket every week. One day he won the lottery, and very soon afterwards, in 1914, when Chaya was only seven, the family emigrated from their home in Lodz, Poland, to the Holy Land.

While settling down in the new land, Isaac gave his money for safekeeping to a religious Jew that a friend from Lodz had recommended. They shook hands on the deal without any witnesses or documentation. Then for a year Isaac worked and searched for the perfect orchard. When he finally found one, he was overcome with joy: the oranges that would soon be his, tasted so sweet, the trees looked so healthy. His dream was finally coming true. He went to retrieve his money but the man denied ever receiving it.

Isaac was shocked; he could not believe that a handshake was not enough to seal a deal between two Jews in the Holy Land – the land to which Jews in the Diaspora had been yearning to return for nearly two millennia. Isaac never recovered from his experience; his heart was broken and he died a few years later.

With a sick and heartbroken father, the family lived in poverty. Grandma Chaya's elder brother and sister worked so she could attend school and she grew to be a beautiful and kind young woman who decided to study agriculture and worked tirelessly in the new kibbutz that she joined.

A few years later she was put in charge of the one-room supply store where kibbutz members came to receive their toiletries. Whenever one of them needed a new tube of toothpaste, she asked to see the old one to make sure it was rolled through and through and there was nothing left inside before giving over a new tube. No one was going to cheat Chaya out of toothpaste.

I have no way of knowing whether Chaya's difficulty in trusting her kibbutz friends about their toothpaste began in her early childhood years, but I had to wonder how her life might have been different had a handshake been enough to seal a deal in the Holy Land.

I might also tell you about Chaya's husband, my grandfather Nahum, a gentle, loving and courageous man who left his family in Russia in 1921 and emigrated to the Holy Land, where he met and married Chaya and lived with her on Kibbutz Ramat Yohanan.

He worked in the fields using mules to plow the land until a few years later, when the kibbutz members decided to buy a tractor. Because of his fine technical skills, Grandpa Nahum was chosen to bring this new tractor to the kibbutz. Overcome with joy at the great honor, he hardly slept the night before.

Early in the morning, he took a bus to the Haifa port where he received the tractor and drove it six hours all the way to the kibbutz. When he finally made it back, it was dinner time. He parked the now dusty red tractor near the dining hall and walked inside. Everyone turned their eyes to see where he would sit and moved closer. My grandfather was a fine storyteller and they wanted to hear what happened. He sat in his usual place and looked up at their expectant eyes, his heart bursting with pride but he was also very hungry because he had hardly eaten the whole day. So he poured himself a bowl of soup and ate while excitedly recounting his adventures, never noticing that he somehow managed to gobble up the entire bowl with a fork instead of a spoon.

My socialist philosopher-artist grandfather Mordechai also deserves a place in my story. He emigrated with his family from Russia to the USA in 1919, when he was 14. At Ellis Island they were told by the clerk that Drachlansky, their last name, had to be changed because it was too long and complicated and Americans would not be able to pronounce it. In one moment, countless years of carrying the name Drachlansky were erased and the family name became Gordon, borrowing from a man my great-grandfather Aaron deeply admired: Aaron David Gordon, the driving force behind practical and labor Zionism.

Yes, I could start with those or countless other stories, but wait – ah – yes, there it is...

Here is where I will begin this story, my story:

Once upon a time, my grandmother Rachel met the woman who changed her life and who years later became Israel's first and only female prime minister, Golda Meir...

In 1921, when she was fourteen, following the pogroms, Grandmother Rachel and her family emigrated from Russia to the United States, where they had relatives. Upon arriving by boat to this strange new land, without knowing a word of English, they lived with relatives in Boston for a few months before moving to their own apartment. Rachel worked in a factory until their financial situation stabilized and then went back to school. In the following years she learned to speak English, worked as a secretary and joined the "Workers of Zion" youth movement where she met and then married grandfather Mordechai. A few years later, when Rachel was 25 and Mordechai 27, Golda Meir came to visit their youth movement in order to convince them to make Aliyah – to emigrate to the Holy Land, Zion, Israel, Palestine. My grandfather was persuaded and very excited to go, Grandma Rachel less so, but she went anyway. After a long boat journey, in 1932, they arrived in Haifa.

Following Golda's advice, they soon joined the nearby Kibbutz Yagur, which was ten years old at the time. At the kibbutz, Grandma Rachel was confronted with the harsh conditions of daily life: their one-room shack with a metal roof that did very little to keep out the heat during the summer or the cold during the winter months; sharing this shack with a third person (because there were not enough shacks) which precluded any chance for marital intimacy; the communal bathroom and showers; the impossibly muddy roads; the scarcity of food (how many times a week can one eat potatoes?); the fear of being attacked by their Arab neighbors – all these hardships were too much for Rachel to bear. And then there was the incessant buzzing of the flies, so many of them that the joke was: *Never kill a fly because a thousand will come to its funeral.*

A year after arriving, she was ready to give up and go back home to her family in America. It was around that time that Golda Meir came to visit. As soon as she saw Golda, Grandma Rachel burst into tears, releasing the feelings of frustration and despair that had built inside her throughout that first year. Golda embraced her, stroked her hair and said fondly: "Oh Rochalle, I know how you feel. I was exactly like you, so happy when I first came to the land of Israel, I just couldn't stop crying."

Rachel looked at Golda in disbelief: *What?*, she thought, yet was unable to correct Golda. She was too embarrassed to admit the pain behind her tears that realizing the Zionist dream was beyond her capabilities, that she just wanted to go back home to her parents where she would feel safe and comfortable. What would Golda think if she told her the truth? What would her husband and all the kibbutz members think? That she was spoiled and weak? No, that would be too shameful.

So, at the age of 26, grandmother Rachel decided to stick it out and stay in Kibbutz Yagur. Perhaps the tears she cried that helped her release some of the pain also gave her the breathing space she needed to continue.

In any case, because she decided to stay, my father was born in Israel, my parents met and created a family, and I am now able to tell you this story, the story of growing up in Israel, a land torn apart by conflict, whose people, Arabs and Jews, Israelis and Palestinians, are longing for healing and resolution.

***

On a bright, pleasantly warm summer day, about a year ago, I decide to visit my grandparents in the kibbutz graveyard. I like entering the sanctuary of tall trees shading this beautiful resting place. I wander through the rows, listening to the birds and the wind rustling through the leaves. There is no one else in sight, only rows and rows of tombstones, some overflowing with red, yellow and purple flowers, others half covered with green bushes.

For a moment I stand next to Chaya and Nahum's gravestones. I breathe deeply and gaze at the familiar names, grayish, weathered by so many cold, rainy winters and hot, muggy summers. I remember how when they married, they took the first letter from each of their first names to create their new last name: Chen (grace).

Then I walk two rows up to visit Rachel and Mordechai. Standing next to my Grandpa Mordechai's grave, I gaze at the beautiful copper mandala sunk into the center of his tombstone. It is one of the numerous copper art pieces he created in the later years of his life on the kibbutz.

My Grandma Rachel's tombstone right next to Mordechai's is engraved with the words: *There is no love that does not know how to cry.* I sit and then lie on her tombstone, looking up at the blue sky, missing her, missing all of them, I do cry for a while.

Afterwards, feeling peaceful, I stand up, knowing there is one more grave I must visit. I cross the path towards the small tombstone surrounded by aloe vera bushes. The name is half hidden but I can still see it between the succulent stalks. It says: *Inbal*.

Chapter 2

Nights in White Satin

1958-1964, Ramat Yohanan

Life is as complex as we are. Sometimes our vulnerability is our
strength, our fear develops our courage, and our woundedness
is the road to our integrity. It is not an either/or world.

Rachel Naomi Remen

My parents were 22 years old and living in Kibbutz Ramat Yohanan when my sister Inbal was born on November 13, 1958. She was a beautiful baby girl with lots of dark hair and blue eyes, and my mother wrote in her diary that she fell in love with her immediately. A few weeks after the birth, she added: "She is finally beginning to gain weight and now weighs 7.33 pounds. Today is a beautifully bright winter day and I am filled with tenderness. Everything is so wonderful, so shiny and pure. People suddenly seem so good, so friendly. Nature is in its full glory and is awaiting you, Inbal..."

A month later Inbal died from heart failure. My parents were heartbroken.

My father could not forget the morning he sat next to Inbal at the hospital, her tiny hand wrapped around his finger. Suddenly he realized she had let go. He called the medical staff, who told him his little baby girl had just died.

So young, so sad, my mother wrote: "I thought I would find solace in my work but I can't meet people, I run away, I can't see and accept them. Being alone with myself is also hard. When will this suffering end? When will I find some peace?"

Following a conversation with my father, she added: "When they came to Jacob to console him on the death of his beloved son Joseph, he refused to be consoled. The commentators tried to explain Jacob's refusal by saying that maybe somewhere inside Jacob knew or actually felt that his son Joseph was still alive. Is this true? Will I find solace only when I accept the certainty of her death?"

They could not bear to stay in the kibbutz with all the memories and heartache. Seeing the places where she walked with her baby girl and the pitying eyes of her friends still holding and caring for their own infants was too much for my mother to endure.

Wishing to escape the memory, they moved to Magal, a new kibbutz, less than a kilometer from the border with Jordan. The kibbutz was on a hill, so close to Jordan that the founders had to make sure none of the buildings were visible to snipers from the town across the border. A few years earlier they had to move the kibbutz dining hall to a different location because once, while they were sitting down for a communal meal, a bullet came through the window and hit a plate.

The adults at the Kibbutz, ages 20 to 30, were struggling. Some were children of Holocaust survivors, some new immigrants or children of those who fought to gain independence and establish the country. When my parents joined, there were only about 30 adult members, a few babies and young children living in the kibbutz. One baby girl, Tamar, was born six months before my parents arrived.

Six months after they joined the kibbutz, I arrived. "You have come into the world," my mother wrote on February 9th, 1960. "We waited for you and will name you Nitsan, blossom, even though from the beginning you look ripe and whole like a flower appearing in all its beauty and yet we, your parents, will always see you as a blossom that will continually be fresh..."

When she returned from the hospital three days later, my mother brought me to the kibbutz nursery to stay with all the other babies. She would visit the nursery a couple of times during the day to nurse and hold me, and took me home every afternoon for three and a half hours. But every evening at 7:30 p.m. my parents would bring me back to the nursery, as did the parents of all the other babies and children. The parents would stay until we fell asleep. Then, they would go to their own apartments in another part of the kibbutz, leaving us little ones in the hands of the night watchwoman, who was switched every week and whose job was to stay up all night and attend to the children in the different nurseries. It was the norm then, enabling parents who worked all day to get a full night's rest while their babies slept in the safest part of the kibbutz.

Perhaps this early experience of being stuck in my crib with no mother or father to comfort me is one of the reasons that I am still afraid of the dark and at times feel that people cannot be trusted and that if I call out for help... no one will come.

In my earliest memories, I am three and a half years old, in my bed, waking up from a nightmare, crying in the dark room. All I want is to be with my parents where I can feel safe. But this "safe haven" is about 300 meters away in a different part of the kibbutz and to get there I have to step outside the nursery and walk along the dark sidewalk all the way to their tiny one-room apartment. Too scared of the dark to go out on my own, I cry until my best friend, Tamar, who is four and a half, wakes up. She slides out of bed, takes my hand, and accompanies me on this nighttime trek.

The two of us step out of the children's house hand in hand, shutting the door softly behind us. Wearing only our pajamas, we walk and sometimes run quietly along the sidewalk, trying to avoid the night watchwoman who in the past caught and took us back. After she did, we would pretend to fall asleep and walk right back out as soon as she left.

When we finally reach my parents' room, Tamar and I are both out of breath. I release the sob I had been holding, let go of Tamar's hand, and run to their door crying, waking them up so they would let me in. Tamar, who is better at hiding her fears and so caring towards her "little sister," as she calls me, walks back to the nursery alone while I cry in my parents' arms, finally feeling safe. Then one of them takes my hand and leads me back on the dark sidewalk towards the nursery. I am lifted in a warm hug and placed into my bed, falling asleep with their hand in mine. Those moments of relief are short but my need for safety is so strong that it doesn't matter.

Years later in a support group for people born on a kibbutz, I heard that so many young children made this night-time journey searching for comfort and safety or, as one of them told me: "I just wanted to make sure my parents were still alive."

When I look back at those early years, I wish our parents would have had a place to share their fears and frustrations without being judged or lectured to, but rather met with compassion and understanding. Having such a place would have enabled them to better see and understand our struggles and fears. Looking back, I am also in awe of the little three-year-old me who rebelled against the norm in her search for solace, comfort and connection, and of her friend Tamar, who was willing to wake up in the middle of the night and walk out in the dark despite her own fears, so her "sister" could reach safety.

Chapter 3

Good and Bad
1965-1967, Magal

The true soldier fights not because he hates what is in front
of him, but because he loves what is behind him.
G.K. Chesterton

It is much easier to hurt someone than to feel something.
Brene Brown

Because our kibbutz was only a kilometer from the border with Jordan, amidst the hum of daily life there was always an underlying fear that someone would be shot by a sniper while on their way to the kibbutz or while working in the fields or that a terrorist squad would cross the border and attack us.

On a sweltering summer day when I was five, the military sent combat engineers to manufacture a bomb after receiving intelligence reports that a terrorist squad was making its way to the kibbutz. Two soldiers were working on the bomb in a room close to the dining hall when they made a mistake in the construction. The bomb detonated, killing them both and sending shrapnel all over, wounding David, Tamar's father, and Haim, my own father, who happened to be walking by. The terrorist squad must have heard the explosion because they quickly escaped instead of attacking the kibbutz. Our fathers were driven to a hospital in Tel Aviv, where they were operated on and spent two weeks recovering. I never heard the story of the soldiers who were killed or their families.

When my father returned with bandages around his leg, I was not sure why or what happened or how serious it all was. Months later he showed us dark spots in his leg and said it was leftover shrapnel. I remember looking at it and thinking how strong my father must be because he had pieces of metal in his body.

Then came the Six-Day War.

The 1967 war began with a siren in the early morning of June 5th, a few months after I turned seven. In the middle of breakfast our caretakers rushed us to the nearest underground shelter. My father, the only officer in the kibbutz and therefore the kibbutz commander, was busy defending us against attacks, together with the military unit attached to the kibbutz and all the other men who had not been drafted elsewhere. My mother, who worked with young children, spent her days and nights in another underground shelter with the children in her group and my two-year-old brother.

The shelters were dug deep in the ground, covered with a huge mound of brown earth and hidden by the kibbutz gardener with flowering bushes. To reach them we had to descend a flight of stairs into a concrete structure with a round ceiling, painted white, whose only light came from a lamp hanging on a white electrical cord from the ceiling. There were no windows. The place was filled with bunk beds, other children, and our caretakers. After a day and a night cramped in the shelter, we were ready for a break.

"Let's play catch," Tamar, the eldest, suggested the following morning when we were allowed to step out of the shelter.

"You're It!" Anat cried to Noga as we ran barefoot on the soft, slightly wet green grass surrounding the bomb shelter. I was squinting in the bright sunlight, laughing as I ran away.

Seemingly out of nowhere, Noga was scooped up, enfolded in a hug and lifted high in the air by a large man in uniform.

"Abba!" she squealed in delight while her father Shimon hugged and kissed her. I stood watching, wishing I was her. I also wanted to be singled out for love, to be the center of attention. Half an hour later, I watched with envy as they walked together hand in hand towards the entrance of the bomb shelter.

The next day Shimon was killed in a mortar blast.

Anat and Tamar's fathers were also injured in the same attack. In a letter to friends who had gone to Argentina for two years as emissaries to bring new families to the kibbutz, my father wrote:

> Magal was under attack for two days. Mainly sniper and rifle fire. Unfortunately, we also got shelled which seriously damaged the mortar

position. It was a sudden shelling, in which Shimon Yudekovik and Danny Swiri were killed, Uri and Pesach were severely wounded, Rami and David Shochat were injured while Daoud and Gabi were slightly injured. Uri lost his jaw, and his life was in danger. Pesach almost lost his hand, but luckily, it was saved. Haya [Shimon's wife] returned with the children to bury Shimon in Tel Hai. And that's not all. In a tough battle over Jerusalem, Noam Kirshenbaum was killed. The atmosphere in the Kibbutz is quite dark in recent days and the people are beaten up by all of this…

Before the war my father, who was the kibbutz shepherd, thought we should befriend our Arab neighbors and often took us to the nearby Arab village of Baqa al-Gharbiyye, where we would eat sweets and try to communicate with the children while he and our host bargained over sheep or spoke about philosophy. I don't remember being afraid on those visits, for our hosts were very kind. But after Shimon was killed, something did not make sense.

My friend Noga left to be with her mother and younger brother and did not return and I had so many questions. Where did Noga go? Why did Shimon and the others have to die? Why were the Arabs shooting and trying to kill us?

Very confused, I decided to ask my father.

Two days following the attack that led to Shimon's death, my father came to visit me in the shelter. His khaki uniform was muddy and there were dark streaks on his cheeks. His Uzi hung from his left shoulder.

He kissed me on the forehead and I asked him:

"Abba, why are the Arabs shooting at us? Are they bad people?"

Stroking my head gently, he said, "Well, Nitsani, it's not so simple. Just as there are good and bad Jews, there are good and bad Arabs. The ones shooting at us are bad, but there are also many good Arabs who just want to tend their fields, take care of their wives and children and live peacefully, just like us."

At seven years old, part of me wanted black and white, good and evil: *Please make this life simple so I can understand what's happening around me.* Instead, what I received was complexity. In the middle of the war, while fighting for our survival, my Abba did not give me an easy answer. Yet his response has stayed with me and guided my path.

Chapter 4

Lost in Translation
1970-1971, Durham

Live abroad, if you can. Understand cultures other than your own. As your understanding of other cultures increases, your understanding of yourself and your own culture will increase exponentially.

Tom Freston

"Welcome, Nishaaan" said the very short woman with peppered white hair who stood by the door when I walked into the second-grade class on that first Monday in September 1970. I looked down at her kind blue eyes and wondered where the teacher was and who was Nishaaan. Then I gazed around the room at the 20 children who barely reached my shoulders and wondered how I would survive second grade at Hope Valley Elementary School in Durham, North Carolina.

That summer, a few months after I turned 10, we left the familiarity and comfort of our kibbutz, our immediate family, all my friends, my school, our country, and moved to the USA so that my father could complete his PhD in Philosophy of Education. My mother was 34 and hardly knew English, could not drive, and had barely finished high school. My two brothers Mor and Neve were eight and five.

After a full year of studying English in the fifth grade of my kibbutz school, "Hello" and "Kiss" were the only words I could remember. "Hello" because it was a greeting I heard when people spoke on the only kibbutz phone and "Kiss" because it means pocket in Hebrew and I thought, *Wow!! It has such a romantic meaning in English.*

Armed with my extensive knowledge of the English language, I arrived with my eight-year-old brother Mor at the elementary school in Durham, as soon as the school year began. Because we didn't speak any English (aside from my two words) Mor, who was supposed to be in 4th grade, was placed in the 1st grade and I, who was about to enter the 6th grade, found myself in 2nd grade. The goal was that once we mastered the English language in a few months we would move to our age-appropriate classes.

Towering above the children was not the only problem I had in the 2nd grade class. My biggest issue was that the woman who greeted me at the door on that first morning, and was at least a head shorter than I, was my teacher. She probably taught 2nd grade, I reasoned, because the children were short, so her height was not an issue until I arrived and then it became a problem. Whenever someone entered the room or when the class went on field trips, they approached me thinking I must be the teacher and asked questions. I would nod my head as though I understood and would try to decide which would be the most appropriate response, "Hello" or "Kiss."

In our apartment in Durham, I had my own room for the first time in my life and a small TV that my brothers and I shared. To have a TV of our own after being used to watching one program, *Mission Impossible*, once a week with all the kibbutz members, was a miracle for us. My parents limited us to an hour and a half a day and being the eldest, I taught my brothers how we could gain an extra half hour by covering our eyes during the commercials. *The Brady Bunch, Dark Shadows,* and *The Partridge Family* were my English lessons, and after a few months my vocabulary increased, along with my addiction to TV.

My second-grade teacher must have noticed my improved English because one day, three months into the school year, she said, "Nishaaan (by now I realized it was my name), the principal wants to see you and test if you can now move up to the 6th grade."

Not sure how to prepare for this exam, I walked over from my class and followed the secretary into the principal's office. He took out a large black book (it may have been the Bible) and said: "Open to page 354."

By then I had learned the numbers and was able to follow his request. When I found the page, he said, "Okay, you can move up to 6th grade on Monday."

That's it? I thought, not quite sure what to say. But as I walked out of his office, a feeling of relief broke through and I jumped and skipped all the way back to second grade.

On Monday I 'graduated' to sixth grade and when I entered my new classroom and felt forty eyes watching me while the tall teacher directed me to sit next to a girl who looked my age, my cheeks grew hot and for a moment I regretted having to leave my post as a look-alike teacher in second grade.

During the first few months in 6th grade, I hardly understood what the teacher was saying. Sometimes I managed to grasp the context and eventually began reading and writing. The only reason I was able to pass 6th grade was that almost all the tests were multiple-choice and hardly any writing was necessary. Luckily, I was not so bad at guessing.

Later that year, my father decided to transfer to Peabody College in Nashville, Tennessee, where he would complete his doctoral degree while working as a school principal in the Jewish Community Center Hebrew School and the Sunday School of a Conservative synagogue in Chattanooga. When the summer came, we packed our belongings into a U-Haul and traveled to the duplex apartment he'd found for us on Signal Mountain, in a beautiful community overlooking Chattanooga.

As we drove through the twists and turns up the mountain, the air became clearer and the bright emerald leaves of the tall trees towering above us shaded the road. When houses finally appeared, the first building I saw was a police station on the right side of the road. Later, I learned that the police station was in that particular location so they could guard the entrance to this mountain community from the "threat" of Black people who lived downtown. A few times Black families had tried to buy houses on the mountain to escape the pollution and dangerous neighborhoods of the city, but each time their houses were burned down by White locals. Similarly, whenever a Black person was spotted driving up the mountain, the police would tail the car to make sure they were just driving through. It was the early seventies; Martin Luther King Jr. was dead and *Black Lives Matter* was still generations away. I, too, was an outsider, so I worried when I heard the stories; but I told myself, *I am white just like them so I will be okay.* And then I did not worry, not until school began.

I have many memories from Signal Mountain Junior High School, including the cafeteria food (which I loved), my failed attempt at becoming a cheerleader, making it to the Honor Society in the 8th grade, my first school dance which I spent hugging the walls, missing my father when he left us to go to Israel for a couple of months in 1973 to fight during the Yom Kippur War, asking to be whipped on my hands like the boys when I didn't do my homework because it was quicker than copying a verse from the Bible 50 times (the punishment for the girls), jogging around the football field, book reports and heartaches. But there is one memory stronger than all the rest – my head-on collision with prejudice.

Chapter 5

Rescuing Beetles in the Deep South
1972, Signal Mountain

*No one is born hating another person because of the color of
his skin, or his background or his religion. People learn to hate,
and if they can learn to hate, they can be taught to love, for love
comes more naturally to the human heart than its opposite.*

Nelson Mandela

Holding a tray carrying a tuna fish sandwich and a chocolate cake with
white icing, I search for a place to sit in the Signal Mountain Junior High
School cafeteria. My eyes wander around the room, wishing there was
somewhere else I could be.

Is there anywhere in this room where the only Israeli – the only Jew – in
the school can feel accepted? Not likely. Even if someone invites me to sit
near them, which is rare, I feel they are just doing me a favor that I don't
truly belong, and then the food gets stuck in my throat because I don't
know what to say and how to be. I cannot stand the discomfort of asking
for help, of owing somebody something.

So, I walk towards the table of the unacceptable. Here sit the strange,
obese, braces-wearing, pimple-filled adolescents and now me – the lonely
Jew, who also happens to have braces and pimples.

As fate would have it, at the table next to us are the school bullies and
each day it's someone else's turn to get picked on. I wish to God today
is not mine. I sink low in my seat, trying to become invisible, and eat as
quickly and quietly as I can, hoping to escape before they even notice I sat
down. No such luck today. Soon I hear them.

"Hey, look at that dirty Jew, see how she eats, yuck!"

And I do feel dirty and humiliated as pieces of food are thrown at me
from the other table. Yet I do nothing aside from trying to disappear,

sinking deeper into my seat. And the other unacceptable? They are looking away. There is no sense of camaraderie, only fear. Each one is scared, probably thinking, *if I speak out, I will be the next victim.*

This happened almost every day for a year. While I didn't get picked on every single day, the fear was always lurking in the background. At times, when I walked home, some of the bullies followed me, throwing small rocks in my direction. Luckily, they almost always missed.

I didn't tell my parents. There was a part of me that felt I was not worthy of being treated differently, that if I was shunned and teased it was because something was truly wrong with me. Perhaps I feared that sharing my pain would make me more vulnerable. What if I was teased about it by my own family? I couldn't risk it. In those painful moments, I left my body so I would not have to feel shame, anger, fear or anything else for that matter. I escaped into my books and television shows, where the heroine was loved and there were happy endings.

During that year I started to cough. The cough went on and on for months and nothing seemed to stop it, not tea with lemon and honey, not antibiotics, nothing. The worst part was at night, when I awakened again and again with fits of coughing. It would get better and then worse until I was exhausted. Just a cough, no fever and no end in sight. Finally, I found a way to stop it by holding it in for as long as I could so the part of my throat that was so irritated would be able to relax and recover. It took a few more days until it passed, only to return every winter for thirty years. Today I believe that because I did not share my feelings with anyone, leaving them painfully stuck inside, my body rebelled and tried to cough them out.

In the middle of that school year was a day I will never forget. I was sitting in eighth grade history class next to Betsy, one of the more popular girls, who was wearing her usual minimal mini skirt. Behind me was Dicky, with his curly red hair, from the bullies' table.

Looking up, I saw Mrs. Garret, our beautiful dark-haired, blue-eyed history teacher, standing by a map of Europe.

"World War II began in 1939 and ended in 1945," she began, "During the war the German Nazis, led by Hitler, brutally murdered more than 6,000,000 Jews and millions more other people."

I was listening intently; she was talking about my people and as the only Jew in the school, I felt special.

"Today, that horrific slaughter is called the Holocaust," she continued.

I knew about the Holocaust from the kibbutz. We commemorated

Holocaust Day every year, lighting candles, hearing stories of those who were killed and those who survived. I was totally engrossed. Then I heard the whispers.

"Too bad more Jews were not murdered in the Holocaust. Too bad you were not murdered." Dicky and Betsy said softly, so only I would hear.

I tried to ignore their whispers as I had ignored all the taunts and humiliation. But they did not stop, repeating those horrible words again and again, louder and clearer. Sweat trickled down the sides of my forehead. I felt invaded, as if the whispers had entered my blood stream and were rushing up into my head. I couldn't stand it anymore and still they continued. My head was spinning, everything went blurry and all I heard over and over was: "Too bad you were not murdered."

Ready to burst, I popped up and screamed, "ENOUGH!!!!" with all the strength I didn't know I had. There was a hush in the class.

For a moment everything snapped into focus and I rushed out of the room. I ran and ran without looking back. That evening I finally told my parents about the harassment and about what Dicky and Betsy had said that day.

They listened quietly and my mother hugged me. I didn't cry, I didn't know how. I just said, "I'm not going back to that school."

"Let me go talk to them," my father replied, and because I trusted him, I agreed to go back the following morning.

The next day in history class Mrs. Garett moved me so I was no longer sitting next to Betsy and Dicky, thank God.

The room grew quiet when my father entered.

I saw my classmates stare at his wild brown hair and beard as if they had never seen an adult man with so much hair. They were probably used to clean-shaven faces, suits and ties, so his tan sweater, his quiet voice and the way he pushed his hair out of his eyes made him seem eccentric. Nobody, including me, knew what to expect. Mrs. Garett smiled and introduced him and then he began speaking:

"I would like to tell you a story about the Holocaust. During that time some people were sent to labor camps where they worked very hard, were fed very little and when they became too weak to work, they were sent to the death camps. One of the jobs at the labor camp was to carry very heavy sacks of cement and sand from a boat on the river's edge to a fortification that sat on top of a hill. With a sack on his back, each person would labor their way up the hill and then run down for another bag. The inmates were exhausted from lack of sleep and hunger, yet the torturous Nazi guards and fear of death kept pushing them on. A few were ready to give up. Then one man noticed that on their path were beetles, some of which had flipped over on their backs and could not turn right side up and walk away. Legs flailing in the air, they were completely helpless."

My father paused for a moment and looked around the room. I followed his gaze. My classmates were leaning forward, mesmerized. Mrs. Garett's blue eyes were shining and focused on him as he continued.

"The man bent down with that heavy load on his back and turned a beetle over. And then he did it again with another beetle. Soon another man saw him and joined in, then another and another. Within minutes all the men were stooping down every few minutes, with their heavy loads, to turn over a beetle and help it on its way. Somehow their load became lighter. On that day everyone finished work and not one person was sent to the death camp..."

When my father finished, the room was quiet. "Thank you for your attention," he said, looking into each of my classmates' eyes before leaving the room. There was a solemn, subdued feeling in the air long after he'd left the classroom. Maybe after that day, there was less taunting. Maybe I became stronger. I am not sure. But somehow, my load did become lighter.

Chapter 6

Standing Up in the Ghetto
1973, Signal Mountain

Dancing is the only art in which we
ourselves are the stuff of which it is made.
Ted Shawn

That same year my family moved to a log cabin situated on a narrow road, in the woods with very few neighbors. The back yard was huge and boasted fruit trees, a stream, a barn for our chickens and enough room for our two cats, Here (as in, "come here, Here") and Dumdum, to roam. The recently renovated 100-year-old cabin had a huge fireplace in the living room, ceiling art, a small kitchen and a tiny bathroom.

I had my own bedroom and when I opened the window, I was overjoyed to find a cherry tree whose graceful branches reached all the way to the dark green window ledge. In the summer I would stretch my arm out the window to pick a cherry or climb into the tree and, despite my fear of ticks, sit quietly looking down into our back yard. Half hidden by the leaves and the height I would breathe in the warm summer air, caress the branches and lean back on the rough gray bark of the wide trunk. *Oh, how I love trees*, I thought, *especially this one*. Extending my right arm, I would pick a dark red cherry and place it in my mouth, feeling its smooth surface on my tongue while swirling it around. Then my teeth would close in and dent the almost perfect roundness as I savored the sweetness of a summer cherry.

From my post I could see my brother Mor step out the back door wearing a superman t-shirt and holding a bowl of leftovers from last night's dinner. He made a clucking sound and soon all the chickens pecking throughout the yard would run towards him and begin fighting over the rice or vegetables that he had tossed on the grass not far from the tree. Without being summoned, Here and Dumbdum would also join the celebration and rub their soft gray furry bodies on Mor's legs asking to be petted.

A few months later, on a winter night, my parents and I sat in the living room listening to music. The song American Pie began playing and a moment later I stood up as if lifted by an outside force and began moving. I had just turned thirteen and had never learned to dance formally. I knew movements from gym classes like jumping jacks and had seen films with dancers, so I moved to the music throwing my arms and legs every which way and enjoying the power the song had over my body. One song followed another as I danced and swirled around the room not wanting to stop.

At some point my father who also loved to dance stood up and joined me. Each of us doing our own dance, not far from one another, we looked over at each other and smiled. My father extended his hand to my mother and she reluctantly stood up to join him. I could see how difficult it was for her to get her body and the music to flow together effortlessly, despite her being so musically savvy. It seemed as if she had to think about each movement before formulating it.

Having very little inhibition in my movements, it was painful for me to watch her making such an effort to do something that for me was effortless. Years later she read me a story she had written of how her experience with dance began and ended:

> Passover dinner had just concluded in the kibbutz dining hall. People moved the tables out of the way and prepared the space for the traditional Hora folk dancing. Along the walls the holiday staff had built wooden bleachers for the audience. It was very noisy, adults and children, members and their guests, a huge crowd. Passover was my favorite holiday. I was ten years old and decided in one moment: *today is the day, today it will happen. Soon the Hora dancing will begin and I will dare for the first time in my life to slip through the dancers into one of the innermost circles so I could try to dance without anyone seeing me. Today I will burst the wall of fear that has held me back. I will go through with it today no matter what!!*
>
> The accordion player was already sitting at the center of the dance floor playing the holiday tunes. My heart was beating fast and my whole body was shaking when I slipped inside and joined the innermost circle.
>
> Suddenly a loud shout coming from the top of the bleachers next to the wall pierced through the music: 'RACHELLA, LEARN TO DANCE

BEFORE YOU JOIN THE CIRCLE!!'

For a moment I stood frozen. *Is this actually happening or am I dreaming?* Then I realized, yes, it's real. Shula, a girl two years my senior, was hollering at me in front of the entire crowd. I sprinted away as fast as I could. The night was dark and not a living soul was on the sidewalks. The children's house was also dark, empty and scary. I felt my world had just collapsed. I fell on my bed and burst into tears, sobbing into my pillow for hours. I don't know how long I cried but at some point, I fell asleep. The following day no one asked what happened or why I ran away.

Since that day I wanted nothing to do with dancing.

I, who loved gym, athletics, ball, and the holiday performances so much, boycotted dancing and movement. It was a choice I made on that miserable night, and I have paid for it throughout my life.

When I danced that evening in the 100-year-old log cabin on the red carpet next to the blazing fire, I did not yet know my mother's story. At one point both my parents watched me moving wildly around the room, not caring about how I looked or what they thought, letting the music lead me and awaken the fire in my heart.

Visibly moved, my mother turned to my father and said: "Let's find her a place to study dance."

Soon afterwards, my parents began driving me a couple of times a week down the mountain and into the city to the *Performing Arts Studio* created by Nancy and Fred Wright. Nancy, 45 at the time, had been a professional dancer, and had lost the ability to walk in a car accident. She then created a set of exercises she called *Preparation for Movement.* These exercises helped her regain movement in her legs, and while I never saw her dance on stage, she did walk and teach some of the movement classes at the studio.

I waited every week for those classes even though some were quite difficult, and I often compared myself to others, feeling I was not good enough.

Seeing my struggles, my father would say: "You know, Nitsani, being the worst in the class is also an experience worth having."

Smiling, I decided to try out for that title.

Nancy's ability to see my strengths and believe in me was extraordinary. In her studio I fell in love with dancing, especially the creative movement classes she taught on Sunday evenings. I was still that same braces-wearing, pimply 13-year-old who had a hard time communicating and connecting, but now I found a way to express my feelings through movement and dance.

There was also a rare class in which all the dancers, professional and beginners, participated together. It was taught by a grey-haired, well-built man, Martin Allen, who was a Quaker which at the time seemed unique.

One day, Martin played a song for us: *The World is a Ghetto* by War:

> *Walkin' down the street, smoggy-eyed*
> *Looking at the sky, starry-eyed*
> *Searchin' for a place, weary-eyed*
> *Crying in the night, teary-eyed*
> *Don't you know that it's true*
> *That for me and for you*
> *The world is a ghetto...*

I listened intently. "The world is a Ghetto" were powerful words for a Jew suffering from prejudice in an all-Christian Junior High.

"Each one of you will improvise to this song alone in front of the class for a few minutes," he told us as a wave of excitement flowed through the room. The professional dancers went first –turning, stretching, kicking, jumping and flying through the air. They looked so beautiful.

I was worried. I had only been dancing at the studio for a few months and had no idea how to follow such powerful performances, especially when everyone was watching. But when Martin called on me, I did step forward, deciding not to try to be like anyone else, since I couldn't, but to dance my own story.

I lay on the floor, waiting for the music to enter me. After a moment I began to move, attempting to raise one hand, a leg, my other hand, my head and each time falling back as though it was impossible, as though there was so much weight on me that I could not lift a hand more than a few inches. I could not raise myself out of this ghetto, this divided world. Still, I persisted, two movements up and one down, slowly rising bit by bit, each time falling back a little less until in one transformative moment I stood up without falling.

Standing alone, 13 years old, facing everyone, I had done it! Perhaps the world was a ghetto, but at least I could stand up within its walls.

In the midst of the applause and tears, I felt "seen".

From that day on, dancing became my way to express sadness, anger and fear, joy and love. My dancing was and still is free, with few inhibitions, and often I wish I would find a way to live my life with the same wild abandon with which I dance.

Chapter 7

The Failure Club
1973-1974, Signal Mountain

There is only one thing that makes a dream impossible to achieve: the fear of failure.
Paulo Coelho, *The Alchemist*

Success is not final; failure is not fatal: it is the courage to continue that counts.
Winston S. Churchill

"You are not welcome into my club because you have not failed yet enough," my father used to say to me with a smile and an emphasis on the word "yet".

"Thank God there is still hope," I responded, also with a smile.

When things got hard for me in school or when my heart was aching because a boyfriend broke up with me, he would add, "Suffering is the only way to learn anything meaningful," this time without a smile.

Looking back, I wonder if his words were one reason why failure, pain, and suffering interested me so much and the reason why, at 12, I read books on the Holocaust like *Babi Yar and Treblinka* that no one else my age was reading.

Then, at 13, we were assigned to report on any book we chose in front of the class. I picked *All Quiet on the Western Front* by Eric Maria Remarque, a German author whose book, published in 1928, had become a bestseller and was later banned and burned by the Nazis when they came into power.

I proceeded to tell my classmates the grueling details of how the hero suffers hunger, trench warfare, the death of his mates, and mortally wounds a man in face-to-face combat. He then has to stay with the man and watch him die a slow death because the constant bombing makes it impossible for him to get out of the trench. I ended my report quoting the author:

"This book is to be neither an accusation nor a confession, and least of all an adventure, for death is not an adventure to those who stand face to face with it. It will try simply to tell of a generation of men who, even though they may have escaped its shells, were destroyed by the war."

When I finished, my classmates were very quiet, as if shocked by the story. I realized that I too knew how to tell stories but was not sure why I chose such pain-filled topics.

When Nancy Wright, my dance teacher, asked each of us to create a dance to a song, I once again chose to focus on the pain of war, dancing to the song *Billy Don't be a Hero* by Paper Lace.

I must have been trying to make sense of my experiences growing up in a conflict zone and living through war. I wanted pain to be something I could handle without running away, and those were my first attempts to bring the pain of war into the open.

Much like the stories he told my classmates on the day after I ran away from school, my father, the relentless philosopher, would often tell us stories, jokes and riddles that challenged us to go deeper into the meaning of things.

"Do you know what eternity is?" he once asked, when the five of us had stopped for a lunch break on a hike up a mountain in Glacier National Park.

None of us did.

"Tell us," I said, knowing there was a story involved.

"Well... There's a beautiful orange and purple bird that sleeps in a dark cave for a very long time," he began. "Once every 1000 years she wakes up and makes her way to the forest to find food to eat. After she eats, she flies over to the mountain you see right here in front of you," he said, pointing to the huge greyish brown rocky mountain almost devoid of trees towering above us. When she reaches this mountain, she cleans her beak on it a few times making tiny pebbles of dust fly into the air. When this bird will have turned the entire mountain into dust by cleaning her beak on it a few times every 1000 years, one day of eternity will have passed."

After he finished all of us were quiet. I looked at the huge mountain trying to imagine it become a pile of dust while only one day of eternity had passed. At 13, eternity was too huge a concept to comprehend, but the story helped.

Emulating my father, I would often tell people stories of my life, especially the moments when I failed and/or suffered and learned something meaningful.

Yet in my desire to reach the end of the story, understand and then explain its meaning to others, I sometimes skipped over the process. What was it actually like to be me in certain moments, to experience what I experienced, to feel the failure or the heartache?

"You know, when I was 14," I once told a friend, "I joined the swim team at the JCC, and although I could definitely swim, I was slow. But since I was on the team, they felt obligated to give me a chance and assigned me to swim the back stroke in one of the local meets. There were six competitors and the distance was 50 yards, one lap – back and forth. I backstroked to one side pretty fast, then turned to swim back feeling exhausted and out of breath. While laboring through the water I heard the splashing of my arms and legs as they furiously beat the surface of the water.

Then I heard a loud and familiar voice soaring high above all the other noise: "You can do it Nitsani, GO Nitsan GO!"

Despite my exhausted state, the sound of my mother's voice encouraged me to swim faster. Beating the water with increased fury, I finally reached and touched the pool's edge and looked around. All the other swimmers had finished well before me and were now sitting and talking with one another near the pool. I looked up at my mother with a new sense of who she was for me. She had kept cheering me on as if nothing else mattered." End of story. Or maybe not.

For many years my new appreciation for my mother was the end of this story. It sounded good, like an important lesson learned, that having someone who has your back, whether you win or lose, is more important than actually winning the race. But years later, when I became more aware of my feelings, I realized that at the moment when I reached the ledge, I was not feeling deep appreciation for my mother, who had cheered me on despite the fact that I was the only swimmer in the pool. In that moment, I actually felt such embarrassment and shame that I simply wanted to sink under the water and never come out. I was not only ashamed of myself for being last, I was also ashamed of my mother who was cheering for me and making a spectacle of herself in front of all those people. When I told the story with my mother as the heroine, it made me feel better about the whole thing– feel that I had learned something meaningful through my suffering – that I had gone through it and come out on the other side stronger.

But missing from my original telling was the 14-year-old girl who felt so ashamed and alone when she reached the pool's ledge and looked around. Going back to her, sitting by her side and hearing her story was something I only learned to do years later when I began a process of emotional healing. Only when I could listen to the young girl I used to be and hold her pain with compassion was I able to let go of the shame and feel truly worthy of my mother's cheers on that day.

Chapter 8

Back in Israel – Who Am I?

1975-1977, Beer Sheva

*The closer you come to knowing that you alone create
the world of your experience, the more vital it becomes
for you to discover just who is doing the creating.*
Eric Micha'el Leventhal

*The hardest question we have to ask ourselves in this life is,
"Who am I?" Ideally, we answer it for ourselves, but be warned
that others will strive to do it for you- so don't let them.*
Karma Brown, *Recipe for a Perfect Wife*

I was 15 and a half during the summer of 1975 when we took our final camping trip cramped together in the VW Beetle with all our gear stuffed into a container and strapped to the roof. We hiked through beautiful parks, streams and forests, sleeping in the huge family tent. And during every visit to the supermarket, my brothers and I still argued which cereal to buy for breakfast: Lucky Charms (me) or Cocoa Puffs (them).

Our trip ended in New York where we said goodbye to relatives and boarded the El Al plane back to Israel. We arrived on a hot and muggy day at the end of July 1975 at Kibbutz Ramat Yohanan where we spent a few days with grandmothers Chaya and Rachel. By that time both our grandfathers were dead.

My father had completed his PhD and received a position in the Department of Education at Ben Gurion University in Beer Sheva. During our five years in the States my mother had learned to drive and speak English, completed a Bachelor's Degree and became a US citizen like my father.

Despite five years of yearning for the kibbutz I grew up in, we never returned to live in Magal. Instead, a few days after landing, we made our way to Beer Sheva, a city close to the desert in Southern Israel with almost no trees, dry heat, wide expansive skies and what my father called "fascist architecture," – buildings that completely ignore their relationship to the environment.

After five years surrounded by so many shades of green, huggable trees and the abundance of rain in Tennessee, this mixture of yellowish earth, large cement structures and scrawny trees was so hard on my eyes. I looked everywhere for small patches of green where I could sit and reconnect to nature and beauty.

Despite the parched earth, my social life was growing in Beer Sheva. I made new friends and suddenly felt attractive. My dark eyes and hair were more the norm and the fact that I was not a blond blue-eyed cheerleader was inconsequential because there were no cheerleaders and quarterbacks in my new high school.

I did feel lost in translation at times.

Once during an exam, Sarah, who sat behind me, whispered: "Hey can you move a bit to the right so I can copy your answers?"

"No" I whispered back, "I can help you study for the test but I will not let you copy off my test."

"Well then," she said firmly, "if you don't help us during tests, nobody will want to be your friend."

I was stunned. In my Tennessee High School there were very strict rules about cheating on tests, and I remember seeing a teacher take a boy he had caught cheating out into the hall, telling him to bend over and then proceeding to beat him vigorously on his behind with a huge wooden ruler. The teachers would tell us again and again to cover our response sheet so nobody will see what we wrote. And here, covering my responses was considered being antisocial.

She was right about some people, but others did become my friends, despite my "antisocial" tendencies. Even though I felt justified, I sometimes felt like a strange bird, not sure how to enter this new environment. Speaking my truth, doing what's right and my father's words about the importance of suffering and the value of failing sometimes helped me feel okay about being different. At other times I just felt so alone.

In addition, most of the teenagers I met were into folk dancing, which felt foreign to me. They had judgments about those people who danced free and uninhibited like me. "You are doing disco dancing," one of them told me. "It's not something we like around here."

But I did not want to change my style of dancing. I felt happy when I danced, beautiful, connected.

During that first year I joined a youth movement – Hashomer Hatza'ir – where I met several young men and women, some of whom later became my friends. In one of the first meetings, I was invited to folk dance with them. The Mazurka was playing and one young man decided to take on teaching me this dance. Zvika had light curly hair, deep brown eyes and a wide smile. When we danced together, I felt he knew what he was doing, and when I made a mistake, we both laughed. Following that one Mazurka dance, I was smitten with him, especially after he walked me home. I hid my feelings, trying to play the role of the cool, collected and confident girl. But after a few days, when he did not try to contact me, I felt so hurt. I tried to connect with him at school, which further alienated him.

I was so ashamed and kept reliving the moment when we met: what I said, or didn't say and should have said, as though that could help in some way. Instead, my relentless thoughts plunged me into pain and darkness. It felt as if someone had turned off the light and there was no more love in the world.

Tamar, my childhood "big sister", came to visit from Magal during one of those "there is no more love in the world" heartache moments, and I remember sitting on the floor unable to communicate, unable to pull myself out of the pit of loneliness. She did not know what to do and how to help. Holding my hand and taking me to my parents' room was useless this time.

Sometimes I think: if only there had been just one person who would have said: "I know you are feeling awful now because your heart is breaking and you think you will never find anyone who can love you. I get it and I'm here for you and want to hear whatever you would like to share. And if you just want to sit quietly, I will sit by your side and keep you company."

Just one person would have made a huge difference.

Eventually the grief and shame would release their hold over my heart and sink back into the basement of my mind.

Later that year, in an English Literature course, I wrote a short piece that my teacher loved and asked me to read in front of the class. It was about a young woman walking on a beach, where she meets a strange looking man. "Who are you?" the man asks her. She tells him her name and what she does for a living but he is not satisfied. Instead, he persists with the same question, explaining, "I don't want to know your name, what you do or have. I just want to know who are you? And why are you here in this world?"

I, too, was searching for the answers to these questions.

Chapter 9

Tummy to Tummy
Child to Adult

*Half of all marriages end up in divorce
and then there are the really unhappy ones.*
Joan Rivers

"I can't understand why you're so angry?!" My mother said vehemently.

"You never understand because you don't see me, you only see the other side!!" My father shouted and bolted out of our kibbutz apartment leaving the door wide open. A minute later, when all was quiet, I slipped out from behind the couch where I had been hiding and looked through the open doorway. He was gone and I had no idea if or when he would come back. My mother was holding and caressing my youngest brother Neve who was crying loudly.

I never saw how these arguments ended, how they resolved their differences, because the following day when I came home in the afternoon from the kibbutz children's house, my father would be there, and everything would seem all right until the next time he bolted.

Once, when I was 24, I remember sitting on the branch of a tree after I also bolted during an argument with Eyal, my boyfriend. I felt he could not see me and the pain was crushing my heart, so I ran away, trying to escape the awful feeling. It did not work. My pain climbed right up that tree with me, lodged inside my heart, and neither of us knew what to do. There was no way I was going to be vulnerable and show Eyal how terrible I felt. I was hoping he would follow me; say he was sorry, and beg for my forgiveness–but he didn't. After a while the pain receded and I climbed back down and walked into his house. He opened his arms and we hugged and never spoke about it. At the time I had no idea how to share my pain openly.

When he didn't bolt, my father taught me some important ways to deal with difficult situations. One of them was humor. He explained that having a sense of humor means not only being able to tell or laugh at jokes, or at something someone stupid does. Mostly it means being able to laugh at yourself.

Once, when we lived on Signal Mountain, my brothers and I made a large sign and hung it in our living room. The sign read: "A MORNING WITHOUT SHOUTING IS NOT A MORNING." When my father saw it, he laughed, knowing we were referring to him.

Later he told us that in their early years of marriage, when they still lived in the kibbutz, they would argue, he would shout and bolt, and my mother would tell him afterwards: "Why can't we be more like our neighbors on the right, they are so quiet?" Six months later, those neighbors divorced. Then she would say: "Why can't we be more like the neighbors on the left? They communicate so well." A year later, this couple also divorced. His point was that getting angry, shouting, and sometimes bolting are actually important ingredients for a good marriage.

I thought they were too until I didn't.

Despite the arguments, for years our home felt like a very good place to grow up in. Our parents loved us, we went on camping trips together to beautiful places, took turns reading Robert Frost poems after dinner, did the household chores together, ate my father's special bean soup and my mother's wonderful cooking, laughed a lot and enjoyed deep discussions about things that mattered.

We often had guests on Friday evenings or went to dinner at friends' houses. When we moved to Beer Sheva, my father's students visited often, to talk and ask advice from my parents. My father and his assistants would sometimes lead workshops in our living room, with the students sitting on floor pillows in a circle on our shaggy black, brown and white carpet, surrounded by wooden shelves filled with books, walls with artwork and a record player that stood in the corner above our huge collection of records. There was no television in that apartment.

At times, as part of the workshops, the students would go out into the Negev desert for experiential exercises that my father and his team created. One such exercise was the Gait of Power based on Carlos Castaneda's *Journey to Ixtlan*, where they would walk with their fingers slightly curled in and notice what shifts in the way they sensed the world. Then they would gather and talk about it.

During those years our home was an exciting place to be in.

My parents also knew how to listen, and I could talk with them about personal matters, even the difficult ones.

Once, when I was sixteen and in love with Avi, the tall, gorgeous 22-year-old life guard at the only swimming pool in town, I walked into my parents' room seeking advice. My father was sitting on his black office chair looking at what he had just written on his typewriter.

"I need to talk to you," I said.

"What's going on?" my father replied, looking up. "Shall I call your mother?"

"Yes." I sat on the couch, which turned into their bed every evening.

I was not sure how to begin this conversation and was fidgeting as I stared at the one thousand or so books organized by authors on the brown maple wood shelves lining the wall right across from the couch.

My mother walked in and sat near me. She seemed curious.

"Soooo?" my father asked. "How was your date with Avi last night?"

"Well... it was good and we talked..." Here I paused.

"And," my father urged me on. "What did you talk about? Are you pregnant?"

"NO!! I am not pregnant!!!" I almost screamed, stunned by the question even though I should have been used to my father's confrontational, 'Let's just throw it all in your face and then we'll figure out how to deal with it' style.

"So, what's the problem?" he asked.

Could this be any more embarrassing? I cringed. But I was there because I chose to be. I chose to confide in my parents something that most girls my age wouldn't because I knew they would listen and help me figure it out.

"So, the thing is... Avi wants us to have sex and I think I do, too," I said, though at this point, with both their eyes on me, I was not sure of anything that I actually wanted. "So, I told him I would speak to you about getting a prescription for the pill."

"And what did he say?" asked my mother.

"He was shocked that I would confide in you but he said 'Okay'.

"And do you love him?" my father inquired while I looked at a tiny piece of paper on the orange wall-to-wall carpet that covered the floor. "Do you want to have sex with him?"

"I am not sure," I replied.

How can I know if I want something I never experienced? And if it will hurt me? Or if something will happen and then Avi will leave me? I didn't know what to say and mostly wished this embarrassing conversation would somehow end immediately if not sooner.

"Well, here is what I suggest," my father, the world's most competent fixer upper, said, while turning to my mother. "Rachella, why don't you take her to a gynecologist so she could get a prescription for the pill? And then, if she decides she is ready, she can begin taking it and be safe."

My mother agreed.

"*Beseder.* OK," I said, and slipped quickly out of their room.

In my bedroom I lay on the bed for a while, trying to recover from the ordeal.

We did go to a doctor a week later and after a checkup he was ready to give me a prescription, but he also explained the side effects that taking hormones could have on my body, and that it might not be good to begin at such a young age. After hearing the risks, I started worrying and decided I was not ready to take the pill for now. I told Avi, and a week or two later he left me. I was heartbroken but my parents supported me and I did not regret my decision.

A couple of years later, after I left home for the military and then the university, things began to change. I heard from my brothers there were a lot more arguments, and when I came home every other weekend the atmosphere was tense. Sometimes, when we sat down for dinner, my father would share something that bothered him in his work at the university and my mother would attempt to show him the other person's side. Then he would say loudly: "Why are you always against me?"

To which she would respond: "I am just trying to show you the other side. Why is that against you? And why do you have to talk so loudly?"

"Because you never understand what I'm trying to say!!" He would shout and end the conversation by stomping into their bedroom.

My mother would look at us, shaking her head as though saying, "See what I have to deal with?" seeming like she had no power in this situation to change anything. Sometimes she would ask me to go to speak with him, and I tried to mediate, listening to each of them, sharing what the other side said, trying to resolve. Usually, it worked, but only for a little while.

If he left the dinner table, my father would leave the bedroom door open and I could go in and speak with him if I wanted to. But once, when I returned home and he walked away from the dinner table, I went to check what was going on and found his door closed. When I knocked, he called out, "Not now!" And I heard him speaking with someone on the phone.

When I was 21, the years of tension culminated in a trial separation and my mother moved out of our apartment in Beer Sheva. My father explained that it would be too hard on him to move in the middle of the academic school year, so they decided she would be the one to move into a small apartment they rented for her in another part of town.

But something else was going on as well. Something hidden in his long phone conversations alone in their bedroom. He was in love, had found his soul mate; and the importance of honesty was temporarily replaced by: "All's fair in love and war."

I remember a desire to be on his side like my mother never was so he would love me. I was also weary of his anger, so when he asked me to go and tell my mother that Rivca, his new beloved, was moving into our home, the apartment they had shared, where my younger brother still lived, I went.

My father, who was and still is so courageous in some things, did not have the courage to tell my mother himself that their trial separation was the end. He could not face her and her pain.

How I wish I had had the courage to say to him: "You coward!!! You go tell her yourself. This is yours. Face up to it!!!"

But I couldn't. Confronting my father and resolving things with him came only years later.

So, I took a bus to her apartment, knocked on the door, walked in, and sat on the ugly gray couch in the almost empty living room. Seeing my mother all alone in her small apartment, that was not our home, broke my heart. Yet I could not hug or comfort her, perhaps because a part of me blamed her for everything that happened, believing that if she had been a better wife we would not be going through this awful situation.

I explained to my mother everything that my father asked me to say and even defended his behavior. I did not want to face or feel my mother's pain, either. I just wanted to escape from that apartment as soon as I could.

I felt so alone and ashamed that the "great home environment with so much love" that I always thought and told people we had was falling apart, and I was not sure anymore what was real in my world and what was an illusion. A month later I broke up with a boyfriend I had been with for three years. I did not talk to anyone about what was going on and felt deeply confused, disillusioned and hurt.

After they separated and my father began living with Rivca, he stopped getting so angry and leaving the room. There was a deep sense of harmony and love between them that still exists today, 40 years later. My mother also found a soulmate with whom she has been for 37 years. I can see they are both much happier than they would have been together, yet sometimes I wonder if there could have been another, less hurtful, way to end their marriage.

Since then, I have had many relationships and have often reenacted within them unhealthy ways I learned at home to deal with difficult situations and conflicts.

Yet there was something my father used to say before they divorced that has helped me in some difficult relationship moments. He would hug my mother or us, smile, and say: "Tummy to tummy all problems are solved."

And while I know that not all or even most problems are resolved with a tummy-to-tummy hug, through the years I have found that the willingness to be present and stay "up close and personal" rather than running away in times of disagreements certainly helps resolve conflicts.

Chapter 10

Sisterhood

1978, Tzrifin

Sisterhood is to be together, feel together,
heal together, and rise together.
Nicolette Bostock

The circles of women around us weave invisible
nets of love that carry us when we're weak
and sing with us when we're strong.
Sark

"Get up, Nitsan, let's go to the bathroom," Lizzie whispers in my ear. "We have something that might help you."

Trying to stifle another painful cough, I open my eyes and look around the huge dark warehouse that is to be our home for three and a half weeks. Fifty beds fill the space and on top of them are young women covered with khaki military blankets, all trying to sleep for a few hours before the dawn wake-up for another day of basic training at the military base in Tzrifin. And I am keeping them awake with my coughing.

Sore throat and coughing, just what I need now in the midst of this craziness when I am so far away from home. Everything is new: sleeping in a warehouse with 49 roommates and tiny mice running under our beds; the daily cleaning of our toilets which are a five-minute walk away; the training in taking apart, polishing, putting together and shooting M16 rifles while scaring each other half to death; trying to follow orders and being punished with 2 a.m. marches around the training field if something is not straight or clean enough. And if that isn't enough, now I also have my damned cough to deal with.

"Come on," Lizzie whispers, again. "We have something that might actually help you."

Out of the 49 young women, Lizzie and Rivki are the only girls I knew beforehand. They were in my class in Mekif Gimel High School in Beer Sheva, but we hardly ever spoke until we found ourselves on the same bus to the induction center on a wintry March day, in 1978, the day we were drafted into the Israeli Defense Forces.

I follow them out into the night, hoping for a miracle.

When we finally arrive at that rundown bathroom that no amount of scrubbing seems to improve, Lizzie reaches into her coat and fishes out a lemon and a pocket knife. She cuts the lemon in half and then painstakingly squeezes the juice into a cup that Rivki seems to have produced out of nowhere. Then she sprinkles salt out of the shaker they pinched from the dining hall that evening and mixes it with her finger. Adding a bit of water from the faucet, she looks at the concoction and then shoves into my face.

"Gargle," she orders, and I do for what seems like hours. "Okay, now you can spit it out," she says, permitting me to spew that dreadful drink into the sink.

Walking back, exhausted, we lace our hands together, laughing at the awfulness of our situation. The next day my throat feels much better and I am so grateful for their support.

It is my first experience of sisterhood as a young adult.

After my cough ended, others began feeling sick and our nights were filled with coughing, toothaches and backaches from endless marching and carrying of equipment. One night Lizzie started coughing so loudly that I worried for her. She cried and told me her lungs were bursting. I took her to the first aid where two young women soldiers had no idea what to do. I fought with them so they would order an army car to take her to the hospital, where it turned out she had pneumonia.

Despite all of the above, I enjoyed basic training, especially helping others and feeling appreciated. I liked finding my own unique path in these special circumstances, wearing the uniform, getting so many letters. After recovering from my cough, I began jogging every day around the marching field with my stick, the substitute rifle for recruits. Instead of sleeping during our short breaks, I would lie on a tiny piece of grass that I discovered in the back of the building and read. Away from the comforts of home, with no men around to divert our attention, and faced with physical challenges that many of us were not used to, we discovered each other. After being so alone for years in classrooms where women competed and gossiped behind each other's backs, suddenly these young women became my allies, my sisters.

Together we complained about basic training, laughed at absurd situations, sang at night when the lights were out, supported those who could not carry their equipment during the treks, cleaned each other's eyebrows, and shared our hopes, dreams, heartaches, and even the letters we received from the one we were currently crushing on. Never before had I felt so good being with women, feeling a member of this tribe, belonging.

Towards the end of our basic training, we were asked to fill in a form with the three top choices of what we would like to do in the military. My first choice, like almost everyone's, was to be in a paratrooper unit with all the cute guys. Teaching was my last choice; and predictably enough, that's what I was assigned to. However, the disappointment around this assignment diminished when I heard that Rivki and Lizzie would be joining me.

Our teacher's course took place at a beautiful college campus amidst gardens and flowers in central Israel where we spent relatively little time studying and mostly enjoyed relaxing next to the swimming pool, flirting with young men who attended the college, and folk dancing at night which by now I had managed to learn.

After the teaching course, we each went our separate ways in the military and did not see each other again for several years. But during those few weeks I experienced how reassuring and nourishing it feels when women support one another.

Nothing we learned in basic training or the teacher's course prepared me for what was to come next: working with children and adolescents from troubled families, being the only counselor for thirty children in a summer camp, teaching disturbed young men only two or three years younger than myself, or being the house mother for troubled teens. I don't know if anything could have prepared me for all that.

Chapter 11

The Purple Hairpin

1979, Ramat Hadassah

Acceptance is simply love in practice. When you love, you accept, when you lack love, you judge.

Abhijit Naskar

"We can't stand having her in our room," shrieked Hannah and Orna when I walked into their room one evening in November 1979. "She is so dirty and our room smells awful," continued Hannah. The room did smell of urine, and all I wanted to do was to walk out and shut the door behind me.

But I couldn't. At 19, as part of my military duty, I was the house mother for these teens from troubled homes who lived and studied in the Ramat Hadassah Boarding School in Kiryat Tivon. The other staff considered my group of 12 boys and three girls ages 14 to 16 the toughest group at the boarding school. Usually, the role of young women soldier teachers was to assist the counselors, since we were too young and inexperienced for the job of house mother. But in this particular group, the house mother had quit after a month because the group was so rowdy, she couldn't take it. So, the director of the boarding school asked me to take her place for a couple of weeks until they found a replacement – which turned out to be nine months later, at the end of the school year. I struggled every day to stay afloat.

On that evening I held my breath so I would not puke and stepped into their room. The fourteen-year-old "her" in question, Leah, was sitting on her bed, head bent, looking at the floor. Once in a while she would raise her right hand to scratch her head. She did not look up at me, and it seemed as though she was not quite sure what to do with the rage directed towards her by her two roommates and was doing her best to ignore it. I wondered if this was kind of treatment she was used to receiving at home.

Without asking for permission, Hannah thrust open Leah's closet and showed me the pile of clothes and sheets that Leah had stuffed inside whenever she experienced incontinence. That evening I learned that Leah often wet her sheets at night and her pants in the middle of the day. If she was at school during that time, she would walk around with her wet underwear and pants, only changing them when she returned to her room at the end of the school day and then throwing the wet smelly clothes into her closet along with the sheets.

Before that evening, I had noticed that during group activities Leah would sit quietly in the corner as though she wanted to disappear into the wall or furniture. Her hair was probably filled with lice, which explained why she was constantly scratching the grungy brown mess on top of her head. Instead of talking when she needed something, she would whisper in a small and whiny voice that made me want send her to a different group – or country.

I felt bad for her but was also disgusted. I had never been a mother and had no idea how to handle an incontinent, lice-infested 14-year-old whom everyone in the group disliked. She reminded me of all the times I had been singled out, teased and disliked, so I did my best to avoid awareness of her presence.

But Hannah and Orna demanded that I do something immediately. They couldn't stand having her as their roommate any longer. "She needs to get cleaned up," they told me. "You can help her."

Looking at the three of them, I suddenly realized I didn't need to love or even like Leah at the moment, but simply do right by her. The next day, I consulted with the psychologist and the local nurse and we devised a plan. First, I brought the whole group to the nurse's office and checked if they had lice, which they did. Then, I lined them all next to the sinks in the large bathroom and supervised as they helped one another wash their hair with anti-lice shampoo and comb it out with a fine-tooth comb.

Next, I began accompanying Leah to the girl's bathroom and would sit outside the shower while she washed, handing her the soap, reminding her to shampoo her hair and wash really well all over as I would a small child. When she came out, I handed her a fresh towel and clean clothes. Every night I made sure there were no piles in her closet and every morning I checked her sheets and had her change them when necessary.

Very quickly something began to shift. A few days after we began this "treatment," I noticed that Leah's hair was combed and that she was wearing a purple hair pin.

"That's a pretty pin," I told her.

"Hannah gave it to me," she said, gently caressing the plastic pin with a shy smile and for the first time glancing up directly at me. I remember noticing her beautiful green eyes, surrounded by long dark lashes.

"That's great!" I said, smiling back at her.

Soon she stopped wetting her pants. Her voice became stronger while asking for something, and at times, I heard her speak angrily towards one of the other group members when they said something she did not like.

A few months later, during the spring break, I began visiting my students' homes. The military asked us to go on these visits so we would have an idea of where our adolescents came from and what they had to deal with when they lived at home.

To reach Leah's home I had to change two buses from the boarding school. Two and a half hours later I finally walked down the street, strewn with garbage and lined with old rundown houses where gray concrete peered through the peeling walls.

Leah's home was filled with dusty furniture, stuffy, smelly, dark and unwelcoming. I sat on the edge of the sofa, not wanting to touch the glass of soda on the table in front of me for fear of catching something. Her mother was the only one at home aside from Leah. She was dressed in an outfit that closely resembled pajamas, her hair speckled with gray, and I noticed a tooth missing when she smiled.

As we spoke, I glanced at Leah, who seemed proud that her "substitute mother" had come all the way to her home to visit her.

I don't remember what we spoke about, only that I couldn't get comfortable, felt on edge, and waited for the moment that I could apologize, step back out into the sunlight, and breathe fresh air. The moment finally arrived and I stood up to say goodbye.

Leah walked me to the bus stop, wearing her shiny purple hair pin and chatting about her life. As I listened to her stories about her mother, her friends, and her neighborhood, something inside me finally opened (it may have been my heart) and I realized how crushed we can be by our childhood and the healing capability that a bit of care and attention can have.

Chapter 12

Searching for Sheik Zaabalawi
1977-1980, Cairo

In Egypt today most people are concerned with getting bread to eat.
Only some of the educated understand how democracy works.
Naguib Mahfouz

The light is reached not by turning back from
the darkness but by going through it.
Leonard Roy Frank

In May of 1980, more than a year and a half after Israel signed the peace treaty with Egypt, my father, some of his students and I landed in Cairo.

Excited and nervous, not sure what to expect, I remember finding it hard to believe that we could walk through the airport without anyone attacking us, stay in a modern hotel rather than the Bedouin tents I imagined, drink delicious fresh mango juice for breakfast, smell the intoxicating scent of black coffee rising from various shops in the street, walk through the lively markets trying on a dozen perfumes while being told by the store owner that I looked like Cleopatra and my companion was most certainly Nefertiti.

Three years earlier I had sat glued to the television at a friend's house, my hands clutching the sides of the chair as I watched Anwar Saadat's plane land in Israel's airport. *Is this for real? Would he actually materialize or perhaps it's just a big scam?* I worried. When he finally appeared in the doorway of his plane, I heaved a sigh of relief. HE IS HERE, in Israel, in our lifetime! After 29 years of wars with our Arab neighbors (Syria, Lebanon, Jordan, Iraq and Egypt), years of pain, fear and suffering for both sides, on November 19, 1977, Anwar Sadat, President of Egypt, came to Israel to talk Peace.

We felt so optimistic in those days, quite sure that something was shifting, changing for the better. The predictions we had heard from adults since childhood: "When you are 18 there will finally be peace, you will not have to serve in the IDF because there will be no more wars" seemed to be coming true. I longed to believe that we had a peaceful future to look forward to.

Peace did not happen so quickly, and I still had to serve in the military. But in May 1980, during my last few months as a counselor in Ramat Hadassah, I was given leave to go to Cairo for a week with my father and a group of his Arab and Jewish Peace Project students.

With 7.4 million people in 1980, Cairo was twice the size of the entire population of Israel. Space was a big issue, especially for the poor.

I remember the huge statues, sculptures and artifacts that were amassed in the Egyptian Museum as if they had just been thrown there for safekeeping, with no consideration for order or the space that these ancient treasures required in order to be truly understood and appreciated.

Outside on the crowded streets, the endless honking seemed almost orchestrated. Because the cars did not stop for traffic lights but rather somehow wove their way between other vehicles in an endless flow of metal, glass and fumes, it was not clear where and how one might cross the street. Sometimes it seemed that the only way to get across a busy intersection was to close your eyes and run, hoping to find yourself on the other side.

The Egyptians we met were very friendly, as excited and curious to meet us as we were to meet them, after so many years of hostility. They were particularly friendly to the Israeli Jews among us, not quite sure how to relate to the Israeli Arabs, whom they often viewed with disdain for betraying their Palestinian brothers and sisters by becoming citizens of Israel while the Palestinian Arabs suffered under the occupation.

Threading its way through the city center was the Nile – the longest river in Africa, a slow-moving river sustaining much of the country and serving as a reflection of the slow pace of almost everything else in the city. When my father asked Anis Mansour, a journalist he met, why things like Buberian dialogue took so much time in Egypt, Anis gazed ruefully in the direction of the Nile and replied: "Everything here takes time; look at the Nile and how slowly it flows…"

One day we hired a small motor boat and began snailing our way along the muddy waters of this huge river. My father was at the helm, gripping the large wooden steering wheel and moving it slowly to the right, then to the left, to avoid other boats and keep us going forward. I was sitting in the middle next to Nuaf, a tall dark-haired young man who was one of the Arab facilitators. The owner of the boat was in the back.

Eventually, my father noticed how once in a while when he turned the boat right it actually moved left or just kept going straight. He wondered what was going on. Looking behind him, he realized the boat owner was using the rudder to navigate the boat and the ornate steering wheel in front was just for show, not connected to anything else.

My father turned to us, and said: "Isn't it interesting how sometimes in life our belief that we are in charge or in control is simply an illusion?"

I smiled and realized once again the beauty of searching for a deeper meaning in our experiences. Other people might have said in their hearts or out loud: "I am so stupid; how could I have thought I was the one navigating the boat?" or "Why didn't you tell me this wheel was not connected to anything?" But for him it became an experience through which he could learn something about life and share his insights with us.

The students in the Peace Project who came with us met and worked in groups at Ben-Gurion University, where my father taught. This was his attempt to educate for peace by teaching Arab and Jewish students to relate to one another dialogically as equal human beings in a society filled with prejudices. The students learned to dialogue through reading and talking about the existentialist texts of Buber, Sartre, Kierkegaard, Kafka and Dostoyevsky and seeing how these related to their lives and to what was happening in Israel.

The goal was to relate to one another not as an IT, an object to be experienced or used, but as a THOU, a being with whom we have a living relationship. Martin Buber was concerned by how often we treat the Earth, one another and God as something to be exploited for our personal benefit rather than a THOU – a being with whom the in between melts and with whom we are fully present in the Encounter, with no agenda.

"What is crucial to understand is that the word pair 'I–Thou' can refer to a relationship with a tree, the sky, or the park bench itself as much as it can refer to the relationship between two individuals" and that an "I–Thou is not a means to some object or goal, but a definitive relationship involving the whole being of each subject." [7]

---

7. https://en.wikipedia.org/wiki/I_and_Thou

At 20, I was just beginning to comprehend the meaning and depth of their Buberian dialogue attempts and was so happy to tag along for the exciting adventure of being in Egypt for the first time.

My father and his students were there to meet Israel's former enemies and try to engage in Buberian I-Thou dialogue with them so that the students would not just experience the places they visited and the people they met as something they did or did not enjoy, an experience that did or did not benefit them in some way, but rather as a heart-opening encounter without an agenda where each side could learn something meaningful.

In his book *Dance, Dialogue and Despair*, my father describes their attempts to encourage dialogue during meetings his students had with Egyptian students, therapists and social workers. In one encounter there were 40 Israelis (Arabs and Jews) and 40 Egyptian participants. They were divided into three mixed groups, presented with questions and expected to dialogue on the topics.

When talking about dialogue, they meant a kind of conversation that is about listening, learning, and the development of shared understandings. In dialogue, "participants focus on their relationship and the joint process of making sense of each other, rather than winning or losing." Buberian dialogue arises from an I-Thou relationship and "has no fixed goal or predetermined agenda. The emphasis is not on resolving disputes, but rather on improving the way in which people with significant differences relate to each other. While opponents in deep-rooted conflicts are unlikely to agree with each other's views, they can come to understand each other's perspectives." [8]

But instead of dialoguing, the Egyptian and Israeli participants in my father's groups tried to convince one another of their opinions without listening to the other side or taking in what they were saying. The encounters ended in shouting matches, each side trying to win the argument while becoming more deeply entrenched in their own opinions.

My father wrote that his attempts to create genuine I-Thou dialogue in his groups with the Egyptians failed.

Yet genuine dialogue did occur during those events, not within the meetings, but in between them, in moments of grace when people chose to be fully present with one another. For example, he writes about Gila, a Jewish woman who said after one large group meeting where dialogue was

---

8. https://www.kaieteurnewsonline.com/2013/07/27/genuine-dialogue/

attempted: "In our group Meliha, an Egyptian woman, was very vicious; she attacked many people. I am not sure, though, that she was playing games (as another Jewish participant had suggested) because her brother had been killed by the Israelis a few years earlier in the Yom Kippur War (1973). After the large group meetings, I had a rare experience with her. She saw that her attacks had upset me and came to me and asked if I see her as a Jew-hater. I answered *YES!* and burst into tears. She hugged me and invited me to visit her." [9]

Other I-Thou moments occurred after the meetings ended, when the Israeli Arabs and Jews sat with the Egyptians in small groups and chatted all night until the early morning hours, hugging one another before leaving. Away from the limelight of the group process, when there was no agenda, listening to their own intuition, the participants were able to sit together, and engage in dialogue.

At the time I was not aware all this was happening, but today I am simply amazed by my father and his team's courage to take groups to Egypt and attempt Buberian dialogue so soon after the peace treaty was signed. No one else was doing it then and very few have done it since.

There was a lot of anger and mistrust but, as he explained, there was also something else: "I ate crap from Meliha like others, I was screamed at like others, I acted mistrustfully like others, I even told Meliha that her rage was something of an act and I hate her for that – and still I know these two evenings were a great event. They were great because after thirty-two years of war, and in the face of all the sick hatred that exists in this portion of the world, forty Israelis and forty Egyptians got together and sat for hours and tried, in their distorted and unsuccessful way, to reach some sort of dialogue. It was great because despite our pain, rage and mistrust, we sat it out till the end and after the first painful evening met again for a second evening. Expressing hatred and rage peacefully, without guns or bombs, is a way of living together. And that we were able to do it, is great."

And yet the main challenge my father never figured out, hence the Despair part of his book, was how to support people in staying connected and maintaining genuine dialogue during challenging circumstances.

His approach helped participants become more authentic, connect with one another and question some of their beliefs. But it did not help them in handling the anger, disillusionment and grief that came up for the

---

9. Dance, Dialogue and Despair.

participants in 1982 during the First Lebanon War. They did not know how to share their feelings authentically and still stay connected to one another. The safe space they had painstakingly created fell apart.

At the time, I too was not aware of the role our emotions played in thwarting or enabling dialogue. But a clue about where healing and transformation that enable genuine dialogue must begin, came to me on that trip to Cairo.

One evening towards sunset we entered the *Cleopatra Cafe* nestled on the banks of the Nile River. About twenty small round glass-covered coffee tables surrounded by wooden chairs were spread throughout the large open space. The evening sun was inching its way towards the horizon, so there was no longer need for the sunshades that stood next to each table. We glanced around and then followed my father as he walked towards a table where a slight, dark-skinned, almost bald man, about seventy years old, with glasses, was sitting and writing in his notebook. As we approached, we saw a waiter refilling a small glass of tea and replacing it carefully on a round plate next to the open notebook.

As soon as he saw us, the man rose and said: "Marhaba. Welcome!" with a wide smile, and extended his hand to my father. It was Naguib Mahfouz the famous Egyptian author, whom my father had been longing to meet since he had read several of his books and taught them to his students in the Peace Project.

Before we arrived, my father had told me: "When Mahfouz wrote in 1975, in his weekly article in Al Ahram, that the Arabs must seek peaceful ways to live with Israel, his books were banned in many Arab countries. But that greatly increased their sales in Egypt and Lebanon. Arabs learned to smuggle along with the hashish that passes from country to country, a few volumes of Mahfouz."

"So, you are here every evening?" My father began.

"Yes," Mahfouz replied, "I like to write in the evenings and this is one of my favorite spots to write in."

Fascinated, I looked at this slight man (who, eight years later, would receive the Nobel Prize for Literature), and thought about one of his stories that I had recently read: Zabalawe. The story is told by a narrator whose name we never know and who is very sick with an unexplained illness. He is searching for Sheikh Zaabalawi, a mystical and renowned healer, whom he hopes can heal him. Again and again throughout the story he nearly finds the Sheikh, only to miss him by a moment or two. Once, he arrives in a bar, hoping to talk to a man who might give him a clue about the whereabouts of Zaabalawi. The man in the bar is drunk and willing to speak with the narrator only if he drinks with him. After a few glasses of wine, the narrator falls into a drunken stupor and has a beautiful nourishing dream. When he awakens his hair and face are wet. The man he was sitting next to tells him that Sheikh Zaabalawi was there just a moment ago, sitting at his table and attempting to rouse him by pouring water on his head. The narrator jumps up and sends people to find the Sheik but it is useless. The story ends, but the search does not.

Who is this Sheikh Zaabalawi and where is he? How did he heal people and why was the narrator unable to find him? I was too embarrassed to ask Naguib Mahfouz these questions, but a clue came a day later when we visited the City of the Dead.

Years earlier, when Cairo was not so crowded, the rich, who felt the dead should be connected to the living, built small dwellings above the graves of their loved ones so they could stay for a few days when they came to mourn them. When Cairo became too crowded, the poor who arrived from the countryside searching for a livelihood took residence in those dwellings above the tombs. In 1980 there were about 100,000 people residing there amidst the stench of sewage and uncollected garbage.

It was not the usual place for tourists to visit, but the Education for Peace team decided we should go there to better understand the challenges faced by the poorest people of Cairo.

On a clear warm morning, the cab drove us from our hotel through dusty unpaved roads into the City of the Dead. As we entered the graveyard dwellings I remember wondering if they ever received mail in this part of the city and if they did what would the sender write on the envelope? Hell St. # 8, City of the Dead? Also, what would the people living there answer to the question of *where do you live?*

Yet as soon as we arrived and stepped out of the cab I forgot about my privileged musings. I realized that for the people living in this place, the name is irrelevant. For them, being able to dwell in the City of the Dead and work in Cairo simply meant survival.

As I walked with the other students on the dusty yellowish roads, smiling, communicating with my hands, sometimes holding my breath to avoid the stench, I saw people with ragged dusty clothes, standing outside their homes, staring at us, some smiling, others inviting us in and all of them very much alive.

Nuaf stopped in front of a young woman who seemed in her early twenties. Her dress was brownish orange with dark stains in several places. Her eyes were bright and when she smiled, I noticed her teeth were brownish.

"Where do you live" he asked her in Arabic.

She pointed to a dwelling situated above one of the tombs and invited us in.

"Do you have water in your home?" he wondered.

She shook her head and pointed to a tap at the end of the street.

Nuaf decided to take her up on her invitation and walked into the tiny dwelling where she lived with her husband, who was working in the city, and her two young children, who peered at us with curiosity from behind her back.

I followed.

In the small dark one-room space, there were mats on the floor and not much else except for a stairway leading down to the tomb. The only way out was the entrance and the air was stuffy. I was afraid to take a deep breath, worried that I might smell a rotting body. My heart began beating quickly and my breathing accelerated. *I have to get out of here* I thought, remembering the bomb shelter of my childhood. Walking hastily back into the sunlight, I took a deep breath and tried to think of something pleasant – a green forest, a stream, a meadow with flowers. I did not want to imagine what it must be like to live there every day.

When Nuaf emerged, we continued walking along the dusty road waving at the children who peeked out. Then, I noticed a sign on one of the grave dwellings and asked Nuaf what it meant.

"It says: Here is buried Sheikh Zaabalawi" he told me.

"Really?" I asked finding it hard to believe.

He nodded and smiled, perhaps also remembering yesterday's meeting with Naguib Mahfouz.

I did not know what to say. That the powerful healer, the sought-after Sheikh, would be right here in the middle of the City of the Dead? Amidst poverty, dust, dirt and all the people who live on top of the graves? What did it all mean?

Unfortunately, Sheikh Zaabalawi, fictional or not, was dead and could not answer my questions or help with our physical, emotional or spiritual healing.

A half an hour later, as we retraced our steps through the dusty yellow street, climbed into the cab and left the City of the Dead behind. Driving through the crowded streets of Cairo and back to our hotel, I found myself thinking about the search for healing.

Is it possible that our healing is found inside those dark corners of our being, our very own cities of the dead, that we fear most to even enter?

We are being challenged by world events, by the tides of history, to develop a more mature consciousness. Yet we cannot do it without facing what hurts. Life is not a piece of tragic fiction, in which at the end of the reading we all get up and go out for drinks. All of us are actors in a great unfolding drama, and until we dig deep, there will be no great performances. How each of us carries our role will affect the end of the play.

Marianne Williamson,
The Gift of Change

Part 2

Creating: Together Beyond Words

Perhaps this story will encourage you to look at that in your life which has thus far remained so deeply buried that it seems beyond words and beyond healing. As you look inward at whatever that may be for you, may the Beyond Words way bring you comfort and hope.

Chapter 13

Ladies and Jelly Beans

1984, Baltimore

In many shamanic societies, if you came to a medicine
person complaining of being disheartened, dispirited, or
depressed, they would ask one of four questions: "When did
you stop dancing? When did you stop singing? When did
you stop being enchanted by stories? When did you stop
being comforted by the sweet territory of silence?

Gabriel Roth

The hot and humid air accosts me as I step out of BWI Airport in late July of 1984 with my father and Rivca, who have flown to Baltimore from Alabama in order to help me during my first days here. I am exhausted. The flight from Tel Aviv to NYC was long and the connecting flight on the tiny plane harrowing, especially when smoke floated out of a hole on the floor of the plane. I am relieved to have both my feet on the ground, concrete, whatever.

I have just finished my BA in Psychology and English Lit a month ago and am ready to begin a Masters in Dance/Movement Therapy at Goucher College. Looking through the car window, I see GREEN in the middle of summer instead of the browns and yellows I have become used to during my last nine Israeli summers.

When we drive into Goucher College the following morning, I stare through the car window at the green fields and the tall trees whose names I don't know but which I am already imagining myself sitting under or hugging. Stepping out of the car, the heat confronts us again. Thank goodness for the air-conditioning in every car and building that make it possible to stay mostly inside in the middle of the day and enjoy being surrounded by shades of green beauty and storybook stone buildings.

The fact that Goucher is an all girls' school does not bother me. I am actually looking forward to the relaxed atmosphere where I will be less engaged in flirting or worrying about how I look and have more time to focus on my studies.

Although I danced for several years and loved it, I did not have the commitment and talent to become a professional dancer. Luckily, a few years earlier I heard from a friend about a profession called Dance Therapy for which one needed a background in dance and psychology and immediately knew: "This is for me!"

Goucher College was the place where women who had studied with Marian Chase, the grandmother of Dance Therapy, taught, and I wanted to be close to the source. Going there enabled me to study with some of the pioneers in the field, amazing women like Sharon Chaiklin, Arlynne Stark, and Judith Fischer.

In those early months in Baltimore, with no driver's license or car or the funds to purchase a car, I became very familiar with buses. I moved around, sleeping in the living room of a Dance Therapy Program graduate, then in the huge empty home of a Jewish family who were on vacation, and finally in the large basement of a cute brownstone on a quiet street, occupied by a single mother and her two young girls. Linda, the mother, had converted to Judaism when she married her ex and happily celebrated both Christian and Jewish holidays with her daughters, Amy and Jenny. I paid rent by cleaning the house and caring for the girls a few times a week.

On the first day of school, I walked into the large, high-ceilinged room on the second floor and was drawn to the view from the tall windows overlooking the tree tops that were still wearing their glorious summer greens. Half the floor of the room was covered with a shaggy turquoise carpet where we danced, and the other half was a linoleum floor where tables and desks were placed during our theoretical classes.

On that morning, eight young women and a teacher sat around a large oval table. Later I learned their names and a bit about them: Debbie, a blonde, blue-eyed girl with a twinkle in her eye; her best friend Kathleen, a redheaded Irish folk dancer and the second daughter in a family of ten; Joan, the beautiful Jewish woman with dark, curly hair who was easily moved to tears; Terry, a powerful ally with a wild sense of humor; Dorothy, a professional dancer, part-German and a perfectionist; Barbara, a funny, deep, kind-hearted woman from Switzerland; Danette, a Native American who seemed like an old soul; and Holly, a Canadian with blue eyes and curly blonde hair who later became my best friend. That first day, feeling self-conscious, I walked in and sat down, looking curiously at the bright eyes of the other young women who would be my colleagues and mates in this journey.

Two months after school began, I wrote to my mother:

I love school!! We have amazing teachers. One of them, Claire Schmais, lives in a log cabin on a mountain in Virginia with no running water or electricity and comes down the mountain once a month to teach us about the language of movement for two full days. We are learning that you can actually help people alter the way they feel by getting them to shift something in their movements. It works and it's beautiful!!

Movement is so basic. It was there long before speech. Babies move and make sounds and expressions before they learn to talk. Later when we grow up and talk to one another we can hide our thoughts and feelings when we speak, but our body usually does not lie about what is going on inside us. Someone may say: "I am not angry," but if you observe them closely you can see tightness in their chest or they might tap their feet ceaselessly. These nonverbal behaviors provide a clue into what is actually going on with them. I am so excited to see that our movements are a much more direct route to our feelings and thoughts than our words!

For work, I am teaching Hebrew in an Ulpan and working in a Chicago Pizza place as a waitress. I also finally have a learner's permit so anyone can teach me how to drive and I hope to have a license in a month.

As part of my training, I am working at the Children's Guild with young children who have emotional issues and am deeply moved by them and by the quality of care they are receiving.

Ima, I am happy you are feeling more confident at work. I remember all your fears from last year. You have come such a long way!!

I miss you and my brothers so much…

Love, Nitsan

In professional terms, I was trying to explain to my mother that Dance/Movement Therapy is based on the principle that a vital connection exists between personality and the way in which one moves, and that changes in movement affect a person's emotional, intellectual, and physical health [10].

One of the most fascinating things I learned during that first year was the concept of "Kinesthetic Empathy" and how it is applied in Dance Therapy. Kinesthetic empathy is part of a sensitivity to the body that dance movement therapists acquire in their training, giving them sophisticated tools to gather and analyze information in order to help people[11]. We were taught to observe the posture, movements, affect, facial expression, and energy level of a person we were working with in order to get a sense of where they are emotionally and physically.

We also learned that the healing process begins when we meet people where they are. Instead of trying to get someone out of the pit they have fallen into, we need to climb down into the pit ourselves so we can get a sense of what it's like for them. We are not asked to fully immerse ourselves in their pain because if we do, we might also be sucked into the bog. But we can metaphorically dip a foot or an arm in that emotional marshland so we have a sense of what it's like for them.

A beautiful thing happens when people feel that we are really there with them, without judgment, without asking them to be different, when they feel "seen" and acknowledged, when they sense our compassion. In that moment they might begin to open up and move a step beyond where they have been confined. Perhaps they might begin sharing what it's like for them in their dark pit, what hurts.

One of our teachers told us a story:

"There was a patient on a psychiatric unit who for years would spend all his waking hours in the day room walking back and forth from one wall to the other. He never communicated with anyone, and when someone spoke to him or tried to make contact he would not respond, but kept walking back and forth.

One day a dance therapist started working on the unit and they asked her if she could do something to help this patient. She decided to try and for a half an hour every day, she would walk with him back and forth, mirroring his body posture as he walked, his pace, the way he held his chest, arms, hands and head.

For a while nothing happened, they would just walk next to each other from wall to wall. After a few days, it became easier for the therapist and

10. https://www.ajol.info/index.php/ejotmas/article/view/163549

11. Akapo, Samson S. "An Overview of Somatics (Body-Mind) Approaches in Dance Therapy." EJOT-MAS: Ekpoma Journal of Theatre and Media Arts 6, no. 1-2 (2017).

she began feeling a sense of connection, a harmony between them. As this feeling grew, she took a risk one day while walking alongside him. She opened her hand and moved it a bit closer to his. For a while nothing happened and they just kept walking. She was not sure he sensed her hand there, open and angled towards his. It was an invitation born out of the trust she felt had wordlessly grown between them.

After a few more trips back and forth she began feeling a warm sensation and soon his hand touched hers. At first it was only a fleeting touch, but then she moved her hand closer and he did not pull back. At some point their hands intertwined and they continued walking back and forth holding hands.

Following that session, step by tiny step their communication grew. First to a word or two then a sentence. It was very slow, but because she met him where he was at, because she stayed the course, a sense of trust formed between them and he began to heal."

Meeting people where they are at and then helping them shift to where you and they would like to go – what a powerful tool, I thought. Yet this ability to create change by genuinely "seeing" people has been known for hundreds of years.

In his story the *Rooster Prince*, Rabbi Nachman of Breslov (1772-1810) writes about a prince who goes insane and believes he is a rooster. He takes off his clothes, sits naked under the table, and pecks at his food on the floor. The king and queen are horrified that the heir to the throne is acting this way. They call in various sages and healers to try and convince the prince to act human again, but to no avail. Then a wise man comes to the palace and claims he can cure the prince. He takes off his clothes and sits naked under the table with him, claiming to be a rooster too. Gradually the prince comes to accept him as a friend. The wise man then tells the prince that a rooster can also wear clothes, eat at the table, etc. The Rooster Prince accepts this idea and, step by step, begins to act normally, until he is completely cured.

The main interpretation of this story is that the prince represents a simple Jew who has forgotten his true self, and the wise man represents a Hasidic Rabbi who has the cure for his soul. Rather than condemn the simple Jew for being non-religious, the Rabbi "descends" to his level to meet him where he is, then shows him how to return to God, step by step, and in a manner that he can accept [12].

In professional terms, what occurred can be described in the following way:

1. The client experiences an embodied emotion.
2. The therapist experiences feelings that are similar but are not an exact replica.
3. The therapist offers a modified embodied and possibly vocal expression of the client's emotional state, which has a regulatory function for the client.
4. The client perceives this; if the therapist is attuned, the client experiences the therapist's expression as congruent with her or his initial feeling state.
5. The client feels 'connected' to the therapist and experiences an enhanced sense of self.

The neuroscientists Gallese et al. (2007) have described this process as an intersubjective model of psychotherapeutic change, with reference to the mirror neuron system. They prefer the term 'intentional attunement' to 'mirroring'[13].

The discovery of 'mirror neurons' by Gallese (2001), offered a neurophysiological basis for the bodily manifestations of empathy, in addition to lending credence to the intuitive use of the Chace (Chaiklin and Schmais 1993) and the Authentic Movement (Adler 1999) approaches in Dance Movement Therapy (DMT) [14].

Being **grounded**, centered and connected to one's body and personal reality in order to be in physical and emotional balance also became part of our studies. In dance therapy and in life, if we want to be present and able to do our best, we need to be grounded. There are many ways to become grounded.

In the Torah, when God speaks to Moses from the burning bush, one of the first things he asks him to do is "take off thy shoes from thy feet, for

---

12. https://en.wikipedia.org/wiki/The_Rooster_Prince

13. https://www.researchgate.net/publication/290857729_Kinesthetic_empathy_and_movement_meta-phor_in_dance_movement_psychotherapy

14. https://www.researchgate.net/publication/233599691_Kinesthetic_ability_and_the_development_of_empathy_in_Dance_Movement_Therapy

the place where you stand is holy ground" (Exodus 3:5). God is about to tell Moses that he wants him to take the Hebrew people out of Egypt. That means to convince somewhere between 60,000 to 600,000 Hebrews who have been slaves for centuries to go to the desert, then travel to the land of their forefathers and to convince the Pharaoh to let them go. That is a huge ask, and in order for Moses to be fully present in the moment when this difficult mission is revealed, connected to himself, to God, to all that was and is going to be, he is first being asked to establish his connection with the ground, the earth, to get grounded by taking his shoes off.

Grounding can be described both conceptually, as one's ability to perceive and to live in 'the here and now,' and physically, as one's contact with the ground (Meekums, 2002). To focus on the present means to pay attention to our body through the senses and through our breathing. Psychologically, grounding can be understood as "a person who is present with him/herself, at home in his/her own body/mind" (Hackney, 2002, p. 236), and who has an active relationship with the earth. It describes the relationship that an individual has with the ground as a foundation or support to become rooted and balanced (Panhofer, 2006).

Some of the things we learned to do in order to feel more grounded were walking barefoot over different surfaces, self-massaging our feet, performing ballet pliés, making contact with another person through the palms of the hands or the soles of the feet, jumping and skipping, all the while paying attention to our feet, legs and weight as well as breathing through "guided visualization" just as Meekums described in her 2002 book *Dance Movement Therapy*.

We also learned that rhythm "grounds or anchors us because experiencing rhythm builds up orientation in the here and now" (Bräuninger, 2014, p. 143). In particular, traditional African rhythms, together with simple and repetitive movements, can be understood as a form of dance therapy. Voice, drums, and barefoot dancing foster rhythmic grounding, which creates a sense of support (Margariti et al., 2012). Drums and percussion remind us of a heartbeat and have either a calming or an exciting effect (Schott-Billmann, 2000). Rhythm also creates synchrony, harmony and cohesion (Stanton-Jones, 1992) and reinforces preventive and reparative capacities and traditional coping mechanisms (Harris, 2007a). Singing along while moving adds strength to the movements, helps to create pauses and to breathe, and gives more unity to the whole group (Margariti et al., 2012). Singing, making sounds, or making percussion with any part of the body, stimulates the production of oxytocin (a hormone also known as the anti-stress hormone), which produces security and confidence (Romero, 2013) [15].

Although I was not familiar with the term "being grounded", soon realized I had learned ways to ground myself long before I joined the dance therapy program. For example, during that first year of school, I was friendly with all the women in my class; we spent a great deal of time together, and while I loved our connection, sisterhood, conversations and laughter, at times I lost myself, my own thoughts and feelings, in the big "us". I became ungrounded. In those moments I would escape and sit on the grass near one of the huge trees growing throughout the campus. There I would write, reconnect to me and become grounded again.

My best friend during those years was Holly. We spoke every day, danced together, ate Friday night dinners complete with candle lighting, blessing the challah I had made and then watching the series Dallas in Linda's family room. I celebrated Christmas of 1985 with Holly and her family in Ottawa. We planned a concert together with all our friends to raise money for the hungry in Ethiopia, and we waitressed at several catering events to pay for our living costs. Sometimes I envied her authenticity, openness, courage, and the way she easily connected with others and knew how to explain things so well. But mostly I sensed with Holly, that I had finally found a Kindred Spirit.

When I shared something painful with her and she said, "Oh honey…" with so much compassion, I felt that I was not alone, that someone was in my pit with me.

"Oh, if only I had the kind of sunglasses that Joan has, then I would truly be happy…" I said to her ruefully one Tuesday afternoon as we sat side by side, bathing in the autumn sun, our backs supported by a stone wall situated between the grassy fields and the spacious balcony of the Goucher cafeteria.

"I would absolutely need Danette's sweatshirt to feel truly happy…" Holly replied with a smile.

Then we both said simultaneously: "Why can't we just be happy now, in this very moment?" We laughed and realized that although it was a long shot, still, perhaps it was an actual possibility, to be joyful, happy, silly, right here, right now, because of and in spite of everything.

15. Grounding: Theoretical application and practice in dance movement therapy Patricia de Tord, MA (Dance Movement Therapy), BA (Communication Science), Iris Bräuninger, PhD, MA, BTD, ADMTE.

That was the moment when *Silly Tuesday* was born. We committed that every Tuesday we would be silly as often as possible, and we enjoyed keeping our word throughout school and way beyond.

The Ethiopia Benefit Concert we planned for weeks never materialized because the well-known band we had invited, who agreed to play free of charge, pulled out at the last minute. Although we canceled the concert, I was worried that some people might not have heard of the cancellation and would arrive to a locked auditorium. So, on the evening the concert was supposed to take place, I drove to Goucher in my ten-year-old Toyota Corolla, aptly named Freedom, that a friend had given me after I learned to drive. Once there, I sat on the edge of the sidewalk and waited for people to show up so I could let them know. I was feeling disappointed and sad that we had not been able to pull it off, that I had not done enough. Then I heard the engine of a car and looked up. It was "Jake," Holly's light blue Volkswagen, driving up. She parked the car, stepped out and came to sit next to me.

"What are you doing here?" I asked.

"Oh, honey... I didn't want you to have to face these people alone," she said.

I was so used to my aloneness in painful moments that it did not even occur to me to reach out and ask for support. But she came anyway, so I leaned my head on her shoulder and cried and Holly just held my hand. When I was done crying, she taught me the speech of the nervous announcer:

> *Ladies and jelly beans, cowboys and itchy bums*
> *And members of the contra banding mission*
> *I stand before you to stand behind you*
> *To tell you something I know nothing about*
> *This Monday which is Good Friday*
> *There'll be a Lady's bridge club meeting*
> *Men only.*
> *Admission free, pay at the door*
> *Bring your seats and sit on the floor.*
> *That's all, thank you.*

I smiled and she said: "Oh, honey... it's *Silly Tuesday*."

I had completely forgotten.

Holly, who remained my friend even though we lived half a world apart, died from cancer in 2014, almost thirty years after we first met. Four months before her death, I took a train from San Francisco to visit her in Berkeley after spending a week and a half with a group at the Esalen Institute in Big Sur. Steve, her husband, picked me up and drove me to their home.

When I arrived, she said; "Hi, honey..." and seemed so happy to see me, so welcoming, like the Holly I remembered, yet so thin and frail. The fireplace was roaring in her living room, and we sat on the couch and talked. She was uneasy, often in pain, and kept moving in her seat, searching for comfort. Finally, she asked me to spread a blanket by the fireplace. When I did, she laid down with her head on a pillow. I sat next to her gently stroking her hair, back and arms. She was crying when she told me that friends hardly ever touch her because they are afraid to hurt her and how she misses being touched and stroked gently.

I laid down curling my body around hers and stroking her hair softly for a long time by the fire while she cried and shared her thoughts and fears. Tears were rolling down my cheeks and I felt so blessed to be given entry to such a vulnerable place with a woman I love so much.

When we said goodbye, I knew and didn't want to know this would be the last time I would be hugging her ever so gently and feeling her breath on that soft place where the neck meets the shoulder.

I love you, Holly, I thought again and again as I made my way on the train back to San Francisco. At one point the train stopped and we were asked to step outside into the dark night and wait for another train. I had no idea where we were and how long this would take, but somehow it did not matter; I was still enveloped in those moments of grace, on the blanket by the fire, holding Holly in my arms.

The last time we spoke was on May 6th of 2014, her birthday, and her voice was weak. She told me she did not know how much longer she had to live. Then she added: "For sure we will meet again someday, honey..." as if trying to console me.

Choked and with no idea what else to say on the phone, so far away with no ability to touch or look at her, I finally suggested, "Let's sing together," and began singing softly one of the songs she taught me when we first met. Soon I heard her singing along weakly.

Today while the blossoms still cling to the vine,
I'll taste your strawberries, I'll drink your sweet wine.
A million tomorrows shall all pass away,
'Ere I forget all the joy that is mine, today [16].

Then, taking a deep breath and hoping she might smile, I began reciting that famous speech: "Ladies and Jelly Beans..."

---

16. John Denver.

Chapter 14

Dance Therapy with Vietnam Veterans
1985-1988, Baltimore

All the sounds of long ago will be forever in my head mingled
with the wounded cries and the silence of the dead...
Charlie Daniels Band

"Psychoanalysis is a guided tour through your own hell," my academic supervisor at the VA hospital, Dr Stephan Warres (Steve), told me during our first supervision meeting in his office. I looked into his brown eyes, saw a smile flicker on his lips and wondered what he meant.

It was my second year of school and I had made a special request to work with war veterans because I thought that would be my focus when I returned to Israel. Arlynne Stark, the head of our program, assigned me to train on the psychiatric unit of the Loch Raven VA Medical Center in Baltimore. There had never been a dance therapist on the unit or in the whole hospital, but Steve, the head of the unit, volunteered to supervise me.

Seeing my surprise, he added: "A journey through your own hell **can** be a cathartic experience. I know because I've been doing it for the past ten years."

He now smiled fully, stroking his short beard which, I soon learned, meant he had a story to tell. His smile was infectious so I smiled back, deciding right then and there that I had no desire for a guided tour through my own hell. Maybe at some point I might be persuaded to go on a short visit of a minute or two, but that would be more than enough.

But I was interested in his stories, his feedback and how he came to have only a leg and a half. I watched him hop around the psychiatric ward on his crutches or limp on his prosthetic leg and wondered what had happened to him. *Was he a war veteran?*

When I finally dared to ask, he told me: "My mother had taken the drug thalidomide for morning sickness when she was pregnant so this is how I was born." I did not know what to say. After a while I stopped noticing it and was just thankful to have him as a supervisor.

Because he was interested in Zen Buddhism and an avid storyteller, I loved going to our supervision sessions and never knew what to expect.

"What can I do with patients who are very resistant?" I once asked him.

"Ohhh that is a good question. Mmm... let's see... Let me tell you about Josh," he said, his brown eyes sparkling, "Josh was in his teens when he became a client in my private practice. He did not want to be there and just sat facing me, eyes half closed, remaining silent throughout the session no matter what I asked or suggested, not one word came out of his mouth. I became frustrated and shared my frustration with his parents but they insisted I continue trying.

So, in the following session I sat facing him, once again dreading those 50 minutes that stretched like hours. Making an attempt to converse, I asked Josh a question thinking that maybe today he will finally respond, but no such luck. I started growing tired, it was after lunch and I looked longingly at the blue couch in my office, wishing I could just lay down for a moment to rest. Then with a stroke of insight or foolishness, I decided to just do it and see what would happen. Nothing else had worked, maybe this would. I looked over at Josh and said: "Listen, I am really tired today so I am going to lay down on the couch and take a nap. Would you mind waking me up when our session is over?"

Steve smiled. "Josh did not respond but looked surprised. So, I rose and walked over to the couch and lay down. A few minutes later he began to talk... I never did get my nap."

I joined his smile, wondering what exactly he was trying to tell me.

I met Steve every week after leading two dance therapy sessions with patients who were an odd mixture of drug addicts, alcoholics, AIDS patients, people struggling with mental illness, and Vietnam veterans suffering from Post-Traumatic Stress. One of the patients described it well when he wrote:

> *There's a squirrel outside my window*
> *Looking for nuts*
> *But he won't find any here*
> *Just people with fear, frustration and anxiety in their guts...*

About twenty patients and ten staff members, sitting squeezed along the walls of a rectangular room, were present at the first ward meeting I attended. The idea was for all of us to get to know one another a bit on a unit where the maximum stay was four weeks, and to talk about issues that arose for the patients and anything else they wished to share.

Sitting across from me was one of the new arrivals, Greg, a young man in his twenties who looked like he was 15 despite his scraggly beard and moustache. He had a small belly and a sweet, endearing smile. His diagnosis was unclear. He was not schizophrenic since he did not suffer from hallucinations, yet he had one clear unbreakable delusion. Greg believed that the rock songs being played on the radio were written about him. During that ward meeting people tried to dissuade him, saying: "Maybe you just identify with the themes..." or "Why about you?" But he remained adamant.

Finally, Steve asked him: "Greg, what about the song *You're so vain you probably think this song is about you* [17] – is that about you?"

"No Dr Warres – that song was written before my time," Greg responded without missing a beat.

"Well then, what would you say," retorted Steve, "if I told you that all the rock songs were written about me?"

"I would say you must be suffering from a delusion, since you know and I know that all those songs were written about me!" Greg replied.

A few minutes later as we got up to leave the room Greg patted Steve on his back and they both laughed. I looked from one to the other not sure what to think, still wondering who **were** all those rock songs written about?

A few days later I "sat in the fire," leading my first Dance/Movement Therapy session with the veterans. "Before it began, I shook with fear, not knowing what to expect," I wrote in a letter to my mother. "What will they be willing to do? Will they make fun of me or ask questions that will leave me speechless? OMG, what have I gotten myself into? They are all men... what will I do if sexual issues arise? I am so scared of being rejected, of feeling like a failure..."

The meeting took place in the dining room, which was another elongated room with small tables that we placed on top of each other by one of the walls. We created a circle with the chairs and sat down for

---

17. Carly Simon.

introductions. One by one all seven men shared their names, why they were in the unit and something else about themselves. I told them about being an Israeli and about dance movement therapy. Then I put on some music I thought they might like and invited them to each lead a movement that the rest of us could follow to warm up and stretch our arms and legs.

Some of them seemed uncomfortable as though they were saying to themselves, "It's bad enough I have to be in the hospital, but now I'm expected to dance to music with a bunch of guys?!"

A few moments after we began moving, one big man with light hair and blue eyes looked directly at me and said, "This is the biggest piece of crap I've ever seen!"

By the time I recovered enough to respond, he had walked out the door. Luckily, the others remained, perhaps because they were curious to see what the strange woman from Israel would do next. When I told my friend about the incident, he said: "Maybe they just liked looking at you, men don't often walk away from a beautiful woman however strange she or what she is doing maybe..."

Thank God for that blessing. In Hebrew there is a saying: *Mitoch shelo lishmah ba lishmah* which means that at times we begin doing something with an ulterior motive, but once we get into it, we discover its worth. And that is what happened with my group. It soon became one of the most popular on the unit because, as many participants said, "It makes me feel better."

I was especially drawn to working with Vietnam veterans, possibly because of my own experience of war and trauma. These veterans accepted me because I was a Sergeant in the Israeli Defense Force, someone who in their minds had also seen combat and would therefore be able to understand what they were going through.

Fortunately, they had no idea that the only time I held a rifle in my hands (aside from when I learned to take it apart, put it together and clean it) was in basic training in a green field during target practice where we all freaked out from the loud noise and the fear that one of the other girls would accidentally shoot us. I never told them my secret and they invited me to attend their private support group.

When I shared this new development with Steve, he smiled while gently pulling his short dark beard. He told me how fortunate and unusual it was that I was invited to attend these meetings. Usually, he said, Vietnam veterans would not let anyone who had not been to Vietnam into their support group because they felt that someone who had not experienced Vietnam could not possibly understand their pain. It struck me how similar people in my country were at times – unwilling to listen to anyone who did not live in Israel.

Steve also told me about his own experience regarding Vietnam: "I spent a year in the Philippines as part of the Peace Corps after completing medical school. On my way back, I had a choice to fly home with a stopover in Saigon or Tokyo. I chose Tokyo, but had I chosen Saigon I could have said to the veterans, 'Yes I was in Vietnam in 1968,' and I would have been accepted, even though my feet would have touched the concrete at the airport for only one hour."

Months later, in a meeting I led with seven veterans, I put on music and asked one of them to lead a warmup movement while we followed. As we began moving, I noticed there was no energy and no investment on their side. It was as if they were doing me a personal favor with each movement and with every stretch. They seemed bored but not relaxed. I noticed tension in the way they held their upper body and moved their feet. Finally, I grew tired of this exchange and voiced my frustration, sharing what I saw happening in the group and how it made me feel.

"Maybe one of you is interested in taking over and leading the group?" I suggested. There was an awkward silence, it seemed they too had noticed how stuck we were. We sat in silence and for a change I did not try to say or do anything aside from breathing and waiting to see what would happen next. After a while one of them spoke up and began leading a movement. The rest of us followed. Nonverbally, through movements and actions, the energy in the group gradually shifted from tense passivity to a more active feeling of involvement. The tension was no longer hidden behind their yawns but came out in playful and competitive movements: pushing against each other, trying to reach higher than the person sitting next to them.

The movements were no longer forced and lethargic, they had intention and direction – they meant something. This powerful change was felt rather than talked about. At the end of the meeting, one of the Vietnam veterans who had joined the group so angry about having to participate looked relieved; his breathing was deeper and some of the holding was gone from his chest. He looked at me and said, "Thank you for asking us to lead the group. I feel better now."

A few weeks later Steve joined me in one of my Dance/Movement

Therapy meetings. Afterwards he wrote in a letter to my teachers at Goucher: "Vietnam vets frequently carry out a search and destroy mission against the very staff that are presumably trying to assist them... Words are bullets in this battle and serve to distance and alienate more often than to provide contact... What is needed is a surprise strategy, one that uses new terrain to bypass entrenched defenses. We have found movement therapy to be a modality that provides unexpected access to hitherto unreachable patients... The tense and enraged Vietnam veteran may be instructed to engage in a sequence of movements. He may first feel his tension grow. Then he may vigorously (aggressively) shake a stretch band or a parachute. Finally, he may let go of the tension. At no point need the tension be named — yet at the end, the veteran may feel able to experience and discuss feelings hitherto resisted. Often a deep feeling of relief and gratitude follows." [18]

After listening to the stories of the Vietnam Veterans in the support group, I began researching what had happened during the Vietnam War and was horrified. In an article I wrote in 1986 about my work, I quoted Karnow who said: "Two and a half million Americans participated in the never fully declared Vietnam war. Fifty-eight thousand came home in coffins, 150,000 returned on stretchers; half a million Americans came back with emotional problems, and the rest, while not clearly scarred by the war itself, were deeply hurt by its unpopularity back home... While in other wars soldiers gauged their progress by conquering territory, in Vietnam soldiers captured and recaptured the same territory and the only measure of success was the body count, the pile of enemies slaughtered." [19]

Arthur Egendorf (1985), himself a Vietnam veteran, described the war in a way that broke my heart:

Many of us experienced horror over the war in Vietnam when we concluded that no political or ideological rationale could justify violence on that scale. The horror grew for those of us who acknowledged our personal complicity in the wrongs. The pain was most intense for those who saw that we had gone to war out of personal blindness — that we gave ourselves to violence to retaliate against past hurts, and that we craved glory to dispel doubts about

18. Warres, Stephan, Movement Therapy for Vietnam Veterans (1986) Unpublished writings.
19. Karnow,1983, Vietnam: A History p.27.

our self-worth.

Creating ways to understand our personal role in the horror reduces its pain. Understanding alone though is insufficient to relieve suffering. The core of the worst horror in war or elsewhere — is the stark confrontation with nothingness, with the utter absence of anything to stand on or provide security for us or for the world we call home. The most thorough kind of healing emerges when we embrace the pain of facing nothingness. Ultimately what we confront at that point is ourselves and how limitlessly and unendingly we are able to care... [20]

When I shared what I was learning with Steve, he told me another story: "While in the Philippines, I met and married a native Filipino woman and brought her back with me to the United States. One day, several years later, we decided to visit the Vietnam Memorial in Washington, D.C. I walked slowly, holding her hand, supported by my crutches, looking at the endless columns of names. Suddenly, a Vietnam veteran in his uniform, saw me with my crutches and Asian wife. He walked up, enveloped me in a hug and started crying on my shoulders: 'Oh God brother,' he cried, 'It is so hard...!!! We've been through so much fucking shit...'

Stunned, I just held him without saying a word."

I looked at Steve, who sat with his half leg resting on a bench, and thought about my own fears and traumas and how sometimes I wish I could trust enough to lay my head on another human being's shoulder and cry about the fucking shit we've all been through.

In the complexity of this world, where often things are not as they appear and there is so much pain inside and around us, I also began realizing that sitting in the fire, where people share and listen to one another's painful stories, suited me; it helped me sense again and again how limitlessly and unendingly we are able to care.

---

20. Healing from the War: Trauma and Transformation after Vietnam, p. 12.

Chapter 15

Prejudice Unveiled

Master's work, 1985-1989, Baltimore

When asked by a reporter if having AIDS was the biggest burden, he has had to bear Arthur Ashe replied: "No, it isn't... It's a burden, all right... but being Black is the greatest burden I've had to bear... Race is for me a more onerous burden than AIDS.[21]

It is already well established that the verb 'to be prejudiced' is hardly ever used in its first person singular – which renders its direct measurement extremely difficult. Yet even without scientific measurements we still know that prejudice has been around for a long time and that it is slow to change.

Roger Jowell

Suddenly I hear music. It seems to be coming from underneath our long rectangular cafeteria table, the table of the unacceptable. I know the song, it's one of my favorites. Someone must have brought a cassette player and hidden it under the table waiting for the right moment, that moment when the bullies would begin picking on us. I hear the first line of the song and feel my body react: *You're just too good to be true, I can't take my eyes off of you...* All the other *unacceptable* have started tapping on the table, oblivious to what is happening around us. Johnny, or Fatso, as the bullies call him, is clapping to the rhythm. Marco, whose face is a minefield of pimples ready to burst, is drumming on an upside-down cafeteria tray. Sue's smile is half hidden with braces and she is almost as big as Johnny but that does not stop her from swaying to the beat like an ancient goddess, and Neil, who looks like he belongs in fourth grade is in this moment, actually singing (who knew he had such a beautiful voice?) while tapping with a fork and a

---

21. Jet Magazine, July 26th 1993.

spoon on the edge of the table.

As if lifted by the energy of all the other hideaways around me and the beautiful song, I am suddenly up on my feet dancing.

You're like heaven to touch I wanna hold you so much. That is my cue, I cannot wait a moment longer. I throw off my shoes, step on a chair, jump onto the table and begin dancing along this makeshift dance floor, swaying and twirling between the plates and trays that people quickly remove so I can come through.

"I love you baby and if it's quite alright I need you baby..." I sing along, pointing at my mates around the table who by now are all dancing and clapping. Their drumming and singing are becoming louder. We have finally joined to do something together.

The students at the other tables turn their heads and are watching us. Some are standing and some have jumped up on their tables to see better, or perhaps they too are dancing -- I can't quite tell because I have just made another sharp turn to the line: Trust in me when I say...

And the bullies are up on their feet, a few of them trying to move forward and mess with us, but the other Unacceptables and I are dancing around them. People from other tables are moving closer. We are being seen and supported and there is nothing those bullies can do to us now.

I dance wild and wacky and move towards Dicky, who is actually a tiny bit shorter than me. I notice it when I look into his green eyes and smile. He tries to remain serious and aloof but my goofy, overdramatic movements, hand gestures, jumping around him, singing the song so out of tune, finally crack his walls.

A smile that begins in his eyes is spreading to his mouth until he cannot hold back and actually laughs. All the other bullies are now laughing too, a joyful laugh, and they have joined the dancing that has spread like a piece of juicy gossip throughout the cafeteria. The unacceptable are in the center and all the rest step in to dance with us as one tune follows another, all of them my favorite songs. This is the day of my redemption; my dream come true.

It never happened, but I keep wishing it had.

Perhaps this dream is what drove me, more than a decade later, to choose transforming prejudices as the topic for my Master's Thesis in Dance/ Movement Therapy. As I began researching the topic, I realized that before considering the possibility of transforming prejudice through movement and dance, I first had to understand what drives us to be prejudiced and what prejudice looks like on a body level. Once I know how to discern prejudice through the body and movements, I might be able to figure out interventions that would assist in transforming it. Knowing what it looked like physically would also help me figure out when a transformation has occurred.

I began with the questions that bothered me.

Why did Dicky and Betsy tell me they wished I had been murdered with all the other Jews in the Holocaust? Why were, I and all the other unacceptable, treated so badly just because we were different in the way we looked, in our religion or in where we grew up? What is the origin of our inclination to pre-judge, stereotype, treat others unequally because of the color, their skin or their religion, their social status or sexual orientation? Are we born with our prejudices or do we learn them from our caretakers and our environment? Why are some people more inclined to behave in a prejudiced manner towards their fellow human beings than others? And how can I intervene to reduce prejudiced behavior?

Today, thirty-five years after I began asking those questions, far more research has been done and the understanding of prejudice has grown tremendously, offering new ways to look at these questions.

I recently learned that our genetic code is programmed with special qualities to ensure our survival. One of them is the capacity for love and connection with other human beings. Rivka Rochkind writes "Humans are hardwired for connection. Neuroscience suggests that we are neurologically wired to connect with others; mirror neurons in our brains are stimulated when we're interacting with other people. Literally, when you are talking to someone, pathways in your brain light up to mirror the emotions and behaviors that this other person is conveying." [22]

This explains our propensity to feel empathy or connection with people who are sharing their emotions, whether they are actually with us or we are watching them on screen or stage, or even reading their story. The same neurons that are activated in the brain of the person who is having an emotional reaction also activated within our brain; we can actually sense what they are feeling, which helps us feel compassion towards them.

Yet even though we are hardwired for love and connection we are also hardwired for other qualities such as classifying, generalizing, making

---

22. April 14th, 2016|Human Behavior, Relationships https://psychcaremd.com/ (hardwired for connection).

quick judgments and other capabilities that have supported our survival for millennia.

Nigel Nicholson writes: "Human beings became hardwired to stereotype people based on very small pieces of evidence, mainly their looks and a few readily apparent behaviors." This is because "classification made life simpler and saved time and energy. Every time you had food to share, you didn't have to figure out anew who could and couldn't be trusted. Your classification system told you instantly. Every time a new group came into view, you could pick out the high-status members not to alienate. And the faster you made decisions like these, the more likely you were to survive." This is why humans "naturally sort others into in-groups and out-groups – just by their looks and actions." [23]

Generalizing and classifying helps us function in our daily lives; when we learn how to drive a car, speak a language or trust unfamiliar people. Without these capabilities it would be very hard to navigate the world.

While both capabilities protect us and are necessary, the propensity for generalizing without enough information can become the basis for our stereotypes and prejudices, sometimes overriding our propensity for human connection. How does our ability to generalize turn into dangerous, prejudiced, racist behavior?

I believe something goes awry when our inclination to generalize becomes intertwined with painful experiences from childhood. Attachment theory teaches us that "early experiences with caregivers gradually give rise to a system of thoughts, memories, beliefs, expectations, emotions, and behaviors about the self and others." [24]

Through research we know that there is a positive association among adults between prejudice, on the one hand, and attachment anxiety and avoidance on the other [25]. Thus, if we did not have a secure attachment relationship with our main caregiver, we are more likely to resort to stereotyping and prejudice when our sense of security is threatened. Our prejudiced attitudes and behaviors are difficult to change because they contribute to our sense of security and well-being. When our emotional wellbeing is threatened by feelings of unworthiness, projecting onto others and stereotyping temporarily helps us feel better about who we are and support our well-being.

---

23. https://hbr.org/1998/07/how-hardwired-is-human-behavior

24. Divorce Doctor, by Francine Kaye, page 140.

25. https://www.researchgate.net/publication/324555251_Attachment_and_Prejudice

According to Hirsh (1955), prejudice allows individuals wounded by particular childhood circumstances to feel less lonely, fearful and anxious by providing an outlet for hostility. Once they release their hostility, they feel better about who they are [26].

These individuals are very reluctant to give up prejudiced beliefs and behaviors because if they do, they might be overwhelmed by an onslaught of painful emotions from their past without the support or knowledge to handle these feelings. Projecting unworthiness onto others is so much easier than feeling those feelings ourselves.

In places rife with economic and social injustice, political unrest and daily violence, our fears and insecurities are triggered and the need for security and a sense of belonging are very present, consequently creating a fertile ground for prejudice.

If left unchecked, prejudiced attitudes and beliefs can lead to horrific consequences, beginning with talking about members of the out-group with like-minded friends and avoidance of people who belong to this out-group, but then if not transformed or at least constrained, prejudiced attitudes and beliefs can lead to discrimination, physical attacks, deportation, pogroms, racial cleansing, genocide and a Holocaust.

After learning all this I wondered, what interventions can transform and heal the underlying emotions so we no longer need to use prejudiced attitudes and behavior to protect ourselves from feeling them?

While writing my thesis, I watched *The Defiant Ones*, a 1958 film where two prisoners, one black and the other white, who hate each other, manage to escape from prison while handcuffed to one another. This forced physical connection gradually evolves into a genuine heart connection and they choose to stay together and support one another even when the handcuffs are off.

Wow! I thought, *that would be one possible way to end prejudice, handcuffing Jews to Muslims, Blacks to Whites, and sending them to survive in the forest with prison wardens and dogs chasing them.*

But do we really need a forced physical connection in order to become aware of our dependence on and connection to one another? Is there an alternative way to awaken this awareness?

I knew that in extreme situations, when our survival depends on cooperation and connection, when we have a common enemy as in wars

---

26. Hirsh, S.G. (1955). The fears men live by. New York, NY: Harper and Brothers.

and natural disasters, certain prejudices no longer serve us. Rather, they become a threat to our survival, so we let them go and are able to see the other person's humanity. And sometimes, due to our ability to generalize, this experience can decrease our prejudice towards the whole group that our new ally belongs to.

But what else can work? Do we need to be faced with dire circumstances to change our attitudes and beliefs? Is there an easier, less painful way to bring about change?

I struggled with these questions as I began writing my Master's thesis, knowing that one day soon I would want to return to Israel where prejudice played a very destructive role. I wondered if I could apply dance/movement therapy in ways that would help to heal prejudices in Israel.

But in order to heal prejudice I had to find out what prejudice looks like in the body so I could search for physical and emotional interventions that might help in changing it. I decided to conduct research that would help me see if there are actually physical attributes of individuals who have a greater tendency towards prejudice.

I began with a test [27] for prejudice that I gave to a group of 150 students, then filmed 12 of them participating in a movement session with simple steps that included the possibility of interactions amongst them. Each student had a number taped to his or her back.

The film with the students moving and dancing was then analyzed by two Certified Movement Analysts, who described each of the participants in the language of body and shape. For example: are their movements more rigid (bound flow) or free flowing (free flow)? Do they mainly initiate their movements from the center of the body (core initiation) or from the outer limbs (distal initiation)? Do they make eye contact?

Then I compared the test results with the CMAs's descriptions to see if there were any movement patterns common to those who tested as High Prejudice (HP) when compared with those who tested as Low Prejudice (LP). Although the sample was quite small and there were only two CMAs who looked at it, I did find certain significant movement patterns, nonverbal cues, which distinguish between high- and low-prejudiced individuals. I found that high-prejudiced individuals exhibit:

A. Very little or almost no shaping or molding of their body to the body of others;

---

27. The Minnesota Multiphasic Personality Inventory.

B. Unclear awareness of space;

C. Unclear awareness of their bodies.

D. Increased use bound flow and passive weight.

Other cues approaching significance were:

1. Most high-prejudiced individuals have a one-unit torso;
2. They initiate most of their movements distally;
3. They have a restricted use of their kinesphere and make almost no eye contact [28].

What did all that mean?

My limited research showed that our movements can actually be used to construct a nonverbal prejudice scale [29]. It was a first step towards seeing what prejudice might look like nonverbally, towards developing interventions which might help in reducing prejudice and then seeing if the interventions actually worked if a change occurs in these measures.

A great deal more research would be necessary before this scale could be used widely but the suffering I had endured as an adolescent began to make more sense. I could see that Betsy and Dicky might have behaved as they did because of how they were treated in childhood, and that finding a way to heal those early wounds might actually help people become less bound, more open and less in need of the defense of prejudice.

Today I also know that had I not personally experienced prejudice, I would have been unaware of how much it hurt and would not have been so passionate in my desire to do something to transform it.

28. See Appendix II for more information.

29. Creating a Nonverbal Prejudice Scale, Master's Thesis, Nitsan Joy Gordon (appendix II).

Chapter 16

Choices
1986-1989, Baltimore

We are our choices.
Jean-Paul Sartre

*The thing you fear most has no power. Your fear of it is
what has the power. Facing the truth really will set you free.*
Oprah Winfrey

It was the morning of July 11, 1986, and I was sitting outside my new boyfriend's apartment reading a book when the phone rang. I had met Brad at a party a month earlier and two weeks later moved in to live with him.

"Hello," I said, a bit out of breath when I reached the phone.

"Hi Nitsani," my father responded.

"Hi Aba, how are you?" I said, smiling. I liked talking with my father.

"I have some news," he continued, his voice shaky. "Neve was severely wounded. He is in the Nahariya hospital."

"What? No!" I dropped to the floor clutching the phone to my ear. "Is he going to be okay? What happened?"

"He was just operated on and it looks like he will be all right. His unit was called from Lebanon where they were serving to abort an attack by four terrorists who infiltrated in a rubber boat along the Mediterranean Sea to Rosh Hanikrah (at the northernmost tip of Israel). The terrorists hid in the cliffs shooting and wounding him and ten of his buddies and killing two of his friends before they themselves were killed. Neve was wounded from shrapnel of a hand grenade they threw which entered his stomach and cut off a toe on his right foot. They took some skin from his hip to close the hole in his stomach and he will probably be in the hospital for the next three weeks."

I was having a hard time processing what he was saying – *My little brother Neve? Wounded?*

"I want to come home. Should I come home now?" I asked, tears running down my cheeks.

"No, let's wait and see what happens," my father replied. And I listened to him."

I am not sure why I listened. Was it because I couldn't pay for the ticket? Or was I worried that if I left, I would lose the relationship that had just begun with Brad? Today it is hard to explain my actions even to myself.

Neve was released from the hospital three weeks later and remained at home where he slowly healed with the support of family and friends.

A couple of months later, after Neve was already home and recovering, I returned to our apartment from teaching Sunday School and found Brad looking dismayed. Apparently, he had received a phone call from my father while I was out. After the usual small talk, my father casually asked when we were getting married.

"And what did you say to him?" I inquired, feeling my chest contract.

"I told him we are talking about it" Brad responded.

"And what did he say?" I pressed.

"He said: What do you mean talking about it? ARE you marrying her or NOT?"

Feeling I had just been transported to the 18th century by my overbearing father's odd sense of humor, I imagined he was probably having fun with this whole incident. Later I recalled having mentioned something to him in our last conversation about *possibly* getting engaged ...

Not yet used to my father, Brad had panicked, stammered some excuse, and gotten off the phone as quickly as he could.

Doesn't he want to marry me? I thought, feeling resentful and disappointed that Brad did not say to my father: "Sure, I would love to marry your daughter (with your permission). I'm so in love with her, I will ask her tonight." Or something to that affect, as it happens in all the romantic novels.

Did I truly want to marry Brad? I don't know. Maybe I did, but I didn't even ask myself that question. I wanted Brad to want to marry me so I would feel loved and desired and not feel the pain of rejection and abandonment. So for the next week, I pouted and moped until it worked. Brad said "let's get married" and I said yes. It was not the proposal I imagined and hoped for but it brought me a step closer to MARRIAGE, which at the time seemed like a "must have" for any girl who wanted to feel good about herself. I called my father to share the news feeling like I had finally "made it", and yet my heart was not bursting with joy.

Brad's family was excited and his mother came to visit with her own engagement ring from her first husband, Brad's father, in her bag to give him in case he had popped the question. Finally, I had a ring on my finger like some of my friends, not the one I would have chosen, but still a ring. We decided to get married in Israel and I remember the excitement and also the constant pressure inside me. *Is this really what I want? Am I marrying the right person?*

Four months later we traveled to Israel for our wedding. When we stepped off the plane both of us were wearing our gift to my father and Rivca, a sweatshirt saying on the front: "Have you read the book?" and on the back *Dance, Dialogue and Despair*, my father's latest book. *That ought to get him on friendly terms with us*, I thought. And it did, he laughed when he saw it.

In our wedding album, there is a photo I call "the morning after", taken on the day following our wedding. Both of us look so dazed, perhaps thinking, "Did we actually go through with it? Was it the right thing to do?"

Although it did not end well, we divorced ten years later, I don't regret my decision. Our time together was full of adventures and I learned a lot. But most importantly our union brought into this world two beautiful children – Shir and Ben – and I cannot imagine my life without them.

There is one more photo in our wedding album that is special to me. It is of my brother Neve caught in the middle of a wild dance, his arms flung to the sides and a huge smile on his face. He is very thin but looks happy. Just five months earlier he had been in a hospital bed, seriously wounded. Seeing him alive and dancing at our wedding was, well... beyond words.

After the wedding we returned to the United States, not yet sure what our next step would be. Two years later our daughter Shir was born and we made a decision: we would move to Israel.

In 1989, when Shir was almost a year old, the news coming from Israel was about the first Intifada, the grassroots Palestinian uprising, and it looked scary. As the date of our move approached, I became more and more anxious: *where was I taking Shir, our baby daughter? Why were we leaving our comfortable life in the USA? Did I really want to do something to reduce prejudice, to advance coexistence and peace? Or was I just trying to please my father by doing what in his eyes was "the right and meaningful thing to do" so I would feel his appreciation and love?* I am guessing, it was a combination of many things.

During the days leading up to our departure, most tangible was the fear. Nightmares and sleepless nights preceded the move. When people asked me why we were going to Israel I avoided their eyes, just as I avoided looking inside myself for a truthful answer. I was going back to a country that from the outside, seemed like a frightening place to be in. And yet, despite the nightmares and misgivings, we made the decision and in August 1989, moved to Israel.

Once there, caught up in daily living, I realized that the news we hear in the media is most often the "Bad News" and there are also many good things happening in Israel, and for a while my fears subsided. We found a tiny one-bedroom house for rent near a green field in Bustan Hagalil, a small Moshav community between Nahariya and Akko, and it was there we spent our first few months in Israel.

Chapter 17

Dance, Dialogue and Hope
1989, Akko

Sometimes we love with nothing more than hope.
Gregory David Roberts

As you start to walk on the way, the way appears.
Rumi

Bustan Hagalil was a small sleepy community nestled among huge eucalyptus trees, next to the Mediterranean Sea, near the 4000-year-old city of Akko, when we moved there in 1989. Having no car, we used bicycles and a trailer to take our daughter to day care in a nearby kibbutz, to shop for produce at the colorful fruit and vegetable market in Akko and to ride through the sand dunes to the city of Nahariya where Brad studied Hebrew and where my mother lived. After working with Vietnam veterans in the USA, I thought of looking for a job with Israeli war veterans, but was led elsewhere.

One bright morning in October 1989, Brad took Shir to day care and I rode my bike to a meeting in Akko. My father had given me a copy of the infamous book from the wedding sweatshirts *Dance, Dialogue and Despair,* and instructed me to bring it to Dr Mariam Mar'i. who had written a chapter for one of his other books [30]. Dr Mar'i was the director of *Dar El Tifle El Arabi* (DETEA), Home of the Arab Child Pedagogical Center, the school for early childhood educators in the Arab community that she and the Akko Arab Women's Association had created.

His book was about his own efforts to work for dialogue and coexistence during the late seventies and early eighties using an approach based on

30. Israel/Palestine The Quest for Dialogue.

Martin Buber's *I and Thou* and other existentialists. The despair came after the First Lebanon War in 1982, when his project began to fall apart.

As I rode my bike through the relatively new part of Akko, I noticed that nothing matched about the buildings matched. Each one was a rundown in its own unique way mostly because of neglect, and architects who had needed to plan quickly for new immigrants flooding Israel after the War of Independence.

I found Dar El Tifle El Arabi in a beautiful stone building directly behind the Akko police station, which sat in an old British fortress next to the beach. While tying my bicycle to the magnolia tree in the yard of the building, I gazed west, where the sparkling blue sea stretched to the horizon.

After stepping through the large wooden door, I was told by the secretary to walk up the steps to the second floor where Dr Mari's office was located. As soon as I walked into her office, I was equally struck by the view of the sea from the tall windows and by the beautiful dark-haired woman sitting behind a large brown desk speaking on the phone. She was dressed in an elegant, perfectly fitting black outfit and high heels and I became uncomfortably aware of my dust covered sandals and the bike helmet I was still holding, but when she looked up, her bright smile and the kindness exuding from the depth of her brown eyes reassured me that I was welcome.

Dr Mari, or Mariam, as she asked me to call her, was the first Muslim woman in Israel to receive a doctoral degree and now taught at Haifa University. She was born in Akko, then escaped with her family to Lebanon right before the War of Independence and returned to Israel during a very short window of opportunity when refugees were given permission to return. Her older brother and sisters had stayed in Lebanon and the family was never given permission to reunite. In an article about her memories of that time, she writes: "One of these experiences was the moment in 1950 when part of the family, including myself, were in the center of a big crowd in Lebanon, waving and bidding farewell to the rest of the family, as the bus took off to bring us home. Not knowing that it meant separation forever. This particular image of me at five-year-old waving goodbye with one hand to my eldest brother, while my other hand was trying to dry the tears that were falling from my eyes, never faded away. Rather, it stayed vivid in my mind through the days and in my dreams at night. I often imagined myself crossing the borders and meeting my brother. At other times I imagined him crossing the border to meet me. Yet quickly I would push this idea aside because I sensed the danger that might accompany it, and satisfied myself by sending him messages and receiving them back through the birds and angels that flew so freely up in the sky and across the borders." [31]

Two years prior to our meeting, Mariam had been widowed. Her husband, Sami Mar'i, was a professor at Haifa University, the director of the Arab Jewish Peace Center and the founder of the Haifa Branch of the Center for Civil Rights. In his writings he claimed that the education of Arabs was a form of systemic control intended to ensure the interests of the Jewish majority of Israel. One night Sami was arrested, interrogated and humiliated. He was accused of meeting with a hostile figure at a conference in Germany two years earlier. He came out of jail a changed man, broken. A year later, he died of a heart attack.

I only learned about Mariam's life months later, when she and I became friends. On that morning I gave her the book my father had sent and asked if she could tell me a bit about the school. She looked at me and smiled.

"When I returned to Israel after completing my doctoral degree in Education in the USA," she began, "I realized there was no program for Arab early childhood educators in Northern Israel that taught Arab women about their own culture and traditions, so they could pass these traditions and heritage to the children they worked with."

"Why is that so important?" I asked, "Why can't they just study in the programs created by the Israeli government for Jewish early childhood educators?"

"Oh..." she smiled holding up my father's book in her hands, "That is the crux of the problem. You and your father would like to enhance genuine coexistence and peace through dialogue, yet you must understand that for dialogue to happen the participants on both sides must feel worthy, that they have something to offer. How can Arab women and men feel like worthy participants if their culture, traditions, language and the way of life they have lived for hundreds of years are dismissed and ignored and they are expected to take on a different language, culture and way of being in the world? How can we feel pride if we continue feeling sorry for ourselves, feeling that we are victims instead of focusing on our strengths and our beautiful traditions, preserving and passing them to the next

---

31. My Experiences Myself by Dr Mariam M. Mari page 1.

generation?"

I was moved by her words. Here was a woman leading an organization that was working to right a wrong that had lasted for generations by following a vision that was both revolutionary and inspirational. She saw into the future and understood what it would take to create a lasting peace and I received my first glimpse of what dialogue, coexistence and peacebuilding would mean for the Arab Palestinian side of the conflict.

As she spoke, I felt that even though I am not an Arab, this was a path that I would love to join. *Supporting Muslim, Christian, Druze and Bedouin young women so they could one day grow into their full potential and power and become our allies in creating a better more peaceful country for all of us? Yes, absolutely, I'm on board.*

When I told Dr Mar'i that I had a Master's Degree in Dance/Movement Therapy, she asked if I would be interested in teaching creative dance or dance therapy or something of the sort to the young women in her school. I immediately replied "Yes," not exactly sure what I would teach but feeling compelled to become involved. She envisioned that my work with the students would help them become more flexible in body and thought and then they would bring this openhearted awareness to the children they work with. It was an innovative concept at the time.

On that day in October of 1989, when I brought the book *Dance, Dialogue and Despair* to Mariam, I had no idea that this gift would birth a program that would include dance and dialogue, and would often transform our despair into hope.

Chapter 18

Mervat's Scream
1990-1995, 2002, Akko

*You teach people how to treat you by what you
allow, what you stop and what you reinforce.*

Tony Gaskins

*Until you learn to say No,
your Yes will never be a real Yes*

Jim Ryan

"I can't believe we're doing this!!" a young woman exclaims while the others giggle and look at me as if I've just landed from Mars.

It's their first meeting and after the opening circle, I asked them to stand up and "follow the leader" who is moving her head in a circle to the Whitney Huston song *"I Wanna Dance with Somebody"*. Perhaps not the best song choice for this group, but I like it, so I thought they might too.

These young women, studying to be early childhood educators at DETEA, never imagined when they enrolled in college that one of their classes would include dancing to Whitney Houston; learning to listen to one another and sharing how they felt without anyone judging, interrupting or making suggestions; and then at the end receiving and giving massages.

How is this even related to working with children aged between six months and four years? they must have wondered.

I was not sure how to explain the importance of our class for their work; I, too, was learning and trying to create something entirely new.

In order to construct a meaningful experience for them, I made sure to have a classroom with no chairs where we could sit in a circle on the carpet. Something about sitting closer to the Earth in a circle rather than behind a desk was already helping us connect. I asked to work with only half a class, which meant 13 women instead of the usual 26. I also insisted on one hour per group, because what can you accomplish in 45 minutes? Mariam agreed; I think she had trained herself to see possibilities where others saw only obstacles. These seemingly technical details provided a setting, a safe haven, where the young women were not lost in the crowd and actual transformation could occur.

I came to work with a bag that included music I love, a parachute, a beach ball, balloons, colorful fabrics, feathers and stretch bands. Very early on I realized many of them were not crazy about my choice of music. Their favorite was Eastern or Arabic music and every time I played it, they broke into a joyous celebration. It felt like home to them – comfortable and familiar.

During the class I would play the unfamiliar music and invite them to try new movements, expand their repertoire, experiment with new ways of moving in space and relating to others. Then I would put on the music they were used to and loved so they could recuperate in the familiar. In order to nurture their connection to one another and to their bodies and feelings we danced, played movement games with the props, and then worked through whatever came up in the group.

Gradually, over the course of a few months, a safe space where we could speak candidly about some of the difficult and taboo issues in our society was created. The women shared openly, perhaps because there were hardly any places in their lives to talk about things that bothered them without being judged, rebuked or even punished. It must have been such a relief to find a space where they could share their pain, their difficult questions, their challenges.

We had an agreement that outside the group they would only talk about their own personal experience, not anyone else's and since most of them came from different neighborhoods, towns and villages, there was less chance that if they did share something about another young woman it would reach people who knew her. Whatever the reason that made it possible, the sharing was deep and personal.

The participating women, who had not been to the military like most of their Jewish counterparts, were 18 or 19 years old, fresh out of high school. Most were looking forward to finding a young man and becoming engaged and often one of the students would show off the engagement ring she had received or photos from her lavish engagement party.

One morning, when one of the more religious participants announced she was engaged, everyone clapped and congratulated her on having achieved this most sought-after goal. Quite big, with only her round face showing under the hijab, she seemed happy as she held up the gold ring she had received from her betrothed at the engagement party.

Over the next few months, we talked about the double oppression Arab women experience in Israel: being treated unequally both by men (and sometimes other women) in their society for being a woman, and by the Israeli Jews for being an Arab.

In the early nineties, it was still rare for an Arab woman to say what she felt and especially difficult was saying the word: "No". So, we practiced, pushing, pulling, and using our physical strength while voicing that one ultimate backbone of our selfhood, the word and concept of NO. "No, it is not okay how you are talking to me right now! No, he is not the man I want to marry! No, this is not what I want to do with my life!" We learned that saying NO to one thing means saying YES to something else. Once the No was spoken, the path to our true Yes became clearer. Many of them shared that they could breathe deeper after pushing or pulling playfully one against the other while saying their YES or NO.

Towards the end of the school year, the recently engaged religious young woman asked to speak with me after class. As soon as we settled on the floor of the old stone building where the classes were being held, she showed me her ring finger. A lighter strip of skin, untouched by the fierce Israeli sun, was the only indication of the place where that gold ring had once been.

"I tore it off," she told me, her eyes shining. "He hit me and called me names even before the wedding, so I pulled the ring off and gave it back to him and told my parents that I will not marry a man who treats me this way." She thanked me for giving her the courage. I pressed her hands with mine and told her: "You are so courageous!!"

Knowing about the horrible possibility of honor killings, I prayed that she would be all right. *Am I going too far, too fast, endangering my students?* I wondered nervously. But we kept going and my students seemed to be all right. Some of them said that this was the only class where they learned things that were actually meaningful for their everyday lives.

Three years later, I was working with another group. During the warm-up (the first part of the session where we start moving and stretching different body parts), I noticed that the young women seemed to be ungrounded and were having a difficult time using the weight effort. In the Laban Movement Analysis framework, the weight effort is associated with asserting oneself and making an impact in the world, with determination and claiming of self.

To help them with grounding, we practiced breath work, stomping, and pushing against one another in the circle and then we moved into playing the Yes and No game. Each woman faced a partner, raising the palms of her hands so they could meet and touch her partner's hands. Standing firm and making eye contact, each pair began pushing against each other's hands while one of them said *Yes* and the other *No*.

"Now see if you can say your Yes or No louder, with more conviction. Try taking a deep breath and let the sound emerge from deep within," I said, demonstrating with one of them.

One of the students, Mervat, an attractive dark haired young woman with clear brown eyes, had a difficult time. Both her No and Yes were spoken softly as though something was stuck inside her throat blocking the path of her voice. Only the remnants of what this voice was or could be made their way through her throat and out of her mouth into our shared space.

Later I learned that she had suffered a leg injury at the age of 12 which left a visible scar. Her worried mother told her that no man would want to marry her now because she was "damaged goods". So young and so nervous, Mervat began praying and asking God to help her find someone, a doctor perhaps, who would understand that it was just a scar, not a sign that something was wrong with her. When she was 17, her cousin, who was ten years older and a doctor asked for her hand in marriage. *Is this the one?* She wondered. *Please God give me a sign*. The answer she received was Yes and at 18, she married him. When we first met, Mervat was 23 and the mother of three children, one of whom suffered from epilepsy.

On that day when I saw the frustration on her face, I offered to take her partner's place and asked if she would be willing to push against me. When she said yes, I began pushing against her: "You can say NO Mervat!!!" I encouraged raising my own voice to invite hers to come out and join.

"Yes!!!" I continued pushing against her powerful hands, looking into her eyes, daring her to voice a "NO." Her classmates formed a circle around us and began shouting, "Go Mervat!! You can do it!!!"

Slowly an aching sound began emerging from her belly, gradually growing into a deep bellow. The pain-filled roar went on and on. The other students giggled at first, perhaps uncomfortable with the depth and strength of her cry. Then, as if responding to an ancient need to voice the deepest wounds that exist in so many of us women, some of them joined in, tentatively at first, and then with more conviction.

Mervat continued on and on until I began to worry that her cry, her scream would never end. It was bigger than anything I had ever witnessed. I pushed against her, lost for words, with awe and appreciation for the unleashed power that later became known as "Mervat's scream." Then it was over. Mervat almost collapsed but we held her up, gently stroking her hair. Later she referred to this encounter as "the day I found my voice."

A couple of months later, on the 25th of February, 1994, the morning of Purim, Baruch Goldstein, a Jewish settler and a doctor born in the US, opened fire from behind and killed 29 Palestinians who were kneeling in prayer at a mosque in the Cave of the Patriarchs in Hebron. One hundred and twenty-five of the roughly 800 praying were wounded.

I heard the news early in the morning before going to work with my Arab students in Akko and felt so shocked and ashamed, somehow partially responsible. I was raised to believe that on some level we are our brothers' and sisters' keepers and instructed in the Torah to seek and pursue peace and justice: "Turn away from evil and do good; seek peace and pursue it" [32].

That a Jew, one of my people, would do something so horrible? It felt incredibly painful to imagine those kneeling in prayer before Allah being shot from behind and to own that my image of being a Jew was deeply tarnished – how could I face my Arab students?

And yet I did. Not only did I go in, but, having learned from my past experience of avoiding pain, I decided to bring what had just occurred into the room.

Most of them had not heard the news, so I told them about it, sharing my horror. Then I passed a talking piece and just listened. At first it was hard for them to share about such an explosive issue. The room was quiet for a few minutes.

Then Mervat spoke up. She began by sharing the pain of being an Arab woman in a Jewish country. The others tried to hush her saying: "Nitsan's Jewish – be careful." But Mervat was not afraid. She shushed them back and explained that it was time to talk. "Nitsan asked and I am going to

32. Psalm 34:14.

answer!!" said the young woman who had found her voice.

Bracing myself, I waited.

"I simply don't understand how people who went through the Holocaust just half century ago can be so cruel and oppressive towards other people," she said forcefully. "The fact that you are Jewish does not make you just or right or the only victims in the world. Why can't you see what you are doing to us? You have no idea what it's like to be an Arab in Israel."

Taking a deep breath, I looked around the room and saw that others were nodding in agreement.

"I hear you and how painful it is for you," I said, looking directly at her and then at all the other women, "and you are right, I don't know what it's like to be an Arab in Israel. We are not the only victims in this tragic situation and cruelty can exist in each of us. But I do have some firsthand experience with prejudice and from that place am asking you to please tell me more about what you are going through here in Israel? I would really like to know."

Then they began to share and I just listened, tears rolling down my face.

When our time was up, I looked around the room and thanked them for their courage. Before walking out the door, many of them came up to hug and thank me.

Afterwards I felt something huge had happened and I was not quite sure what. I felt so relieved that I had faced my fears and opened an issue that was so difficult for all of us. After that meeting I knew that I wanted to work with Mervat.

A year and a half later, when we began the Arab-Jewish groups for kindergarten teachers, she became an assistant in the group and later one of the facilitators. During the years she worked as a facilitator, she, like the rest of us, experienced both personal and interpersonal changes. Her effect on her community was clearly visible late one night, in June of 2002.

Eight years after she first spoke up in class, Mervat and I were invited to the United States together for a four-week workshop/lecture/fundraising tour to share our peacebuilding efforts. I came to pick her up in a cab on our way to the airport at nearly one in the morning. The second Intifada was going full blast and suicide bombers frequently exploded themselves in various parts of Israel. As the cab entered her street and slowly approached her building, I wondered why so many people were out on the sidewalk near her house at such a late hour of the night.

Fearing something terrible had happened, I was relieved to see, when we came closer, Mervat and her suitcases in the middle of the crowd. She was smiling and hugging the people surrounding her. "What happened?" I asked her as soon as she climbed in. "Oh, it's all our neighbors, they just came down to bid me goodbye and wish me luck. They think I am going to the United States to bring peace and they want to make sure I have a good send-off..."

I looked at her, stunned, as she opened the window, shouting goodbye to her "fans" and waving her hand.

At that moment I saw how the transformation of one person can affect many. I realized some people here in Akko actually believed in what we were doing and that in the context of the conflict around us, it meant something important to them. Their belief in us and our work refueled my desire to continue seeking and pursuing peace.

Chapter 19

When We Listen
1990-1991, Abirim

Listening is the oldest and perhaps the most powerful tool of healing. It is often through the quality of our listening and not the wisdom of our words that we are able to affect the most profound changes in the people around us. When we listen, we offer with our attention an opportunity for wholeness. Our listening creates sanctuary for the homeless parts within the other person. That which has been denied, unloved, devalued by themselves and others. That which is hidden.

Rachel Naomi Remen

"Shushki, play nice," I tell my two-and-a-half-year-old daughter. She is fighting over a toy with her new friend Maya, the three-year-old daughter of our neighbors from the caravan[33] next door in the small community, Abirim, that is now our home.

When I first saw Abirim, on a bright summer day in 1990, nestled on top of a mountain amidst green oak trees, with a spectacular view of the Mediterranean Sea stretched to the horizon, I knew immediately *this is where I want to live...*

We then went through an acceptance process that included tests and meetings with five of the thirty families who lived on the mountain. Once accepted, we moved into a tiny 120 sq. foot caravan with two bedrooms, a bathroom and a small kitchen/living room area. The neighboring caravan was the home of Michal, Amiram and their daughter Maya, who became Shir's friend.

Shir and Maya spent most days playing outside on the grass or inside one of the caravans. But right now, they don't look too happy.

Shir is trying to pull a doll out of Maya's hands, screaming, "It's mine,

---

33. "Caravan" in Israel refers to a small portable building or mobile home.

mine!" as though her life depended on having that raggedy doll all to herself.

"Share," I urge. "She's your friend, share with her."

But Shir is relentlessly pulling and screeching while Maya holds on with quiet determination, showing no sign that she will ever let go of this sorry-looking doll. She seems unfazed by Shir's screams and is looking curiously with her beautiful bluish-gray eyes at her friend, as if wondering what she will do next.

Shir is getting more and more upset and is now hitting Maya with her small fist.

"Enough!" I shout, feeling embarrassed by my rowdy daughter and scaring Maya, who let's go. Shir grabs the doll with both hands and proceeds to hit Maya on the head with it.

Maya bursts into tears and runs out the door to the neighboring caravan while I shout, "SHIR, you can't hit your friend! You are going to your room now for time out."

I lift her as she struggles to get away and take her to her room, shutting the door while she continues screaming. Overwhelmed, I make it to the couch and collapse. I don't know what to do and how to make her behave with her friends. *What will the neighbors think of me now?* A moment later Shir walks out, crying, "Bamba, I want Bamba!"

Great. Now she wants comfort food. How do other parents deal with this so much better? Why is Maya not hitting and screaming? I am such an awful mother!

A knock on the door shakes me out of my current state of self-loathing

"Come in," I say, looking up as Amiram, Maya's father, walks in, carrying Maya in his arms.

Now I will have to get Shir, who is still pulling at my pants with her endless Bamba demands, to apologize to Maya, whose face is buried in her father's shoulder. I look down in embarrassment.

"It's hard, isn't it?" I hear Amiram say. "Don't you sometimes just wanna throw them out the window?"

I smile and my throat tightens. Someone is actually seeing me, my struggles, and I don't know what to say. Yes, there have been times, especially after nights with too little sleep and too much nursing, coupled with "terrible twos" tantrums, that I felt ready to shake her or simply resign my post as a mother and admit defeat.

"Throwing out the window has not occurred to me, but now that you mention it... that might actually be a good idea..." I finally say, smiling, feeling a momentary relief for having retrieved a wisp of humor from my mind's lost and found bin.

"Listen," he continues, searching for my eyes, "I am opening a parenting class that might help you deal with these difficult moments. It's going to be on Tuesday evenings at 8:30 p.m. in our living room. Why don't you come and join us?"

By that time, I had seen that Maya's parents had a unique way of being with their daughter, and with both our girls when Shir was there. Amiram loved playing and going on adventures with them, and whenever one of them was upset, he would not try to distract her with toys or food. Rather, he would stop everything and support her in releasing those emotions. This might be the reason (if truth be told) that Shir enjoyed going to their caravan much more than Maya enjoyed coming to ours. *It was so hard sometimes; maybe there was something I could learn from them that would help me be a better mother.*

In that moment I decided to go.

Amiram's class was my introduction to Reevaluation Counseling (RC) and it changed my parenting and my life.

In the first class, Amiram told us the story of how RC originated. "In the 1950s Harvey Jackins, who developed RC, worked in a factory with a man called Tom. One day Tom was fired from his job and then his wife left him. Harvey was worried about his friend so he went to see him in his apartment. When he walked in and saw Tom sitting on the living room couch, his eyes red, Harvey could tell that Tom had been crying for hours. He greeted him and sat by his side, but Tom did not even look up.

"After a while, frustrated that his friend spent so much time doing nothing but crying, Harvey decided to give him a pep talk: 'Hey, Tom, listen to me,' he began, 'you know I care about you but what you're doing right now is not helping. You gotta get yourself together man... You gotta go out there and find another job! That is the only way to get your life back on track!'

"Tom just continued sobbing. Harvey saw his advice was not heeded or even acknowledged so he gave up trying to do anything and just sat nearby while Tom cried.

"One morning, a couple of days later, Tom got up, washed his face and said to Harvey: 'Thanks man, I feel better now. I'm going out to look for a job.'

"Harvey was mystified. He had no idea what happened. How had Tom, who looked so depressed a couple of days earlier, become so full of energy and ready to go back out and face the world when all he did was cry? What brought about the change? This experience led Harvey to explore the value of crying and emotional discharge.

"While I cannot vouch for the absolute accuracy of my memory of this story," Amiram concluded, "I can absolutely vouch for the value of crying."

I don't remember crying much before RC. Mostly I tried to hide my tears. In my teens, I would sometimes get very angry with my mom for borrowing my clothes without asking permission even after I told her quite a few times to ask before borrowing. My anger would soon turn into tears of frustration, especially when she said things like, "I don't understand why you're getting so upset, it's only a sweater," emphasizing the 'so' as if she wanted to delete my "messy" emotions.

As a dance therapist, I learned to talk about my feelings but hardly ever cried. When I felt heartache, I usually sank into a cave of loneliness and shame. My mother and father never cried in front of us. Being vulnerable was very difficult before I began RC.

From Amiram I learned that Reevaluation Counseling, or *Listening Partnerships*, as we began calling this practice after reading Patti Wipfler's booklets for parents, is an agreement between two people to take turns listening and sharing what is going on in their lives. Wipfler adds, "In our many years of work with parents, we have found that if parents take regular turns listening to each other, each parent makes dependable gains in their lives. The time to explore thoughts, set goals, and work through the tensions of everyday life helps parents care more effectively for themselves and their families. *Listening partnership*s are a simple and rewarding way to give and to get the support we parents need as we meet the challenges of nurturing our children." [34] Later I learned that this tool is extremely helpful for anyone, not only parents.

I remember the mixture of awkwardness and relief I felt when I first realized someone was actually listening to me. I could say anything I chose about my life or be silent and that person would still be there with their full and compassionate attention focused on me.

At first, I didn't trust it. How could it be real when for so many years

34. Listening Partnerships for Parents.

there were less than a handful of people who really saw me and just listened, lovingly, non-judgmentally, without giving advice, just wanting to know more? When have I listened like that to anyone? I was always worried that my raw pain and unsightly thoughts – my jealousies, shame, anger and criticism of myself and others – would be judged and that anyone who really knew what was going on inside me would not love me. But in RC it was different.

The guidelines were key. We learned that a listening partnership between two people is a sacred space. We were instructed that anything our listening partner shared with us was not to be mentioned to anyone else, not even to our partner when we saw them again. When sharing with others, we could only bring up **what we ourselves had spoken about.** If for some reason, it was very important to mention what someone else had said, we needed to first **ask their permission.**

In Amiram's class, I began to connect with Liry.

I had first met her while walking with Shir on the gravel road connecting the caravans in Abirim. She was outside her caravan, nine months pregnant, and bending over to clean the wood stove she and her husband had just purchased from a second-hand shop to keep them warm during the cold winter months. We said hello and smiled at each other. Neither of us knew that our meeting would be the beginning of a friendship that has lasted over thirty years.

When Amiram's class began, I was the pregnant one and Liry was trying to survive the first year of her son's life. Her honesty, rolling laughter, emotional openness, and contagious excitement about so many things impressed me deeply and filled me with envy – she was someone whom everyone, including me, couldn't help liking. Only later, as our friendship deepened, did I become aware of her struggles.

Her father, whom she adored, left her mother and married another woman when Liry was six, and the wound of that loss was so painful that for years it colored her relationships with men and physically weakened her heart.

Leah, Liry's mother, a Holocaust survivor, was six herself when her own mother disappeared after going to visit a relative in another Russian town. Her father was taken later, and she and her brother managed to escape the Nazis with their uncle by going to Siberia.

Knowing Liry's challenges helped me feel more comfortable sharing my own trials. I knew that, although we lived in the same community, the next time we met on the sidewalk or in the playground she would not ask, "How is it going with your husband?" or anything else I mentioned in our Listening Partnership. Nor would I ask her, "Has your neighbor apologized yet?" if this was something that she had shared during her turn.

My stories and struggles were safe with her, as hers were with me. And as we shared, as I saw my different partners' vulnerabilities and heard them cry or express anger about what bothered them, it became easier for me to open up. I realized how similar we are in our struggles and began feeling less alone.

In Amiram's class we learned to listen. We also learned that what challenges us as adults is almost always connected to our past, to the times in our childhood when we were hurt by the behavior of our parents, teachers and others around us who, for the most part, had no intention of hurting us, but did so because they themselves were confused and hurt.

"When children get hurt by thoughtlessness, mistreatment or circumstances, they are saddled with emotional tension caused by the hurt. Children interpret incidents that hurt them in a very personal way. They assume that the troubles that befall them are a sign that there is something very wrong with them. Unhealed hurts leave scars in the form of rigid, irrational behavior." [35]

Liry and I would practice our Listening Partnerships in one of our caravans or during our evening walks after the children fell asleep, sharing the challenges and frustrations of the day. With her loving attention during these "sessions", as we called them, I learned to cry, and it was such a relief. After a good cry it became easier to breathe; there was less tension in my chest, my anxiety subsided, and I felt more self-compassion. The more I cried, the easier it became to cry whenever something touched or hurt me.

One sunny morning, a few months after we began Amiram's class, I was sitting in our caravan with a cup of tea, enjoying a moment of quiet after the rush to take Shir to the daycare in our community where she spent a few hours every day.

Deep in thought, I jumped when I heard a knock on the door, almost spilling my tea on the floor.

"Come in," I said.

Liry entered, looking frazzled. "Do you have a few minutes? I'm going crazy here..."

---

35. Listening Partnerships for Parents, page 1.

"Sure," I said. "What's up?"

"I urgently need a session," she said.

"OK no problem, the house is empty, we can sit in the living room. I'll get everything we might need." I grabbed some tissues (for possible tears), my clock (to tell the time for switching) as well as some extra pillows (for punching).

Liry settled on a large puffy pillow in the living room and I sat facing her, looking into her eyes as Amiram had instructed and waiting for her to share when she was ready.

"Our neighbor called the police on us," she blurted.

"Why? What happened?" I asked, surprised.

"Nothing major. My little Shachar cried this morning. I knew he was not hungry or wet, or in pain. It started when I put away the Bamba. He ate half a bag and wanted more and I said: "No more Bamba right now" and then he began screaming and crying. I had a feeling it was not just about the Bamba but also other frustrations he had, so I just held him while he cried for a really long time. I guess it got on my neighbor's nerves or she thought I was hurting him so she called the police."

Here she paused, her eyes tearing up, and I reached over to hold her hand.

"When the policeman arrived Shachar was already playing with Shmulik, laughing, rolling on the carpet and pretending to be a very strange animal. The policeman looked at my laughing toddler and husband, smiled, apologized for the intrusion and left. But I'm still feeling shaky inside."

At this point, after several months of Amiram's class and much practice, I knew that I should not try to stop whatever she is feeling by telling her: "Don't worry about it, it's going to be OK, shush no need to cry...!"

Neither should I give her suggestions like: "Maybe next time you should shut the windows when he begins crying."

Also, it would not be good to interrupt with my own stories, as in: "You know what this reminds me of?"

And I should definitely not judge or criticize her saying: "You shouldn't take these things so personally."

Or ask questions that only satisfy my own curiosity as in: "Do you know which neighbors called the police?" or, "What time did it happen because I think I saw a police car drive by when I walked Shir to kindergarten?"

The goal is not to take her out of what she is feeling at the moment,

but rather to help her go deeper into the source of her angst.

To accomplish this goal, aside from continuing to listen compassionately, I could now do one of two things. I could show her I get it, as in: "Wow, sounds like you had a really tough morning..." and wait to see if she wants to share more. Or I could support her going deeper into why she felt like she was going crazy and was so upset. I chose the second option.

"What was most difficult for you about everything that happened?" I asked.

"There were moments when I just didn't know if Shachar was ever going to stop crying, if this would ever end and I felt so helpless..."

"Has there ever been a time in the past when you felt this kind of helplessness?" I continued.

"Yes," she said. "When my father left us."

"Oh..." I replied, taking a breath, my heart aching for my friend. "Tell me more, what do you remember?"

Liry cried as she shared everything she remembered from the day she found out her father was leaving. I listened and held her hand, knowing that at the time, when she was so young, overwhelmed and alone, there had not been even one person in her life who said to her: "You look upset, sweetie... Would you like to tell me about it? I am here for you."

Because if there had been even one person, she would not be feeling so much pain today.

A trigger from a current event had hijacked her to an event in her past that she was too young and alone to handle at the time, but in this moment, she was not alone. I was with her and the intelligent, warm and loving woman she had become was also present. Liry cried as she saw her younger self, her little girl, on that day feeling so helpless and alone.

"Is there something your little girl wants to say or request now that she couldn't then?" I asked her.

Liry nodded through her tears and spoke, her voice cracking. "Ima, I need you to see me, to tell me it's going to be OK. That I will be safe and loved even when Aba is not here and that it's not my fault he left us." She sobbed, looking at me as though I was her mother.

I held her hand, not trying to make her feel better, just making room for those feelings she had not been able to articulate when she was only six.

After a while her crying subsided. Eyes shining with tears, she met my gaze, not as her mother anymore but as her friend.

We hugged and then continued to the final stage of the process, called 'present time.' I asked Liry questions that would help her return to the here and now, so she could continue with her day feeling centered and present.

"Can you tell me three lies about Abirim?" I inquired with a smile.

"Sure... it's very crowded, there is a wide river running through it and all the children have green hair..." she replied, laughing.

I laughed with her. "Great! And so true... And what are you looking forward to doing today?" I continued.

"Taking a long walk in the forest with Shachar and Shmulik... And of course, my dance class this evening," she said, and then, "Thank you, I feel so much better."

We chatted for a few more minutes, then we switched and she listened to me.

After Liry left I looked in my booklet at how Patti Wipfler summarizes the steps of Listening Partnerships:

- Respect your listening partner, and the power of your own attention.
- Pay attention to your partner's issues, not your own, during her turn.
- Identify the upset that your partner has chosen to work on.
- Help your partner to release the emotional tension she talks about [36].

Reading it, I thought of the huge transformation that can happen when we listen in this way to one another, and how much I would like to share this gift with others.

---

36. Listening Partnerships, page 5.

Chapter 20

For Crying (and Laughing) Out Loud
1992, Abirim

People cry not because they're weak but because they've been strong for too long.

Johnny Depp

Crying is how your heart speaks when your lips cannot explain the pain you feel.

Anonymous

When Shir begins to wail I think of the time my brother Neve said: "Don't you just hate it when the child of the family sitting next to you on the plane begins crying while you're stuck in your seat, a seatbelt around you, trying to rest and all you hear are loud screams?"

If he were here now, I would show him that in this case we are that family disturbing all our neighbors on the flight to Baltimore, Maryland, to visit Brad's family. I would also tell him that, luckily, when I get stuck alone next to a disruptive family like us, crying no longer bothers me so much.

It is as if all the tears I cried over the past two years have dissolved some of the limestone that accumulated on the walls of my heart and now my heart is more open and accepting towards crying children.

But Neve is not with us on this trip, so I stop the conversation inside my head, pick up my wailing three-and-a-half-year-old daughter and stroke her light brown hair, letting her know that I get how hard it is for her right now. After a few more minutes of crying and annoyed looks from exhausted neighbors on the seats behind us, she falls asleep in my arms.

Taking a deep breath, I feel gratitude for my RC training.

In the RC class, I learned that when a baby is born, she is born with the ability to love anyone regardless of the color of their skin, race or religion. She is born curious, with a zest for life, with shining eyes, an open heart and great intelligence. And she is born with an innate ability to heal from most of the hurts she will inevitably endure.

And then, like all of us, she gets hurt, for the most part not because those around her are trying to hurt her, because they are confused, have been hurt themselves and have not been able to break the cycle and transform their inner pain so they transmit it.

Some examples of the ways we hurt babies and children begin at birth in the hospital, where the baby is often greeted with a slap, poking and prodding and taken away from the mother. As children grow, they may experience corporal punishment, feel fear, see their parents fighting, be lied to about things like death and sex, have to sit quietly behind a desk for hours and years in school when the best learning involves movement, have people talk above their heads as though they cannot understand, and be criticized and given negative feedback so many more times than positive feedback.

Most of these hurts would not be carried over to adulthood if children were allowed the release and relief of using their natural mechanisms to heal from them. Crying, laughing, shaking with fear, yawning, sweating and speaking quickly as we do when we are angry are mechanisms that have been around for thousands of years. They are the body's natural way to recover and return to balance after we've been hurt.

Crying seems to be the most controversial of these bodily reactions to hurt and stress, yet according to research it has been found to be immensely useful.

In 1996, when Shir was eight and Ben was five, I read an article in Mothering magazine by Ellie Becker that described research on the value of crying and emotional tears. She explains that the biochemist William H. Frey II, who conducted research about the content of tears, knew that nature phases out biological functions that are no longer necessary for survival. Crying and emotional tears have not been phased out and he wanted to understand why. "What is the reason we have the ability to cry and what is the physiological purpose of tears?" he asked in his research. He began studying crying and tears in 1979 and in 1985 published a book called: *Crying: The Mystery of Tears*. In the book he explains that "emotional tears carry away harmful chemicals produced in response to stress, and thereby play a central role in restoring the chemical balance of the body."

According to Frey, 'Crying it Out' is not just an expression; "it may be a literal description of what occurs as the body rids itself of stress-induced chemicals. Holding back tears, on the other hand, may impede the body's return to equilibrium after stress."

Amazingly Frey found a different protein content in emotional vs. irritant tears (induced by dust or cutting onion). "Human tears contain the endorphin "leucine – enkephalin" as well as a hormone called adrenocorticotropic (ACTH). The endorphin is thought to affect pain sensation and to modulate stress-induced changes in the immune system, while the hormone ACTH is released from the pituitary gland and is an indicator of stress." [37]

In other words, according to Frey emotional tears help in easing the pain, in maintaining the balance of the immune system and in releasing a hormone that the body produces in times of stress, thus functioning as detoxifiers and playing a central role in restoring the body's chemical balance. So if adults teach children to suppress their feelings and not to cry, they are doing them "an excessive disservice by robbing them of one of nature's adaptive responses to emotional stress." [38]

My own ability to cry and release pain related to my past hurts improved my relationship with Shir. I felt immense relief when I understood that sometimes babies (as well as children and adults) need to cry and be held lovingly as they release the frustration, sadness or hurt they are feeling. There is a type of crying that babies have that is not about being hungry, thirsty, or in pain. It is about the release of stress and other emotions that have built up inside, emotions the body wants to let go of in order to return to a state of balance.

"Young children are not able to say directly: 'Mommy or Daddy, would you listen to me for a moment? I am very upset'," Amiram explained in our RC class. "Instead, they show us how they feel when they begin to behave irrationally, asking for things that are usually not allowed, testing boundaries."

In those moments many parents, including myself before RC, try to pacify their children with diversions such as food or toys, or threats, in order to gain another moment of "peace" for themselves and their surroundings.

---

37. Mothering, Winter, 1996 by Ellie Becker.
38. *Ibid.*

Sometimes we try to explain to our children rationally why they should behave differently, but since their emotions are in the driver's seat, their rational mind cannot hear us. Until those emotions are addressed, rational explanations will not be heeded.

What if we could stop everything else we are doing in those moments when our child is behaving irrationally and hold him or her, saying "No" to the irrational request yet listening as they express their frustration about our decision and perhaps about many other things that upset them that day?

Expression of frustration and hurt does not look "good" by our usual standards and it may include tears and screaming. Yet if children do not learn to release their pain in a safe, loving place, they may end up acting it out as adolescents and adults in destructive, hurtful ways.

I learned that it is so hard to listen to our child cry when we ourselves had no support for crying as young children. It is also hard to listen when we are exhausted by lack of sleep and other worries or when we have more than one child or need to work or are a single parent. I realized that what parents need most is support and someone to listen to them when they are upset so they can continue to be loving and nurturing parents to their own children.

After several months of experiencing deep listening to my hurts, listening without judgment or interruptions, my ability to listen to the pain of others increased and crying and tears stopped bothering me. On the contrary, when someone who had been holding their pain inside started crying in my presence, I felt a deep sense of relief – "Finally..." I would say to myself.

My relationship with Shir was changing too. Instead of blocking her release of emotions, I learned to hold a space for her to discharge her upsets, as others in Amiram's class held space for me to do the same.

Parenting was no longer such a daunting, mysterious, never-ending endeavor and my confidence increased because I knew that when I messed up and felt emotionally overwhelmed, I could reach out and get support, release my feelings and regain my clarity.

Now when Shir cried I tried to remember that "when a child cries, throws a tantrum, or sometimes trembles and struggles, to expose and offload her bad feelings during her upset, she's doing her best to dig herself out of an irrational state" [39]. And that if I am able to support her during times of emotional stress, there is less chance that scars will be formed and more chance that her behavior will remain rational and flexible when faced with challenging life issues as an adult.

Instead of trying to bribe Shir with food or toys so she would do or not do something, instead of sending her to her room when she was misbehaving, giving her time out when she was upset or taking away some privilege, I would say NO when necessary and then lovingly, determinedly hold a space for whatever emotions came up.

For example: "No you can't have ice cream before dinner." Loud scream... "It is OK to be angry, Mommy will be here with you, but no ice cream before dinner..." More screaming. "Yes, you are upset and it is very frustrating but still you cannot have ice cream before dinner."

Sometimes it was very hard, her screams very convincing. She kicked, pushed, and tried to bite me as two- or three-year-olds will do when angry, but I kept holding her gently yet firmly from behind, avoiding her biting and kicking, and whispering how much I loved her and how I would never leave her no matter how angry she became. Gradually her kicking and pushing would subside and she would cry for a while until she relaxed into my arms and sometimes fell asleep as I held her close to my heart. A few hours or minutes later (depending on the circumstance) she would be back to her loving, joyful, curious self, running around the house, playing and laughing with Maya.

When the other facilitators and I led workshops and taught the basics of RC we would ask participants: "When was the last time you cried?" Most women said: "In the past week or month." Men would usually say: "When I was at a funeral of a family member a few years ago and even then, it was just a few tears rolling down my cheeks."

"Where do you cry?" we continued our inquiry. "In my room, alone where no one can see me" – was the usual response or "Never in front of the children."

"How do you feel after you cry?" we persisted. "Better, more connected, as though a fog has been lifted from my head and I can see things more clearly." "I feel more compassion for others." "I feel a sense of release and relief," were the answers.

If crying helps us – why do we try to hide it? Why is it still considered

39. Patti Wipfler.

by most people as something that one should control, withhold, and never share with others? Why is it considered a sign of weakness, especially for men, that is only sanctioned in certain places like funerals? One of my Arab students once shared: "I go to many funerals of people I don't know because there I can cry openly."

Jennifer Hansen from Enlightened Solutions, a holistic addiction recovery center, writes: "When emotions are held back, such as swallowing or holding back tears, the emotional energy gets congested in the body. Rather than having that flow of emotional force circulating and completing its cycle, it gets stopped up." [40]

I believe there are two main reasons why people hide their tears and do not cry in public places. The first is **confusion** about the importance of crying out loud. Parents and society are sometimes confused and believe that every form of crying is a call for help and that when they stop the crying it means that now everything is alight. Yet, as Frey showed us, there is a type of crying, whether it is our own or the crying of others, that is not about expressing a need but rather about releasing stress and emotional pain accumulated inside us. When we stop this type of crying, we are actually doing a disservice to ourselves and to others.

The second reason why we hide our tears is for **protection**. Crying is considered a sign of weakness, vulnerability and helplessness. We believe that if people see us in our weakness, they will use it against us. Sometimes this is true: our crying triggers responses in people that are based on how they were treated when they cried at a young age. But at other times, our vulnerability awakens empathy and invites connection, helping those around us to open up as well.

In RC we believe that what hurts children the most is being alone when they feel bad. For many of us, when we felt hurt, upset, vulnerable, as young children, there was not even one person who said with compassion; "I see how hurt you are, you can cry or get angry, I will be here supporting you."

Instead, many of us were criticized when we expressed our emotions: "Go cry in your room," "You are too old to cry," "Boys don't cry," "Stop whining," "If you don't stop crying I will give you something to cry about!" and more. People often reacted as though these feelings were bad and not a natural part of our reactions to life's challenges.

---

40. https://www.enlightenedsolutions.com/

And so, we grow up feeling lonely and not loved for who we truly are.

When there is no emotional release, there is no relief and the painful feelings that made us want to cry in the first place just build up, one on top of the other, until they hurt so much that sometimes we can explode. This explosion can hurt ourselves and others. It is an example of pain that has not been transformed being transmitted.

RC became a key component in the Together Beyond Words approach because it is a simple and very useful tool to release daily upsets so they do not drive our behavior. In a region that has been in a state of conflict for over 100 years, where trauma is so prevalent and gets triggered by daily challenges, it is crucial to have such a tool so we can remain centered and open-hearted.

Chapter 21

When Touch Can Heal

1996, Tuval

*As a community, we create a lot of space for fighting and
pushing back, but not enough for connecting and healing.*
Tarana Burke

*Loving touch, like music, often utters
the things that cannot be spoken.*
Ashley Montagu

*Touch deprivation is a reality in American culture as a whole.
... It's not just babies needing to be touched in caring ways or
the sick. It's not just doctors and nurses needing to extend it.
It's all of us, needing connection, needing to receive it,
needing to give it, with genuine happiness at stake.*
Rev. Anthony David in *"The Power of Touch"*
by Nora Brunner

"Ima!" I hear a voice calling from the bedroom.

"Ima come here!!"

It's 7:30 a.m. and I am in Metulla, a town located on the northernmost
tip of Israel at the Lebanese border, where my daughter Shir and her
husband Tom live with their two children, my grandchildren.

Shir has just walked out the door to take one-year-old Shalomi to
daycare and Tom is in Tel Aviv. I am alone with four-year-old Danielle,
folding a mountain of laundry piled on the dark brown living room sofa.
I have been waiting for her to wake up so I can take her to kindergarten
before I drive back home.

When I walk into Danielle's bedroom, she jumps into my arms.

"Mommy is not here," I tell her while kissing her forehead. "She took

Shalomi to daycare and is going to work afterwards."

Holding her in my arms, I walk over to the sofa and push the folded laundry out of the way so we can sit down. I lean back on the sofa cushion and she relaxes into my arms.

In the mornings Danielle loves to cuddle; in fact, it's probably the only time during the day except bedtime that she asks to be hugged. The rest of the day I am lucky if I can kiss the top of her head, she is so busy playing. But mornings are a time for physical connection, a time of grace.

"Savta, I love hugs in the mornings," she tells me.

The fragrance of the lavender shampoo that I used to wash her hair last night has lingered and I breathe it in while kissing her dark blond hair. Her cheek feels so soft against mine as I gently wrap my arms around her and say: "You are so wise. Hugs in the morning are the best way to wake up. I wish everyone would wake up to a few minutes of hugs every morning."

I am hoping she will never outgrow this desire.

So many years ago, the caretakers at the kibbutz nursery told my mother: "You should not touch, kiss, hug or hold your children too much... it will spoil them." That is how she was raised and also how she raised me. I wondered what the people who said this to my mother meant by "spoil". Did they mean the child might get used to hugs and kisses, closeness and intimacy? Might even grow to like these caring gestures and feel comfortable with them? Or might grow to need them and become soft-hearted, weaker? I am not sure.

I just know that gentle, loving touch, caressing and hugging were rare in my childhood on the kibbutz. The moments when it did happen are engraved in my mind. Like my first through fourth grade teacher Ruti, who would bring her forehead close to mine to rub noses, or when my younger brother Mor and I lay inside a hammock on both side of my mother, our skin touching, feeling her warmth and listening to stories about her escapades with her kibbutz classmates during April Fool's Day.

When I grew up, I found it difficult to hug people. In the junior senior prom when I was fifteen, my date put his arm around my shoulders and I had no idea what to do. Should I sit still or move? I was not sure, so I just sat there like a statue waiting for it to be over. When I was sixteen and a girl from high school came over and hugged me, I was uncomfortable and thought her really strange.

Wafa, an Arab Palestinian colleague who facilitated groups with me once shared: "When I was seven years old, my mother asked me to bring lunch to my father at his workplace in the old city of Akko. Walking over, I ate a pita sandwich she had prepared for me. When I arrived and gave him his lunch, he noticed a piece of food on my cheek and reached over to remove it with his hand. As his hand brushed against my cheek, I realized it was the first time I ever recalled him touching me."

When I heard her story, my heart ached for that little girl whose only memory of touch from her father was a brush of his hand against her cheek, and for the little girl inside me who longed for touch and at the same time had trouble receiving it.

After reading some research, I understood that touch is such a basic human need, so much so that babies who are not touched can develop physical and psychological problems or even die.

In a Huffington Post article from 2011 author Maia Szalavitz writes: "Babies' brains expect that they will experience nearly constant physical touch, rocking and cuddling: without it, they just don't grow. And without receiving kind empathetic care, they are less likely to behave that way towards others as they get older." [41]

Of course not all forms of touch are beneficial, as Cari Romm writes in a 2018 article from the Cut in New York Magazine: "Touch can be invasive and it can be violent. But affectionate touch, in particular, is a necessary ingredient for humans to thrive – and when we go without it over an extended period of time, the physical, mental and emotional consequences can be severe and long-lasting." [42]

As I began writing about touch, I realized that over the past few years the importance of "a little bit of human touch," as Bruce Springsteen puts it, has become a controversial issue and not easy to write about because so much of our news is filled with sexual abuse and harassment cases and because so many of us have #MeToo stories. But when reading a letter by Ann Wild in the Washington Post, I could also feel "that we are headed toward becoming a society in which everyone is scared to touch another person to offer a sign of affection and support for fear it will be misinterpreted." And that even while applauding the #MeToo movement, "we need to recognize that not all touch is sexual and that human touch is vital for our well-being." [43]

41. https://www.huffpost.com/entry/how-orphanages-kill-babie_b_549608

42. https://www.thecut.com/2018/06/the-lasting-damage-of-depriving-a-child-of-human-touch.html

43. https://www.washingtonpost.com/opinions/metoo-is-a-good-thing-but-so-is-human-touch/2019/04/04/dd1aea2e-563a-11e9-aa83-504f086bf5d6_story.html

Loving touch is key here; "loving" does not have to mean "sexual", but it always means consensual. Much like Listening Partnerships, affectionate or loving touch also involves respect for boundaries, and respect for privacy. Both are intimate in different ways, and require mutual trust to varying degrees between the people involved.

During the period of closures and isolation due to COVID-19, so many people longed for touch and connection because loving touch enhances our well-being. According to research, when we are touched lovingly the level of the stress hormone cortisol decreases and the immune system actually becomes stronger. In addition the level of serotonin, the natural antidepressant and pain reliever, increases as well as the level of oxytocin, the bonding and love hormone. With the frequent lockdowns and quarantines of the pandemic, we were missing that loving touch more than ever.

In my adolescence and early twenties, touching others, especially men, was confusing – *Was my touch too soft or too firm? Do they really like it or are they uncomfortable? Is every touch sexual or is there a touch that can be just nurturing?* I was searching for answers --- but where to find them? Most people did not talk openly about these things.

Studying dance therapy in the United States surrounded by women who were comfortable hugging one another helped. I began feeling more at ease with being hugged.

Being in a relationship with a man helped, too, and with the birth of my daughter and later my son something opened inside my body; I loved touching, holding and hugging them. They slept near us in the family bed and when they were away from me as babies, I felt physical pain.

In 1996 I decided to learn more about touch and joined Avi Grinberg's school for Holistic Reflexology. Six times a year, I would meet with about thirty other students and our teachers for a week of classes. Half the time would be spent in a classroom and the other half in a very large room with high ceilings, light blue carpet and floor-to-ceiling windows overlooking the green hills of the Galilee. Along the windows were massage tables where we practiced the techniques.

Avi Grinberg, who studied many different forms of massage, realized that emotions are held in the body. He also noticed how many of us try to run away from painful feelings such as fear, sadness, anger, loneliness and pain. When things become uncomfortable, people make small talk, walk away, ignore the situation, drink, smoke, eat, take drugs, shop, etc. We find

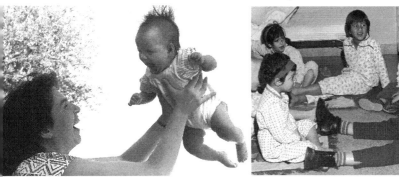

1. A moment with my Mum. (PS)
2. Listening to a bedtime story in the kibbutz nursery. (PS)
3. Our Family in Signal Mt., Tennessee.
4. During the Six-Day War. (PS)
5. A moment with my Dad. (PS)

Photos Credits: Gal Mosenzon / Magical Children of Light (GM) - Aviv Perez (AP) Joshua Yelin / *Pashi* (PS) - Gilad Reshef (GR) Assaf Pocker (ASA)

1. Graduating from Goucher College with Holly and Barbara.
2. Our first Arab/Jewish group.
3. On a tour of the old city of Akko. (AP)
4. Arab and Jewish children playing together in Akko kindergarten. (AP)

1. With the President of Israel Yitzhak Navon and Alan Slifka at donations award ceremony.

2. Silvia Margia leading a group. (GM)

3. Mariam Mar'i Ryan at DETEA.

4. Our group at Esalen. (ASA)

5. Efrat Ashiri & Richard Schwartz with one of our groups at Esalen.

1. In a workshop in Israel with Marianne Williamson (second from the right), and Noa (center).

2. A Listening Partnership.

3. Osnat Arbel & Einat Bronstein teaching us IFS Level 1 in Nazareth.

4. Leading a group. (GM)

1. Strength can connect us. (GM)
2. Empowering women to use their voices, Mervat vs. Gita.
3. Feeling our strength while staying connected. (GM)
4. Developing trust.
5. Pulling away without letting go. (GM)

1. During the first year teaching at DETEA.

2. Our first group. (AP)

3. Playback Theater at Oranim College. (GM)

4. Why ? (GM)

5. Playback Theater at Beit Berl College.

6. Playback Theater at Metullah. (GR)

1. Supporting one another.
2. A moment of grace.
3. Healing Touch. (GM)

4. Liry (Jewish) and Silvia (Christian Arab) during a Listening Partnership. (AP)

1. Our Tel Hai Playback group.
2. Mary, Miri and Rozit during a workshop.
3. With Paula D'Arcy at Esalen.
4. Two Playback Theater actresses (Yoli and Tasneem).
5. Ann Bradney during workshop. (GM)
6. The center of the circle. (GM)

an "exit," as the author and couple's therapist Harville Hendrix calls it.

But what if we looked at these emotions more objectively, befriending them and trying to understand why they have come up into our awareness at this time? What are they trying to tell us? And can we learn to stop our automatic reaction to a situation and create a space for something new?

In the Grinberg approach, the person giving the massage is called the teacher and the person receiving is not the client but the student, who is there to learn more about the emotional and behavioral patterns hidden in their body and what they can do to transform them. We began by learning how to become aware of a person's physical and emotional strengths and challenges by looking at and touching their feet. This foot analysis guided us to which body part to work with and what kind of touch to use. We learned how different qualities and types of touch can support the process of returning to a balanced state.

For me, the best part about our meetings was the opportunity to be in a safe setting where I was encouraged to touch, where I was touched and where I could explore what type of touch felt good and what did not, how to feel comfortable with touching others and how to let them know what I needed.

On one of the first days, the teacher asked half the group to lay on the massage tables, while the rest of the group were each assigned to stand near one of the tables. We were asked to massage the person's back for five minutes without specific instructions. "Just become familiar with your partner's back" was what they told us.

After five minutes we were instructed to move to the bed on the right of us and now touch this person's back for five minutes. We moved around the room in this way for about thirty minutes and then stopped to notice what had accumulated in our bodies after massaging different people. Then we switched and the ones on the tables stepped off and took our places. This exercise helped me feel the differences between people's backs and begin to get a sensation of the kind of touch that each back needed. When I lay on the bed, I felt various people's hands and the sensations that came up for me with each set of hands.

After a few weeks of classes my awareness of the wellspring of emotions and sensations stored in my body, which would bubble up in response to the different types of touch, increased. We were encouraged to release these emotions, and since we all worked on massage tables in one big room, the crying, laughing, or shaking with fear of some would reverberate around the room, assisting the release of suppressed emotions in others.

Encouraging the release of emotions did not mean allowing these emotions to control our behavior or debilitate us but rather that experiencing our feelings can help us become more present.

One day, while we were working in pairs to practice a certain technique, it was my turn to be on the massage table first. Yuval, a tall young man with curly brown hair, worked with me and something came up. I started crying uncontrollably. Soon my body began shaking and energy seemed to be flowing out of every pore. I could not stop it and was encouraged not to fight it, just be in it and feel everything. When it was time to switch places and work with Yuval, I was still shaky and crying.

I left the classroom to wash my face but the tears kept flowing so I sat outside, not sure what to do and how I could return to work with him. One of the assistants came out to look for me.

"What's going on?" she asked.

"I can't go in there and work with Yuval now, I'm a mess." I whispered through my tears.

"You are not a mess," she responded, "You are just very open. Go in there with this energy and use it. It's good energy and you can continue crying as you practice the technique on him."

I went back into the room to the massage table where Yuval was lying on his stomach (thank God I did not have to face him) and began practicing the new technique we had just learned while my tears flowed. At some point I forgot the tears and everyone else in the room and what they might think of me and began enjoying the energy flowing through my fingers while I touched Yuval. It was as though some inner source of aliveness had opened within me and was flowing into his back and shoulders. The feeling was so good, so powerful that I did not want the massage to end. When we stopped Yuval continued lying on the bed for a while. Later in the cafeteria he came up to hug me and told me how rested and connected he felt.

As part of my studies, I began practicing the healing touch on several friends and people I met in workshops. Someone had only to mention that they had a headache and I would be there, sitting behind them and asking permission to massage their temples and possibly help their headache disappear. At one point, when trying to figure out how to advertise my private practice in holistic reflexology, I imagined writing an ad saying: *a crying reflexologist in search of a client who needs to cry.*

Very soon I incorporated the healing touch at the end of all the courses and workshops I taught for Palestinian Arab and Jewish kindergarten teachers.

It was usually their favorite part of the meeting, the part they wished could last for hours. I realized the depth of our longing as women to be nurtured and touched and how it connects us to one another.

Years later I read about the research that Shelley Taylor, PhD, conducted at UCLA with five of her colleagues. They discovered a new response to stress and threat, in addition to the freeze, fight and flight, that is more common in women and named it *tend and befriend*. Women developed this response because *fighting* an enemy might endanger them, especially if they had children with them or were pregnant, and if they tried *fleeing* with their young children their pace would be slowed considerably by the child's smaller legs and feet or by carrying their baby. Women required a different approach to threatening, stressful situations and since oxytocin, the bonding hormone, was more readily available to them, they were able to develop *tend and befriend* which refers to "nurturing behaviors – the "tend" part of the model – and forming alliances with a larger social group, particularly among women –the "befriend" part of the model." [44] Perhaps this is why women find it easier than men to form circles across political, religious and national lines where they could befriend and tend to one another.

In our groups, women loved the tending and being tended to. I encouraged them to ask for the kind of touch that actually felt good to them. Asking for what we need, physically and emotionally, is often difficult for us women, and yet is so crucial to our empowerment and liberation.

Years later, in 2002, while on a lecture workshop tour in the USA with Mervat, I received a very valuable lesson on how the need for healing touch extends across cultures and continents and can appear in the most unexpected places.

We were invited to meet the director of a foundation who might be interested in donating funds to TBW. As we entered the tall building where her office was located, we were stopped at the reception and asked where we were headed. After we gave her name, the receptionist called up and her assistant came to escort us upstairs.

---

44 - BETH AZAR Monitor Staff July 2000, Vol 31, No. 7

Nervousness rose up from the center of my stomach when the assistant knocked on her office door and ushered us into the spacious room where the director was working on some papers behind a large dark brown desk. She invited us to sit on two chairs facing her, and when I noticed the gray professional looking suit and skirt she was wearing along with the high heels I became even more nervous. I knew it was up to me to do the talking, at least in the beginning, and was not sure what to say. When she looked up, her beautiful, welcoming smile and caring eyes helped me relax a bit.

A while later, as I was sharing information and answering her questions about the organization, I noticed she was massaging her left shoulder with her right hand as though it hurt.

"Are you OK?" I inquired

"Yes. I think it's just a tight muscle in my shoulder."

Immediately my desire to heal the world one massage at a time kicked in and I offered her a massage. Surprisingly, she agreed and a moment later she lay on the bluish office carpet, her head on a pillow, while I massaged her shoulders and temples and Mervat massaged her feet.

Mervat and I looked at one another in disbelief. *Is this actually happening or did we conjure it?*

Twenty minutes later she opened her eyes, thanked us for the massage and said it helped. We continued talking for a bit and before we left, she invited us to submit a proposal. That unusual meeting began a connection that has lasted for over fifteen years: the foundation supported several of our projects, she and I became good friends, and she even participated in one of our workshops calling it later 'the most profound healing work on a human level that I have ever witnessed.'

But on that day as we stepped out of the foundation's office, I looked at Mervat and smiled, feeling elated and blessed to be a woman and able to "tend and befriend" [45] even in the most unlikely situations.

---

45. https://taylorlab.psych.ucla.edu/wp-content/uploads/sites/5/2014/11/2011_Tend-and-Befriend-Theory.pdf

Chapter 22

Birthing Together Beyond Words
1994-1996, Akko

*The dormant power of women together is the untapped
resource needed by humanity and by the planet.*

Jean Shinoda Bolan

In 1994, three years after I began working with Mariam at Dar El Tifle
El Arabi (DETEA), I received funds from the Global Fund for Women to
conduct a year-long research study about the efficacy of the approach
I was developing. At about the same time, Mariam Mar'i met Alan Slifka,
who had just founded the Abraham Fund, the first nonprofit organization
dedicated solely to furthering coexistence between Israel's Arab and Jewish
citizens.

Alan believed that we must learn to coexist or we will cease to exist.
When he heard about Mariam's work he approached her and suggested
that she create a coexistence project at her school and his non-profit would
consider funding it.

"No," she responded, "we are not ready. First, we as Arabs need to take
care of our own needs, learn about our own roots, culture and traditions.
Only when we feel that we have something to offer and that we are more
equal can our coexistence work begin."

I did not know about their conversation when I began conducting my
research.

I was trying to find out if the approach combining Dance/Movement
Therapy and Listening Partnerships, which I had begun to develop, was
actually making a difference for the women studying to be early childhood
educators who participated in my classes.

When I asked them how they felt in the closing circle at the end of the
class, many responded: "This is my favorite class in the college," or "It's the

only class where I learn things that actually make a difference in my life," or "It's the place where I can be myself, share the things that bother me and not feel judged."

I was curious to see if their testimonials on how meaningful the class was for them would also be visible on a body level.

In September of 1994, we filmed two separate groups going through a Dance Therapy session led by Orit, another dance/movement therapist. Then, during the school year, I worked with only one of the groups, the experimental or research group, while the control group took all the same classes as the research group at DETEA but did not work with me. At the end of the year, we filmed each group again in separate sessions with Orit.

Afterwards we sent the film to a Certified Movement Analyst (CMA)[46] who was blind to the purpose of the study and to which group was the control or the experimental. Each participant had a number taped to her back so that the CMA could describe her movements referencing to that number.

The CMA's impression from the pre-intervention film reflected what I had been sensing for a while. She wrote: "In particular, I am struck by their lack of weight effort, or the passive attitude towards weight expressed mostly in limpness. Whenever weight effort appears it is usually light. Appearance of strength is rare. In the LMA framework weight effort is associated with asserting oneself and making an impact in the world. It is about determination and claiming of self. For some reason the women do not assert themselves through movement." [47]

This makes sense, I thought. The weight effort has to do with feeling grounded and being able to assert oneself and my students often appear ungrounded, afraid to voice what they really feel and have a difficult time saying No. It makes sense that these behaviors would be reflected in how they move. The Laban Movement Analysis (LMA) method also talks about direct and indirect movements in space. What the CMA noticed in both groups before the intervention was that "their movements lacked spatial awareness and spatial intent."

---

46. According to the Laban Institute "A CMA is a skilled movement professional trained and certified by the Laban/Bartenieff Institute of Movement Studies (LIMS®) and has a highly refined understanding of the patterns of movement through the (Laban Movement Analysis) LMA lenses of Body, Effort, Shape and Space. As a Movement Specialist, a CMA uses his/her comprehensive knowledge to identify movement patterns and convey the 'what' and 'how' of any human movement."

47. Yahav, D. (1995). Movement assessments of two groups of Arab women from Acco. Unpublished manuscript.

I remembered noticing in my groups how difficult it initially was for the participants to honestly express their thoughts and feelings, and how eager they were to please, to give in and to be nice, perhaps especially towards me because I am a Jew and maybe there was fear involved. They would try to get their needs met in other, more roundabout ways and hardly ever took a stand.

The CMA added: "In the meeting the women in both groups (control and experimental) seem to feel intimidated, shy, embarrassed, closed and insecure about what they need to do. They giggle a lot, have limited eye contact with one another and are not open to interaction among themselves."

What happened at the end of the school year?

Of group 1 (control group) who met for regular classes at DETEA throughout the year but never with me, the CMA wrote: "Although the women seem to feel more comfortable with each other, they are not really engaged in the session. They still giggle and do not interact freely with one other. When moving with the scarf, they are dependent on the teacher's directions and are not open to explore other possibilities."

For group 2 (experimental group) who worked with me, she wrote: "In addition to feeling more comfortable with each other, they become engaged with the lesson much faster... The group tends to be more dynamic and Effort and Shape qualities appear more frequently. In the locomotion part, they are creative in interacting with each other. Moving with a scarf, they seem to take more initiative in exploring independently creative possibilities. They are aware of the imagery suggested by the various ways of using the scarf and are willing to develop it further as a group." [48]

What changed? Not much in the first group, though after spending a year together they did become a bit more comfortable with each other. But there was a dramatic shift in the experimental group – they became more open to a new way of interacting; they were less self-conscious and felt comfortable enough in their bodies to begin a creative exploration in movement to unfamiliar music with a teacher they had only met once during the first meeting at the beginning of the school year. They were also comfortable enough to create a group improvisation – a wedding scene. But most importantly, the Effort and Shape qualities – like weight and use of space – appear more frequently. The women were both more grounded,

---

48. *Ibid.*

allowing them to be more creative, and more direct, which enabled them to interact in movement with each other.

Because many women living in this part of the world are still oppressed and otherwise abused, regaining the use of the weight effort can lead to their ability to create real lasting changes in their lives.

Barrky (1980), who worked with abused women, noted: "Without active use of weight there is little hope that these women will ever be able to stand up for themselves" (p. 135) [49]. Chang and Leventhal (1995) describe what happens to a woman who is asked to push against a partner and realizes, with the support of the therapist, that she is not a "push-over". These interventions encouraged her "to interact more assertively with the important figures in her life and begin to perceive herself more positively" (p. 62) [50].

Looking at this evidence, I concluded that the method I used had created some body-level changes connected to changes in feelings and attitudes. Amongst the changes were an increased sense of comfort with themselves and their bodies, an enhanced ability to creatively interact with others, an increased openness to new and unexpected experiences and empowerment.

Based on this study, I decided it was time to take another step. I spoke with Mariam, who was excited about the results and said: "I think the time has come for a coexistence project."

I agreed. Both of us thought it would be amazing to use this approach that helps young women feel stronger and better about themselves and more open, direct and honest in their interactions with others to do something for coexistence and peace.

A few weeks later, Alan Slifka and other donors of the Abraham Fund came to visit DETEA. Mariam asked me to lead a session for them so they could experience what it is that we do. Soon they too were dancing, listening to one another, sharing stories and even messaging each other's shoulders. Afterwards Alan came up to thank me and I sensed immediately how special he was: a man, a very wealthy business man in his sixties who was willing to walk into a strange room and begin dancing

49. Barrky, C. (1980). A comparison of the movement profile of battered, ex-battered and non-battered women: A pilot study. Unpublished master's thesis. Hahnemann Medical College, Philadelphia, PA.

50. Chang, M. & Leventhal F. (1995). Mobilizing battered women: A creative step forward. In F. J. Levy, (Ed.). Dance and other expressive arts therapies: When words are not enough (pp. 59-68). New York: Routledge.

with a group of his colleagues, share stories and play games. I was amazed.

We wrote a proposal for a project that would include Arab and Jewish kindergarten teachers and in September 1995 it was approved. We named our first group *Creativity, Attention, and Connection*. Later it evolved into *Together Beyond Words*.

From the beginning, I knew this group would be led by an equal number of Jewish and Arab women facilitators and that Liry would be my partner in this venture. I searched for and quickly found two Arab women who were happy to work with us – Wafa and Mervat. Wafa was a teacher at the College and Mervat, the one who found her voice a couple of years earlier. Finding facilitators was the easy part – now we faced the challenge of finding kindergarten teachers willing to participate in this new and innovative program.

Most of the Arab teachers for the first group signed up after I led a workshop at one of their monthly meetings with their superintendent. Finding Jewish teachers proved more difficult. I tried going to one of their meetings and telling them about the workshop but most seemed unimpressed. I could only guess as to why: perhaps because they had been through similar workshops before or because they were part of the privileged Jewish majority and had less of an incentive to try to connect with their Arab colleagues. Whatever the reason, I was running low on options.

That is how, one warm sunny afternoon in the fall of 1995, I found myself facing the fence surrounding a Jewish kindergarten in Akko, preparing to scale it.

I'd thought I would just stop by and talk to the kindergarten teachers, but I had not taken into account the high fence surrounding each kindergarten. The only way to get in would be to climb over it. I looked around, hoping for a different solution, a miracle perhaps, but no help came. So, I tightened the bag on my shoulders and began climbing. A moment later I was on the other side. I rang the bell and when a teacher answered I introduced myself and began explaining about the new group for Arab and Jewish educators and the wonderful opportunity it presented.

Even though Akko is known as a town where Jews and Arabs live together, the kindergartens are for the most part separate, with Jewish teachers for Jewish children and Arab teachers for the Arab ones. With every teacher I approached, my explanation of what we were trying to do improved a bit.

"Why would I want to join this particular group?" they'd ask.

"Look, I know how hard you work," I'd say, looking directly into their eyes, "I also know that being with children all day is exhausting and going to a workshop afterwards where you would be sitting and looking at a teacher for three hours is probably the last thing you want to do after a full day's work, even when there are continuing education credits involved. But this workshop will be different, it will be fun, healing and nurturing. You will come out feeling much better and more energized than when you came in and you will be doing something meaningful for coexistence at the same time." After working with the students in Akko for a few years I truly believed this would be so.

I must have said what they needed to hear; my efforts paid off and by February 1996, we were able to assemble the first group of 24 Jewish and Arab Kindergarten teachers for a 56-hour, four-month course.

Chapter 23

Our First Meeting

Winter, 1996, Akko

> [...] peace comes by following three paths. The first is to make peace with ourselves – all of ourselves. The second is to make peace in ourselves with the significant people in our lives. The third is to find our own experience of Peace with a capital P.
>
> **Louise Diamond,** *The Courage for Peace*

On a chilly afternoon in February 1996, Mervat, Liry, Wafa and I – two Jews, a Christian Arab and a Muslim Arab – begin facilitating our first group using a new approach based on our shared knowledge.

Twenty-four kindergarten teachers from Akko and other parts of the Western Galilee drift in slowly, placing their shoes on the floor outside the meeting room and their bags and coats inside. From the way they greet each other I can tell that some of the women know one another well and others have only just met.

Half of our meeting room has a light tile floor, used mostly for the movement part of the meeting. The other half is covered with a flat light blue carpet, on which we sit during the opening and closing circles and when we're in a listening partnership. For the healing touch, we have thick comfortable mattresses and have asked the participants to bring towels and scarves from home that they can put down on the mat beneath their heads.

We invite them to sit on the carpet in a large circle around an altar centerpiece, an orange-red scarf arranged around a white candle in a glass holder, matches, and a heart-shaped piece of rose quartz. Wafa greets them and asks for a volunteer to light the candle. One of the women makes her way to the center. She lights the candle, looks up at all of us and says, "I am so happy to be here."

Then Liry begins. "There is only one candle in the center of our circle and we all see it, yet each one of us sitting here has a slightly different perspective of this one candle depending on her location in the circle. In order to actually see the whole candle, we need the perspective of each one of you.

"The same goes for our experiences of living here in Israel. Without hearing your different experiences and points of view, we will never be able to understand the full picture. Every woman who is sitting here is important for putting together this human puzzle, each one of you through her unique experience contributes to the understanding of the whole."

I can see the light of the candle reflected in some of their eyes as I gaze around the room, taking in the presence of each of the women. Some are nodding, others seem reflective and one woman has tears in her eyes.

Wafa picks up the rose quartz lying at the altar and says, "I am going to pass this heart stone around the room now and would like to ask each of you to tell us your name, where you're from, the kindergarten you work in and what made you decide to join this group..."

As the heart stone passes from one to another, gathering the warmth of each pair of hands, I listen to their words:

"I was curious and attracted by the experiential nature of this course," one woman says.

"I just needed the credit hours of the Ministry of Education," another replies. "But now I'm starting to feel curious."

"I really want to get to know my colleagues from the other side of the conflict," was a response that came from both Arab and Jewish women.

After each woman speaks, Wafa thanks them for sharing.

Once the stone has made its way around the full circle and back to me, I share about myself, then say, "We have begun getting to know one another mostly through our words. Now let's see if we can get to know one another and the space we share in a way that is nonverbal, beyond words."

In the spirit of meeting them where they are at and transitioning slowly, I ask them to sit back-to-back with one other person. I put on the song "Lean on Me" by Bill Withers, and watch as they arrange themselves in pairs.

"Now take a deep breath and notice how the place where your backs are touching feels... Keep breathing and begin to move, allowing your backs to get to know each other. Imagine you're a puppy that's turned on its back in the grass and is twisting from side to side to massage and scratch its back... Great! Now slowly bring your hands towards your partner's. Touch her hands gently as though you are saying hello. See how it feels to touch and be touched. Are you touching gently or firmly? See what feels good and adjust. Then slowly lift up your hands together through the sides of your bodies as high as they will go without letting go of each other until you are both stretching together. You may want to try and lean from side to side, or one of you may reach with her arms towards her feet while the other can relax over her back, feeling the stretch in her chest and arms. Yes, that's it. Great!"

Around me I hear ohs and ahs and "Wow, it feels so good!!"

"OK, now come back to center and let go of your hands, take a deep breath and imagine, just for a moment, that the woman whose back is against you did something that irritated you this morning, that you are upset with her and that right now is your opportunity to push against her and show her just how upset you are."

As they push against each other, I hear laughter and find myself smiling with them. The room is alive with playful, childlike energy that has broken through the need to be in control, to be nice and friendly.

"Relax for a moment," I continue, "and see how the spot where your backs are touching feels now. Breathe into the place of connection. Does it feel different from when we began? See if you can find a way to stand up together without losing that place of connection and without the help of your hands."

Some of the women are able to do it at once while others need several attempts before they find a way to stand up together. All seem energetic, lighthearted.

For the next 20 minutes we continue to move and dance, transitioning into the mirror exercise and a group warmup where each woman offers a movement and the rest try it on. Then we dance together, each time with a different partner, to the beat of Cyndi Lauper's "Girls Just Wanna Have Fun."

The room is bursting with energy and laughter as women twirl around one another, bumping hips, following a leader, breaking into small groups and lacing their hands in pairs or dancing in a circle, square dance style. When the music ends hands are clapping and a sigh flow through the entire room. "When was the last time I danced and played like this?" I hear someone say.

"Walk around the room for a moment and catch your breath," I tell them. As they walk, I add, "Now face another woman for a moment, gently close your eyes and notice how your body is feeling right now. Where do you feel energy? Open your eyes slowly and look at your partner for a moment. If you feel moved to say or do something, say it and/or do it and then sit down facing her on the carpet. You have ten minutes to share anything that is coming up for you."

After all 24 participants have returned to the circle, Wafa says, "Let's hear a few of you who would like to share. What came up for you during the movement and listening?"

"I work as a kindergarten teacher all day but I just realized that I hardly ever play with them or with my own children. It's fun playing"

"I remembered some of the tag games I played in my childhood."

"I felt heavy in the beginning, as if some force was pulling me towards the ground and I didn't want to get up. I was resentful for having to move and get up, but when we started pushing back-to-back forcefully something shifted and I began feeling energetic again. Afterwards the rest was fun."

"It was wonderful to meet a woman who has worked in Akko for as long as I have and we never even spoke. I am looking forward to getting to know her and the rest of you better."

As the women continue to share, I look around the room again and notice they are sitting a bit closer than they had in the beginning. Some are leaning towards each other, smiling and talking. Something in the group's energy feels more open.

Mervat speaks. "Today we will try to understand in more depth the meaning of Peace because we feel it's an important basis for the work we are doing here with you. So, I want to ask you. What is peace?"

"When there is no war."

"Quiet. Calm."

"Getting along with people"

"Having no intruding thoughts"

"Yes, to everything but there is more," Mervat responds. "Liry, can you share what you wanted to say?"

"Yes," Liry says. "The Hebrew word Shalom, *Peace*, comes from the root shalem, meaning "whole." *Oseh Shalom – He who makes Peace in the heavens, may He make Peace on us and on all of Israel* is a prayer and a song we sing on Friday evening after lighting the Sabbath candles. And," Liry says as an aside, "I would add that maybe the He can also be a She and perhaps He or She can also make Peace on all the world, not only on Israel, while they're at it.

"But what does it mean to make Peace in the Heavens?" she continues. "Last I checked there was no war up there... The Jewish answer is that, in the heavens we have opposing elements: water (rain), fire (sun and stars), earth (planets) and air, that coexist in harmony. A state of harmony between opposing forces/elements, where each one maintains its essence without negating the other, is the definition of Peace."

Women are nodding. It makes sense to them.

"But how can I create a state of harmony between opposing forces outside me when so often it feels like I have a war inside?" says Hussniah, a full-bodied Arab woman with brown hair and a beautiful smile.

Wafa looks at her and at the others. "Tell us about the wars you have inside you, what do you mean?"

"I have no peace or quiet even for a moment because I am constantly thinking of what I still need to do today or about something I did yesterday that was stupid," replies Hussniah.

Others begin to chime in as well.

"I spend so much time comparing myself to others and often feel I am not good enough."

"I hate my hips."

"My stomach is too big and I look really awkward when I dance."

"I eat too much and want to stop but can't."

"Sometimes I suddenly feel bad or sad or anxious and am not sure why."

"I am very angry with my father for some of the things he did to my mother but can't find a way to tell him."

"My children sometimes drive me nuts."

"I am so tired of trying to be nice all the time and worrying about what people think about me."

"Yes," I agree with all their examples. "Did you know that we have about 50,000 thoughts a day?"

They look as surprised as I was when I first heard it. I answer the unasked question: "Yes, someone actually measured it. How many of our thoughts do you think are positive? How many are like Liry's son who, at five years old, would say, 'It's so good I was born because I am so cute and everybody loves me'?"

They guess but for the most part already know the answer.

"At least 80% of our thoughts and feelings are negative and sometimes it does feel like a war is going on inside our hearts, brains and souls between positive and negative emotions," I resume. "It is just like that fable about the Native American grandfather and his grandson who are sitting outside by the fire at night looking up at the stars:

"'Did you know that sometimes I feel as if two wolves are battling over my heart?' begins the grandfather, 'One of them is full of anger, fear, worries, hatred and thoughts of revenge while the other is loving, kind, compassionate and forgiving.'

'But who will win?' asks the grandson, looking worried.

'The one I feed,' replies the grandfather."

There is a sigh in the room; the story hit home.

"But why is it so important that we feed the loving wolf? What happens if we feed the other?" Mervat asks the group.

"Then we risk bringing more hatred, revenge, anger and fear into the world, hurting not only ourselves but everyone around us," someone replies.

I nod in agreement.

Some of the women are changing their positions, stretching, looking behind and around them and whispering to one another, as if they have had enough sitting and talking in a circle and want to share what is coming up for them. Wafa notices and suggests, "Let's take a short break and then find someone you don't know really well and sit facing them. One of you will share whatever is present inside her right now that she feels moved to share and the other will just listen. Don't interrupt, ask questions or make suggestions. Let her try figure things out for herself within the caring space of your attention. Imagine your listening is a spotlight of compassion and she is on stage trying to bring her most authentic voice forward. The quality of your spotlight can make a huge difference. Try looking at her as you listen and if she is comfortable with it, you may even reach out and hold her hand so she can feel as well as see that you are with her.

"You have ten minutes each to share. Even if your partner does not want to share just sit quietly with her, making no attempt to fill the silence with your own words. Being lovingly present with someone as they try to figure things out even when they are quiet is a huge gift. We will tell you a moment before your time is up so you can be prepared to switch."

This is our first meeting and we still have not explained the "how to" of *Listening Partnerships*, but as I look around the room, I realize it is possible that we have an inherent knowing of how to be there for one another when given the opportunity and supportive space.

When the time is up, we return to the circle.

Mervat asks, "Does anyone have something they would like to share with the group? You may share anything of yours but do not share something your partner said to you without asking their permission."

A chorus of replies begins.

"I don't remember the last time that someone really listened to me like that."

"I began feeling so sad, I am not sure why but tears were flowing down my cheeks."

"At first I didn't trust that she would really be there for me but then I let it go. It just felt good to be able to share with someone who actually listened."

"When she spoke, I realized that I have very similar issues and it made me feel less alone."

I feel touched by their responses and want to hear more, but we are nearing the end of the meeting so we ask them to return to their partner, take a mat and have one of them lie down on her stomach while the other sits next to her.

"Take a moment to breathe, focus in, see what you are present to as far as thoughts, feelings, any discomfort in the body, energy and just breathe and keep noticing," Liry instructs.

"Now, if you are the one giving the massage, place your hands somewhere on her back where you feel moved to touch and stay in that place for a moment as you breathe. Let the warmth from your hands seep into her back and become aware of the beautiful being that is laying underneath your hands. Think about all the good she does in just one day, every day. Just notice her. Then begin massaging her back in the way you like to be massaged. The woman who is receiving, please let your partner know if you would like a different kind of touch – firmer, lighter – and if there is a place on your back or shoulders that hurts and needs special attention."

I put on Enya's *Shepperd Moons* and watch as the Arab and Jewish women nurture one another. It feels as though in this moment we are existing in an alternate universe, a sacred space.

After they switch and the massage time ends, I see them hugging one another and talking. We invite them back for the closure.

We are standing in a circle, shoulders touching and Mervat asks each one to share one word that expresses how she is feeling right now.

"Peaceful", "Connected", "Love", "Friendship", "Wanting more", "Relaxed", come the responses.

Before leaving, Wafa tells them what Virginia Satir said about hugs: "We need four hugs a day for survival, eight hugs a day for maintenance and 12 hugs a day for growth." She invites them to get some of those hugs right here and now. Most of them are walking around the room, hugging one another as "Stand by Me" plays in the background and I feel a mixture of relief and joy. They keep talking and it seems like they are having a difficult time leaving the room, breaking the connection.

When they finally leave, Mervat, Wafa, Liry and I gather to talk about the meeting. We all feel relief that our first meeting is over and joy that it went so well. When we think about what worked we come up with a few insights:

1. **It is important to begin with an awareness of where they are at, what they need and what they have in common.** Because women work so hard in their kindergarten jobs and at home with their children, they hardly have time to take care of themselves and their needs. This is common for both Arab and Jewish women. All of us need to be heard, to share what bothers us, to take care of our body, release emotional pain, play and laugh, cry and get angry without hurting ourselves and others and to be nurtured. Creating a common space for all that is one good way to enhance connection.

2. **Listening and being listened to helps develop compassion for ourselves and others.**

3. **Empathy, compassion and caring are intertwined.** When women become aware of their similarities and begin to feel empathy towards one another, they begin to care about what happens to the other and a relationship develops.

4. **When we care about someone and they get angry about what happens to them, it is easier for us to listen to them.** This ability to care that comes from knowing the story of the other can serve us on the days when things become very difficult in the outside world and especially regarding the conflict.

The system divides Arabs and Jews from kindergarten to high school. We lead separate lives, live in different communities and our children play in different playgrounds and go to separate after-school activities. We, therefore, have very little awareness of each other's lives and stories – what makes the other cry or laugh, her rituals, holidays and daily activities, what she was like when she was young, what games she played, how she fell in love or met her husband, what her parents and grandparents experienced living here and so on. Most of us do not know what messages "the other" received from her parents or society about being a woman. What happened to her family in the Nakba or Holocaust? And so much more. We just don't know and when we don't know it's easier to project negative qualities and harder to care. When we do care about a someone or some people and we see them unhappy or suffering, then we try to do something to help.

One of the first clues that we were onto something important came from Hussniah, the Muslim Arab Kindergarten teacher with big brown eyes and a huge smile who participated in this group. A couple of months after the group began, she shared a story with us: "My kindergarten of 24 Arab children is located wall to wall with a Jewish kindergarten that has 24 Jewish children. I have been working there for ten years and even though I know Nurit, the Jewish kindergarten teacher and have met her in our in-service training it never occurred to me that the Jewish and Arab children could play together both inside the kindergarten and outside in the yard. But after participating in this group and getting to know all of you, I decided I would speak to her and suggest that we open the gate in the yard's fence which separates the two kindergartens and let the children play together on both sides so they can get to know each other. Nurit agreed and this is what we have been doing since." She looked around the room, smiling brightly at all of us.

I could not quite believe her story; it sounded too good to be true, too picture perfect, so I decided to go and visit the kindergarten and speak with the Jewish teacher. I came over one day and actually saw both Arab and Jewish children playing together on both sides of the fence. The Jewish teacher invited me to her kindergarten and as we spoke, she told me: "When Hussniah suggested this, it suddenly dawned on me that this was actually a possibility. I have no idea why we waited so many years to try it."

I was not sure that ten years from now, the young children would remember they had played together, but something about the possibility that participating in our program was making almost immediate changes in the world outside gave me hope.

Chapter 24

The Second Intifada...
and We Continue to Meet

2000-2002, Akko

*Brothers [and sisters], love is a teacher; but one must
know how to acquire it, for it is hard to acquire, it is dearly
bought, it is won slowly by long labor. For we must love not
only occasionally, for a moment, but forever.*

From the words of Father Zossima in
The Brothers Karamazov by Fyodor Dostoevsky

"Marhaba," Wafa says, welcoming us with a smile as we walk into her small second-floor apartment overlooking Ben Ami, a main street in Akko. I look at her more closely after we hug and notice that her eyes are not smiling. Nahawand, our assistant facilitator who is a kindergarten teacher in the old city of Akko, is already sitting on the couch and Mervat is standing by the small balcony, looking out into the street. It is October 2000 and just yesterday the street was full of Arab rioters who threw rocks at both Arab and Jewish shops, breaking windows and shouting after they stormed the police station. The police responded with tear gas and rubber bullets and the mayor was wounded when someone threw a rock at his head.

Our group had been canceled for the week but Liry and I decided to visit our colleagues and see how they were doing in the midst of all this. As we drove into Akko with Amiram, our RC teacher who came to support us, I looked around warily, ready to duck if a rock or a Molotov cocktail was thrown in our direction.

Between 1996 and 2000, Liry, Mervat, Wafa and I had worked with three more groups. There was no longer a need to climb fences or convince kindergarten teachers to join our workshops – now they heard about it through word of mouth and signed up.

Then in September 2000 came the Second Intifada, the Palestinian uprising caused by the failure of the 2000 Camp David Summit with US President Bill Clinton, Israeli Prime Minister Ehud Barak and Palestinian Authority Chairman Yasser Arafat and the failure of the peace process itself. The Second Intifada began with a visit of Ariel Sharon, who later became Israel's 11th prime minister, to the Temple Mount, which is also the Al Aqsa Mosque complex. The visit triggered violent protest which the Israeli military suppressed with rubber bullets and tear gas.

Later, as the Intifada progressed, there were high numbers of casualties among civilians as well as combatants. The Israelis engaged in gunfire, tank and air attacks, and targeted killings while the Palestinians engaged in suicide bombings, rock throwing, gunfire and rocket attacks. The death toll, including both combatants and civilians, is estimated to be about 3,000 Palestinians and 1,000 Israelis, as well as 64 foreigners [51]. It was a scary time to live in Israel, and all of us felt it on the day we met in Wafa's apartment.

After hugging Wafa, Nahawand and Mervat, Liry introduces Amiram and we all sit in a circle of pillows on the floor.

"Let's stretch a bit before we begin," I suggest. I am nervous about being in Akko and about what our Arab Palestinian colleagues are going to say. *The stretching might help in getting me and the rest of us into our bodies, grounded and connected to our emotions,* I am thinking.

We stand up to stretch. Liry shakes her body, making loud AAHHHH sounds which encourages the rest of us to do the same. After a few minutes, feeling more centered and connected, we sit back down.

I look around and begin speaking: "We came today to hear what is going on with each of you during these riots."

"Yes," Liry adds, "we are worried. Please tell us how you are doing, we would really like to support you in whatever way we can..."

We decide to divide the time so that each one of us can share something that is coming up for her. Amiram agrees to do whatever is needed to support the process.

There is a moment of silence as we focus in and then Nahawand begins to share: "The children in my kindergarten did not want to go out to the playground today even though there is a high stone fence around the kindergarten and no one from the outside can get in. They are so scared

---

51. https://en.wikipedia.org/wiki/Al-Aqsa_Intifada

from the loud noises of shouting, throwing rocks, glass breaking and the shooting. They asked me if their parents will be alright. Some of them clung to their parents and cried so much when the parents left. Most of the day they just stayed close to me and my assistant and when I had to go to the bathroom, they stood outside waiting until I came out. It is so hard for me to see how all this is affecting them. Why do they need to suffer? They are so young..."

I listen, not sure what to say; the others also seem at loss for words. We just move closer, touching Nahawand's back, holding her hand while tears run down her cheeks. After a while she opens her eyes and looks at us. "I'm so sorry it's like this," I say as I lean in to hug her.

A few minutes later it is Mervat's turn to share and I take a deep breath, knowing it will probably be painful to hear what she has to say.

She chooses Amiram as her listening partner (the one she will focus her eyes on when she talks) and the rest of us create a circle around them. Gazing at Amiram for a moment in silence, Mervat seems to be connecting to an inner fire before beginning to speak:

"We are regarded as second-class citizens and treated in ways that you would never allow in your own communities. How dare you?" she says loudly, forcefully. "My brother was caught and beaten by the Jewish police even though his only crime was to be driving with a friend from Nazareth to Akko." Mervat is shouting now. "How could you? Would you sit quietly if this was happening to people in your families? To your brothers?" She begins sobbing while Amiram holds her hand. I am taking it in and for a moment I am able to listen, really listen without arguing or feeling guilty, just feeling what it must be like to be her.

Finally, her sobbing subsides. She looks at Amiram who opens his arms. Mervat moves closer so he can hold her while she cries.

It's now Wafa's turn and she asks Liry to be her listening partner.

Wafa looks at Liry as if testing her and asks: "Are you going to leave me if I tell you how bad it is and how angry I am?"

Liry does not respond. She does not say: "No, of course not, I am never going to leave you," because who can promise that?

She does not try to make Wafa feel better or less alone. She just holds her hands and looks into her eyes as if saying: "I am right here, right now, and I care."

Wafa continues asking and asking the same question until she bursts into tears. Liry moves closer, wrapping her arms around Wafa's shaking shoulders and whispering into her ear, "I am here now no matter what you say or feel or how upset and angry you become. I am staying with you in this moment." Wafa's sobs increased and I feel choked – am I crying too? After a while her sobbing subsides.

Then it's Liry's turn. Speaking to Wafa, she says: "I am so scared. We live only four miles from the border and I am afraid that we will need to leave our home again if the fighting escalates, if Katyusha bombs are fired at us from Lebanon. My children are so young and every time I hear a loud noise or something in the news about the fighting in the North, I am terrified…" Liry is shaking as she speaks and Wafa hugs her.

Even though I live in the same area and am often very scared to drive on the road with my children or alone imagining a bomb might hit the car, I block these feelings. In Amiram's class we learned that fear and terror are the most difficult emotions to feel, especially alone. And although I am not alone now, I am not courageous like Liry and do not feel comfortable enough to share my fears.

When Liry stops shaking in Wafa's arms, the others hug her and then it is my turn.

I do not know what to say. In this moment it is easier to listen than to be vulnerable and share something that actually hurts, scares or angers me. I am still trying to take in all of what has been said. I take a deep breath and look at them.

Finally, the words just come. "I don't know what to say. Inside me there's an emotional turmoil… I just want to sit here quietly in your presence and feel whatever comes up. I don't want to have to talk or explain or worry about what you might need from me, think about me or how to make sure all of you are okay. In this moment I don't want to care about all that, I don't want to care so much about anything…"

By this time, I am crying and they are sitting around me, their hands touching my legs and back reassuring, supporting. And I realize that there is no pressure to be something that I am not, that the only pressure comes from within me and that I can actually feel whatever I choose to feel. Just the realization that I can stop, breathe and be me as I am and that they care, touches me so deeply that I cry and cry.

Then we all hug and just before we leave Liry asks if we can each share in a few words how we are doing right now.

"Less alone," Wafa says.

"Seen," says Mervat.

"That maybe there is hope," adds Nahawand.

"Deeply touched," replies Amiram.

'That I can't wait for our next group," Liry says with a big smile.

"Ditto on everything you said, plus I feel so happy that we came here," I add, my eyes still wet.

A few minutes later we leave to go back home. I am not looking around to check for rock throwers and Molotov cocktail hurlers. Somehow, I know we will be all right.

In the next couple of years, the conflict within Israel becomes more severe. Every day the news is worse. The Israeli army has entered refugee camps – at least 21 Palestinians have been killed in the two camps, two of them children, aged 10 and 11 years. At least 230 people were wounded and many more people are suffering. A suicide bomber explodes on bus 16 in Haifa, killing 15 Israelis and wounding 40.

And yet we at Together Beyond Words continue to meet.

A 19-year-old Palestinian explodes and kills nine Jews, including four young children and two babies, and wounds more than 11, at a Bar Mitzvah celebration in Jerusalem. One whole family is wiped out. The wife was scared to come to Jerusalem but the grandmother convinced her to make the effort. Now they are all gone. A missile apparently meant for a Hamas activist kills his wife and three children and two other students who were in the area. Another shell hits an ambulance, killing the Red Crescent worker inside. A young Palestinian woman, whose brother was killed a month before and whose fiancée was killed a week ago, explodes near a checkpoint killing two soldiers. A Palestinian man enters a restaurant in Tel Aviv, shooting and throwing hand grenades until he is finally killed by a Druze policeman.

And yet we continue to meet.

People are depressed, hopeless, feeling as though their life is on hold – waiting. Waiting for the government to do something, for international powers to do something, for somebody to do something. Many do not listen to the news. They can't stand to listen anymore.

We continue to meet.

We get emails from friends here and abroad telling us that coexistence efforts have failed and are of no use – that the Arabs and Jews will always hate one another.

We continue to meet.

Ariel Sharon tells us that we are dealing with bloodthirsty people and that we should be prepared for an extended battle with many casualties. Avigdor Liberman, minister of infrastructure and Benny Ayalon, minister of tourism, suggest that we bomb Palestinian markets and city centers.

And yes... we continue to meet.

Why? Why did we continue to meet? Why did we continue with our efforts for coexistence and peace along with the growing Peace movement in Israel?

We continued and still persist because in times like these, as Alan Slifka said, we either try to build bridges towards genuine coexistence and peace or we don't. And if we don't, we risk falling into the abyss of hatred, revenge, violence, death, destruction and hopelessness. Building bridges helps us to maintain faith that things will get better.

In our meetings, when we move, dance, play, cry and laugh together, when we ease each other's aches through massage and listen to one another's stories and most painful feelings, we come closest to actually experiencing the possibility of how we can live together peacefully and we realize what needs to be done in order to begin the healing process.

Perhaps the most important reason we continued to meet is because of our children. Because we are mothers, educators and caretakers, constantly around children who were born into an environment filled with violence and who live with deep-seated mistrust and fear. Through our meetings we are attempting to ensure that the children we work with will have had the benefit of a different experience, of learning that peaceful coexistence is possible.

In our 2002 group, Fanny, a pretty dark-haired Jewish teacher from Kibbutz Metzuba, which is about a mile and a half from the border with Lebanon, missed one of the meetings. When we spoke to her best friend Iris, who was also in our group, she told us what happened: Fanny's son who had just turned 14 was waiting at the kibbutz gate for his girlfriend, Atara also 14, who was on her way to visit him. Atara lived on another kibbutz and her mother Lin was driving her over. He waited by the gate at the set time and an hour passed and still they did not show up. He walked home to try to call her but there was no answer. Then he found out that two men from the Palestinian Islamic Jihad had infiltrated into Israel through the fence from Lebanon, hid in the bushes next to the road, then shot and killed both Lin and Atara as they drove by in their car.

Shocked and saddened, we, the Arab Palestinian and Jewish facilitators, decided to visit Fanny at her kibbutz. When we arrived, she invited us to sit on her front porch overlooking the surrounding hills that seemed so green, so innocent and beautiful in the setting sun. Fanny cried and shared the pain her son was going through and what she felt. We held her and listened. Our visit encouraged her to return to the group the following week.

During that meeting, she spoke about what it felt like to have a fourteen-year-old son who just lost the girl he loved: "I want to comfort him but do not know how. He often tells me, *'Mother don't get too close to me, because you may lose me too,'* which is so awful to hear... He visits the graveyard every week and stands by Atara's tombstone talking to the young woman he loved, still loves, while I stand at the gate, not sure what to do. Sometimes I just cry."

By the time she finished her story, all of us were weeping with her.

Holding her close, with tears running down her face, was another member of our group – an Arab teacher from Akko.

In that moment I felt that, although we had resolved nothing, had not found a miraculous solution that would bring peace, had not found a way to make Fanny's son or Mervat's brother feel better, still we were not arguing, not trying to convince one another of our truth and not competing about who suffers more. We were simply women of different ages, cultures and religions sitting close to one another on the floor of a century-old building, feeling our grief, together.

Part 3

Transforming: Emotional Pain into Understanding and Empathy

Only when we are brave enough to explore the darkness
will we discover the infinite power of our light.
Brené Brown

Below are stories from our workshops and
meetings over the past fifteen years, as TBW
developed beyond a group of kindergarten teachers
doing work based mainly on dance/movement
therapy, listening partnerships and healing touch,
to include a much broader range of people
and methodologies.

Chapter 25

Esalen

2006, Big Sur

In every moment, the Universe is whispering to you.
You're constantly surrounded by signs, coincidences,
and synchronicities, all aimed at propelling you
in the direction of your destiny.

Denise Linn

"I'm so nervous," I whisper to Jerry, my second husband, right before we knock on the wooden door of the garden cottage nestled on a cliff overlooking the Pacific Ocean at Esalen.

"I know," he whispers back, squeezing my hand warmly in his, "but go ahead and knock anyway."

A woman with a bright smile opens the door. "Welcome!" Nancy says. We hug and I feel so happy to see her, even though we've only just met.

"It's so good to have you here," she adds.

"It's great to be here," I say, and mean it.

"Go ahead and make yourselves comfortable. The leaders who will be teaching this week are over there in the living room. Why don't you pour yourselves a glass of wine and join them?"

Jerry's hand is reassuring on my lower back as we walk towards the living room.

I am not sure how to do this mingling thing. Jerry seems better at it and is already speaking with some people so I just stand next to him, checking out the small, cozy living room filled with wooden chairs, two couches, brown and green, small tables and shelves loaded with books. I look with amazement at the women and men standing, sitting, talking, drinking wine, eating grapes and cheese with crackers... *What exactly am I doing here with all these renowned leaders? How did I even get to be here and staying in the same house the world-renowned Fritz Perls had stayed in when he taught Gestalt here? Is this a dream?* I pinch myself. No, it's quite real.

Jerry and I were married a year earlier and maintained a long-distance relationship between Israel, the United States, and New Zealand where he also lived some of the time. In early 2006 it was my turn to visit him in California. Because I only had two short weeks for this visit, I was longing to be in a place where I could rest and get away from the intensity of living and working in Israel. So I decided to write a letter to the Esalen Institute. I had never been to Esalen but saw the sign on Highway 1 several years ago and had heard about this center for personal and social transformation from Jerry. I sent an email saying I would be happy to lead a workshop that would give participants a taste of the peacebuilding work we have been doing here in Israel in exchange for staying a few days at Esalen to recharge.

I was not sure they would respond – in fact, I was pretty sure they wouldn't – and yet Nancy, the director of programming, did respond, inviting me to stay and teach at Esalen for five days. So here I was, in February 2006, at Esalen for the first time.

Standing next to Jerry, with zero experience in cocktail parties, I feel a bit lost. Luckily, we are soon asked to sit down and introduce ourselves. The butterflies in my stomach make it difficult to focus on what everyone is saying.

Finally, Nancy turns to me and asks: "Nitsan, please tell us about yourself...?"

I share the story of my encounter with prejudice in junior high school in Tennessee, my Master's Thesis on Prejudice, my yearning to do something for coexistence and peace when I returned to Israel in 1989 and what we have been doing since.

When I finish talking there is a moment of silence. Glancing around the room, I see people wiping tears from their eyes. A part of me wants to disappear, to escape the vulnerability my words created, and yet when people approach to talk, I enjoy the delicious, warm feeling of being "seen" and appreciated.

One of the people who approaches me is a pretty, red-headed woman with a bright smile who introduces herself as Ann Bradney. She looks into my eyes and says:

"Your words touched me deeply; I want to work with you."

Having no idea what she means by "working" with me, or how pivotal this moment would be in my life, I nod my head and say "Sure," thinking she is probably just being nice.

A year later, when we began working together and became friends, Ann told me about her life and the motivation for her words that evening.

"I was born and grew up in Jacksonville, Illinois, the second of four sisters. My mother had a violent temper and I was so terrified of her, not only because she often hit me, but mostly because she cut me off whenever she was angry. The feeling of being disconnected and abandoned was even more terrifying than the corporal punishment and I never knew when and if she would return to connection. To avoid these painful emotions, I began using drugs and alcohol at the age of thirteen and was on a path of self-destruction for years until I found Core Energetics and began the deep emotional healing work that changed my life.

"After studying Core Energetics, I became a practitioner. Years later I felt something was missing for me in the model and I developed my own approach that I call Radical Aliveness. It was born of a strong desire, a need, to work not only one-on-one or with small groups but to do something bigger to make this world a better place. The work I developed moved beyond psychology and was about always including the world and the social context in what we are processing. When I heard you speak and share your story, I felt a powerful calling to become involved and work with you."

At that cocktail party in 2006, I had no idea where this synchronicity would lead us. Later that evening, when Jerry and I said goodbye to Nancy and thanked her, she said: "Nitsan, let's meet tomorrow morning on the lawn, I would like to talk with you about something."

The following morning at 10 a.m. I found Nancy sitting on the green grassy cliff towering above the Pacific Ocean. I was told one could see whales and dolphins gliding along the shore but noticed no telling sprays when I looked towards the shining blue waters. Glancing behind us, I saw the mountains reaching up into the clear blue sky, the wooden cabins snuggled between the trees and the organic vegetable garden, and I thought: *does one ever get used to such beauty?*

"Have a seat," Nancy offered, pointing to the wooden lawn chair next to her.

I did and for a moment neither of us spoke. I enjoyed the warmth of the sun on my back and the clear air that made it possible to see far beyond over the ocean.

"What you said yesterday really moved people," Nancy began, "so

I want to share with you a dream I've had for years. I was reminded of that dream when I first received your email asking to come here and again when I heard you speak last night."

She looked at me as if checking I was actually there and then continued:

"My dream is to bring a group of Arab and Jewish women from Israel to Esalen so they can experience this healing place together and go through a workshop that would provide them with peacebuilding skills they would then take back home to Israel. I wonder if you can help me realize this dream?"

I closed my eyes, trying to take in what she just said. *Is this for real?* I thought. *Did she actually ask if I could help her realize a dream by bringing a group of Arab and Jewish women to this incredibly beautiful place for a workshop?*

I pulled a piece of grass from the lawn and rubbed it between my fingers. No, this is not a dream.

"Yes!! Yes!!" I replied excitedly, opening my eyes and meeting her expectant gaze. "I would love to do it. But tell me more. How many women could I bring? For how long? What would be the cost?"

"Oh... how about 20 women for a week and Esalen would cover the cost of their stay here?"

I looked at her in disbelief, not quite sure what to say.

Coming back to Earth, I remembered the long 27-hour trip from my home in Israel to Esalen and pressed my luck: "A week would not be enough because of the jet lag. We would need more time. Just recovering from flying halfway around the world takes a couple of days so if we want the experience to be truly beneficial, we would need a more extended stay."

"Fine," Nancy replied, "I will check my calendar."

"Great, unbelievable, amazing!!" I gushed, trying to hold back on the superlatives so she would not change her mind.

"Oh, by the way," she said, "Do you have any idea who you would want to work with the group while you're here?"

"Eh... No..."

"Well, why don't you check our catalogue; we have amazing leaders who come here. Once you choose, I could talk with her or him."

I was never good at choosing ice cream flavors, so choosing from a list of great facilitators? I was clueless.

"Who do you suggest?" I inquired.

"How about Ann Bradney? She wants to work with you and she is great," Nancy replied.

"OK," I answered, trusting her intuition. Something was happening here that was bigger than anything I had ever imagined. It felt as if we were guided, supported. How else could I explain what transpired in those days, and in the years that followed?

Chapter 26

Gather the Women

2006-2007, Big Sur

Each time women gather in circles with
one another, the world heals a little more.
Anonymous

I am grateful to be a woman. I must
have done something great in another life.
Maya Angelou

After returning to Israel, my colleagues and I gathered a group of women teachers, facilitators, and activists who were interested in participating in the Women's Peace Leadership program with the in-depth workshop at Esalen.

In January of 2007 our organization, Together Beyond Words, brought the first group of Arab Palestinian and Jewish women to Esalen, where we worked with powerful leaders such as Andrea Juhan, Leah Green and Ilana Rubenfeld. But in the workshop with Ann Bradney my heart cracked open. In a letter to friends dated February 2007, I wrote:

"To be present and feel our pain was very difficult. We tried escaping to other things. Esalen has so much to offer. But then Ann Bradney came and created the safe haven we were all yearning for. She invited our pain, our anger, our grief – whether it was messy, ugly or seemingly endless – it was welcomed into our shared space. She knew that only bringing it out into the open can create a possible transformation, healing.

"What most of us experienced was something that was truly beyond words. Ann would focus on one of us and this woman's pain would create a chain reaction, sometimes touching just one other person, at other times involving the whole group in a communal outcry of agony "Enough! We cannot stand it any longer!!! How much more suffering? How many more need to die?" We cried for ourselves, for each other and for that painful reality we were born into and have been living in for so many years. We cried for the pain of the mothers. For Palestinian women seeing their husbands and sons taken away, not knowing when they would see them again. For the Jewish mothers who after so many years of ancestral persecution just want to find a peaceful place where they can live and safely raise their children, for those who lost their home in Bulgaria, Romania, Germany, Poland, Russia, Iraq, Morocco, Israel or Palestine. For those who are still carrying keys to homes they once had and hoping to return, for brothers and sisters, husbands and parents touched and hurt by this conflict. For families lost in the Holocaust, in the years of struggle, in prisons and compounds and families living in refugee camps across the border. At the end as my eyes wandered around the room every woman was either hugging or being hugged. Holding or being held. The pain and love intertwined."

Our 2007 experience was so powerful, so life changing, that we asked for and received an invitation to bring another group to Esalen in January 2009.

When we returned people asked me: Why take a group of Arab Palestinian and Jewish women all the way from Israel to the USA for a workshop instead of holding the workshop here in Israel?

Emerging from the depth of the experience, I tried to form the words:

"When we are away from this part of the world," I said, "we are able to do our deepest, most life-changing, healing work for a couple of reasons. First, because living in Israel is very stressful and as women we are constantly caring for, nurturing, "putting out fires" and making sure everyone is OK. Some of our participants have two cell phones so they would never miss a call. In our workshops, during every break, they run to check messages.

"At Esalen, away from that level of stress, with no cell reception, they are able to see that it is possible to live differently, take the time to relax, care for their own needs and go deeper into what really hurts.

"Second, in the United States our hosts and leaders do not know which ones of us are Jewish and which are Arab Palestinian, so they treat us all as equally foreign. Since this is often not the case in Israel, it enables the Arab Palestinians to express themselves more fully and openly. The women return to Israel deeply connected to one another and with a drive to work for change. These reasons make the trip worthwhile."

Financially, the Women's Peace Leadership Program with the trip to Esalen was challenging because it included scholarships for women who could not pay for their flights and the costs of working with the women for a few months prior to the trip and afterwards. In 2007, our support came from the Krieger and the Shapiro Funds, but in 2009 Paula raised the funds for our trip.

Paula?

"And now let's welcome Paula D'Arcy," the speaker was saying as I walked into the huge space of the San Antonio Convention Center on March 9th, 2007.

After our first journey to Esalen in 2007, I took a sabbatical and was living in Austin with Jerry. It was then that friends invited me to join them for a gathering of women from all over the world in San Antonio.

The speaker continued: "Paula D'Arcy was only 27 when a drunk driver killed her husband and young daughter as they were driving back home from a day on the beach. She herself was three months pregnant during the accident and was not harmed. In the midst of her crushing despair, and to her complete amazement, she discovered a presence within her that responded to her fearful cries for help. Her anguished heart was met by a great tenderness and wisdom, which she grew to recognize as transcendent love. Over time — knowing that pain was not the final say and did not have absolute power — she was able to find her way back to the light. Please join me in welcoming Paula D'Arcy" [52]

The person on the stage was joined by a small woman (maybe five feet) with short black hair, beautiful shining eyes and the warmest smile I had seen in a long while. As she stepped on a block to reach the podium, I felt a sense of awe.

"Hello and a huge welcome to each of you... to all 1100 women who have traveled from all over the world to join us here today. I am so happy to see you!!!" She paused for the enthusiastic applause, then continued:

"I would like to share a story with you, the story of what prompted this conference...

"Several years ago, I was assisting the leader of a vision quest. Each of the participants chose a power spot to be on their own in nature for a few days, away from other participants. The leader would visit them once a day to see how they were doing and I was in charge of keeping the fire going

52. http://www.redbirdfoundation.com/learnmore

in the gathering place where the vision quest began and would also end. On the evening before the end, at sunset, I went for a walk on the hills surrounding the camp. The leader said he would join me soon.

"I walked in slow meditation on the path, looking at the bare hills colored orange by the setting sun. A bit later I heard footsteps behind me. I thought it was the leader so I did not turn around, believing that in a moment he would catch up. But he didn't and the sound of footsteps continued so I finally turned to see who it was.

"I saw hundreds of women from all over the world, wearing their traditional costumes in so many different shapes and colors. Astounded, I looked at them as they walked together behind me. It seemed as if they wanted to tell me something, ask me to do something. I stood for a long while watching them until the sun set and they disappeared into the hills. I had never seen such a vision before."

"The following evening the vision quest ended with a gathering around the fire where each participant shared a moment that was especially powerful during his or her time alone. When the talking stick reached the last participant, Lucy, she said:

'The most powerful moment for me was yesterday. At around sunset I had a vision of women from all different countries in the world dressed in their traditional garb walking on the hills over there.' I looked where Lucy's finger was pointing. It was the exact place where I too had seen them.

"Overcome, I was at loss for words. We had both seen the same vision at the same time. What did it mean?"

Paula stopped talking, her unanswered question suspended for a moment amongst us. Everyone was silent. I sat on the edge of my chair, entranced, waiting for her next words.

Paula continued. "Years later I understood that the women from our shared vision were asking me to create a gathering for women, sisters, from all over the world so they could meet one another, talk, listen, speak their truth, share their struggles, be acknowledged for their strengths, learn from one another and in this way support each other's empowerment and liberation.

"Once the realization came to me, Beth, my daughter and I assembled a group of friends and together we worked very hard to make it happen." Paula paused again, allowing her words to sink in. Then she continued:

"Please take a moment to look at the women sitting next to and around you. They have made the journey to be here from all over the world. This conference, which we decided to name *Womenspeak*[53], is the gathering prompted by that vision I saw so many years ago."

I looked around the room at the hundreds of women sitting next to each other, many of them wearing their traditional colorful garb. Paula had realized her vision and I knew I had to meet her.

During one of the breaks, I walked up to her, introduced myself and asked if we could talk. She agreed to meet me in Austin where both of us were living at the time.

A few weeks later, Paula came to visit. Between stories about our lives, tea and cookies, I felt I had found a sister. When I told her about our Women's Peace Leadership Program with the training in Israel and the retreat at Esalen, I also mentioned that we had been invited to bring our next group to Esalen in January of 2009.

"Where will you get the funding to do it?" she asked.

"I am not sure. Do you have any ideas?"

"Yes," she said, "let me look into it."

On a warm evening, a few weeks later, the phone rang while I was hanging the laundry outside.

"He-llo," I said a bit out of breath.

"Nitsan it's Paula, I found a donor for the Peace Leadership Program at Esalen."

"Really?" I said finding it difficult to take in and then "Wow! Paula that is so great. We are doing it Yeah! Yeah!, Yeah!" I was dancing with the phone. "Will you be able to join us while we are there as one of the leaders?" I inquired pressing my luck.

"I will do my best to be there" Paula said.

And she did.

---

53. http://www.redbirdfoundation.com/womenspeak

Chapter 27

Armed with Love

2009, Big Sur

I refuse to accept the view that mankind is so tragically bound to the starless midnight of racism and war that the bright daybreak of peace and brotherhood can never become a reality... I believe that unarmed truth and unconditional love will have the final word.

Martin Luther King Jr.

Operation Cast Lead, the war between Israel and the Hamas in Gaza, erupted a few days before the group arrived at Esalen in January 2009. Luckily, most of the Arab and Jewish participants lived in the Galilee and Central Israel, where bombs had not landed so far, and they were able to leave their homes for the journey, albeit with great trepidation. One Arab Palestinian participant, who lived in a Southern Israeli city bombarded throughout the war, stayed behind with her family, waiting for a ceasefire so she could join the group. The ceasefire finally came – on the day we flew back home to Israel.

Ann, who returned by popular demand in 2009, had been to Israel in 2008 and worked with our groups. She volunteered her time and helped us go deeper into our healing work than we had ever dared before.

Every morning at Esalen we began sitting in a circle on floor pillows on the light blue carpet at Huxley, a large meeting room next to the dining hall. The 4x4 foam cube, bataca bats[54] and garden gloves that Ann had placed in the corner of the room would be brought to the center of the circle when necessary to assist us in expressing powerful emotions.

"*Radical Aliveness* teaches us how to be effective, influential leaders in a

---

54. A uniquely designed bat, half covered with foam and used in our groups to hit the foam cube and express strong feelings safely.

new socio-political environment where we are all connected, where we can all participate, and where each individual is needed to create the wisdom of the whole," she told us one morning.

"What do you mean?" Liry asked. "How is it related to what we are doing here?"

"Good question," Ann replied. "Do you remember how we said that within this room **every feeling is welcome** and the only rules are that **we don't physically hurt ourselves, anyone else or the space that we are in?**"

I looked around and saw the women were nodding.

"When feelings begin to move through our bodies with greater freedom," Ann continued, "when there is permission to show our anger, hopelessness, grief or shame in a safe and supportive space, then our inner system begins to shift."

"I do feel better after I cry or express my anger physically without hurting anyone, but what exactly is the shift?" Noa wondered.

"The shift is about becoming more authentic in sharing what we feel both inside and outside the group. Also, we become more comfortable with 'messy' emotions, such as screaming, shouting and crying. That means we can stay present and in our leadership, even around powerful emotions, and move to intervene in ways that support healing.

"Finally, expressing what we feel brings us closer to a deep place of awareness and connection. That is why during the workshop I will not be the only one leading the group. Any one of you who is in touch with your feelings and/or the feelings of someone else in the group can be in your leadership, impact the group and move us all a step forward in the process of healing. Together we will create a space where we are all connected, we can all participate, and where each one of us is needed to create the wisdom of the whole."

I sensed her words entering my heart and I could see the other women were also aware that something meaningful had been said. Still it seemed these words needed to be embodied in an experience before we could fully grasp their meaning.

"There is so much I don't know about what you are going through because I have never lived in a war-torn country, but I do know what it feels like to be terrified and from that place of knowing would like to hear whatever you are ready to share. I honor you so much for being here and willing to express your feelings in a safe way rather than act on them in the world outside... So please let's bring it on!" Ann said passionately.

Yes! I thought feeling excited.

"I have asked Paula to start us off," Ann told us, gazing around the room at our expectant faces.

Paula stood up looking energized.

"Shalom and Salaam everyone, it's good to see all of you here this morning," she began. "Let's stand up and stretch, we have been sitting awhile..."

We stood to stretch and I looked over at Paula, wondering what would happen next. "Now begin walking around the room. Walk as though you are soldiers going to a battle, to war."

To show us what she meant she began stomping, her feet banging against the grayish-blue carpet. We joined her and stomped all around the room, smiling when we encountered each other's eyes.

Gradually, with Paula's encouragement, we became more involved with the stomping. Looking around, I noticed the smiles had disappeared. I wondered why we were doing this; it seemed so senseless, much like the stomping around the parade ground of my military days. Suddenly Paula, who was standing in the center of the room, cried:

"ENOUGH!!!!!"

I froze, as did the others. We turned and stared at her. *Why was she shouting? What's going on?*

Looking at her closely, I realized that her shout, her scream was not only her own. She was screaming for all of us and for all those who couldn't. The children, the women and men who were caught up in endless, senseless battles. There must be a way out of this madness.

Even though it was quiet now, Paula's shout was still present, vibrating in the silence around me. Feelings that I didn't want to feel about the war back home and the fear for my children and family began rising from a dark and hidden place in my stomach, pushing their way towards my throat.

"Now see if you can walk as though your feet are flowers gently seeding the earth." Paula said softly.

Some women began to cry.

After a while we stopped and stood facing the center. Paula walked inside the circle, looking at each of us with her beautiful brown eyes. I felt shaken.

When we sat down, Ann looked around at each of us and said, "Who would like to share something that is coming up for you?"

There was a moment of silence, of trying to find the courage to speak. But our emotions were not so guarded and as I looked from face to face, eyes were shining and cheeks were wet. Ann saw it too.

"Oh you guys," she said, gazing compassionately at those who were crying, "if your tears could speak, what would they say?"

Women began to speak of their children and their fear of war. I was touched that they were able to talk about what I could not yet put into words.

Then I looked at Radwa, her beautiful young face showing underneath the black hijab. She was not crying. She seemed restless. Ann saw her restlessness and asked: "Would you like to share what is going on for you Radwa?"

Looking directly at Ann, Radwa erupted in anger: "What about the women in Gaza?" she said vehemently. "Do you think they don't cry out in pain as they give birth to their children? Do you think they don't breastfeed them? Or get up at night to care for them? Love and worry about them? Send them to school and try to protect them? What about families who have lost their children? How would you feel if you were living there and getting bombed by such a powerful military?"

The room grew quiet and Ann invited her to work in front of the group. Radwa was reluctant but Miri, one of the Jewish participants, encouraged her, saying, "Please speak your truth, Radwa, I must hear it if we are ever going to fully connect to one another!"

Ann gestured towards the large foam cube and two women carried it to the center of the circle and handed Radwa the gloves to protect her hands and a foam bataca bat.

With Ann's encouragement, Radwa began hitting the foam cube using the bat. Her screams of rage became louder and louder. She screamed about the anguish of women and children in Gaza and the anger of Arabs in Israel who have been mistreated for so long. Around the room women were crying, others holding them. Some women sat at a distance hugging pillows, as if protecting their hearts from this powerful emotional onslaught. Miri, standing nearby, was whispering encouraging words in Radwa's ears.

After hitting and screaming for a while Radwa looked exhausted, as though all her energy had seeped out through the red bataca bat. She sank her head unto the large cube and began sobbing with pain that must have been buried underneath her anger and was now pouring out through the cracks of her broken heart.

Women edged closer, placing their hands gently on her back and guiding her unto a mat. Lying down, her head in someone's lap, she was touched and caressed by Arab and Jewish women, comrades in this healing journey, who spoke of their love and appreciation for her and her unique voice.

Although I felt the power of the moment and was so grateful to Radwa for finally bringing the horror of living in Gaza and the pain of being a second-class citizen in Israel into the circle, at that moment a part of me was also angry.

Ann saw me and said, "Nitsan, is there a voice coming through you that needs to be spoken?"

I thought of the words of Riane Eisler, whom the group had met at the beginning of this journey in a small library near her home in Carmel. Looking at us, she had said, "We will only be able to stop the cycle of violence by paying attention to the most fundamental of human relationships – the one between women and men – because violence between nations is directly connected to intimate violence."

I remembered my own painful experience with intimate violence and began speaking. My voice was shaking: "Thank you Radwa for your courage to bring the suffering of the Palestinians into our circle. But I miss hearing your voices screaming against oppression by men that so many of you and hundreds of millions of your sisters are suffering from. Why are you not screaming for the women who have to hide every part of their bodies but their eyes? Why are you not screaming against honor killings and intimate violence, the stoning of women, the selling of young girls as sex slaves or genital mutilation? Why are you not screaming against your community who tells you whether or not you can drive, what to study and who to love and marry? You have a voice!! Band together with other Arab Muslim, Bedouin, Druze, Jewish and Christian women and use it to cry out both against the suffering of the Palestinians in Gaza and in Israel and against your own suffering as women in a world dominated by men!!"

The words spilled from my mouth like a boiling fountain but as soon as I spoke, I was overtaken by fear and shame. *What have I done? I am a leader here and now they will hate me and stop expressing what they really feel around me.*

Yet when I dared to look around the room instead of anger, I saw them nodding their heads. Some came up to me and held me close. Eyad, a Muslim leader, said: "Go Nitsan!!! We need your support to make our voices heard louder."

At that moment I was not sure who needed whose support more but I felt good for not holding back. Sharing my anger and still being accepted and even appreciated helped me feel so connected to them and was more healing than words can describe. I realized what Ann meant when she said that each one of us can contribute to the wisdom of the whole.

Someone was holding me from behind and crying, I felt her warm tears on my neck. Turning around, I saw it was Noshene, a pretty young woman with dark curls who grew up in Iran and now lived in the United States.

"I was born in Iran," she said, tears running down her cheeks. "I was forced to wear the abaya and study only certain religious texts. At some point I realized that the government and oppressive social institutions that are run by men try to divert our feelings of anger at the system, towards outside conflicts such as the Iran-Iraq War in order to distract us women from struggling for our own liberation."

Yes, I thought, *that must be what Riane Eisler called "weapons of mass distraction".*

Later, some of the Jewish women protested that the voices of the women and children from Southern Israel who live and suffer tremendously under Hamas's bombing were missing in the process. Ann, who could see the evolution of our group and was grateful that the Arab Palestinian voice was finally coming out so powerfully, replied, "There will be a time in the future to hear the other side, but for now, without the Palestinian women's open and honest voices you will not have partners for Peace...!"

By the end of our time at Esalen, a warm sense of comradery connected us. Through the guidance and support of Ann, Paula and other women from the United States who had joined to hold a space for our work, we were able to feel our pain together and emerge stronger and more connected.

On our way home we spent one last night in a motel at Monterey luxuriating in the warmth of our togetherness. It was then I heard the news.

I was standing in the doorway of one of the rooms, chatting with the three women inside. At some point, one of the women looked at an email and paled. Sounding shocked, she said:, "Bessan was killed a few hours ago." I froze in place as she began sharing the details of the story. Unable to move, I just stared at one spot on the wall and shook uncontrollably.

Bessan, her two sisters and a cousin had been killed in their home in Gaza. Some of us knew Bessan personally because of her involvement in the Creativity for Peace summer camps that were led by women who had trained with us. I knew her because she had been with my daughter in those peace camps and on a trip across the United States a few years earlier. Bessan was the daughter of Dr Izzeldin Abuelaish, a well-known physician from Gaza who was the only Palestinian doctor to work in Israeli hospitals. During Operation Cast Lead, Dr Abuelaish was regularly interviewed on Israeli television and radio. Since no Israeli journalists were able to report independently from within Gaza, Dr Abuelaish was one of the few Hebrew-speaking witnesses who told of the Palestinian suffering under fire. Four months prior to Operation Cast Lead, his wife and the mother of his eight children died from cancer, leaving Bessan, the eldest, then 21, as the main caretaker of her sisters and brothers, the youngest of whom was six years old.

On that day four young women were killed by Israeli shelling of their house. When the Israeli military tried to explain the shelling of this particular house, they said they were targeting armed men shooting from nearby. Dr Abuelaish responded, "There were no armed men in our house. My daughters were armed only with love."

The horror of the four young girls slain, their bodies torn apart in seconds and the screams of their father on national TV when he reached the room and saw them lying on the floor in pools of blood, were unbearable.

One thousand three hundred and eighty five Palestinians, many of them civilians, and thirteen Israelis were killed in Operation Cast Lead (operation, war, assault – how does one decide how to name these things?) and many more were wounded.

Radwa's words and Bessan's image never left me during my journey home. I cried and shook so much on the plane that when we reached Austin, the stewardess arranged a wheelchair to escort me out. When they brought me to the luggage claim, weak from hours of crying, with so much extra baggage in my heart, I had zero desire to claim anything.

A few days later, I realized that our journey through the painful emotions at Esalen had armed us with love, opened our hearts and taught us to hold a safe space for pain and grief. I prayed we would stay alive long enough to share these gifts with others...

Chapter 28

The Way Back Home

2010, New York

The way back home is the way back into our own hearts.
Cathy Johnson

At first, she just showed him her identity card.

"No, you can't go in," he said. "Not today."

"But I must go in today!" Aya tried to control the urgency in her voice. "They are burying her tomorrow and if I don't see her today, I will never be able to see her again." Her composure was breaking and tears welled up in her eyes.

Aya's grandmother had lived in Al-Boreij, a refugee camp in southern Gaza. Her grandmother was the one who had raised her, had been more of a mother to her than Aya's own. All Aya wanted was to be able to go into Gaza and be with her family as they sat around the body and mourned the woman she loved so much. She longed to touch her grandma's hand and see her beloved face one last time.

So she tried again. Facing the Druze Israeli soldier at the checkpoint, Aya uttered a word that was not easy for a young, proud Bedouin woman to use when facing a man: "Batrajak," she said. Please. "Please, I must see her one last time." She knew she was begging and might hate herself later but the urgency was too strong to deny and she had to do something, something that would change his cold gaze, something that would open his heart.

But it was no use. "No" was the answer and nothing was going to change it.

Feeling defeated and very angry, she drove back to her home near Beer Sheva in Southern Israel. Two days later she was finally given permission to enter Gaza. Clutching her grandma's photo in her left hand, Aya stood next to the mound of freshly-turned earth in the Al-Boreij graveyard and all she could feel was immense anger, anger at everything and everyone. She especially hated the endless conflict and oppressive government that had denied so many of her people their rights for so long.

Now, months later, at the Omega Institute Retreat Center in Rhinebeck, NY, thousands of miles away from that day, Aya found herself in a beautiful, spacious room with a wooden dance floor surrounded by large windows that let in the autumn sunlight. Gazing out, she could see the leaves of the forest shining in greens and reds, gilded by the early morning rain as the sun shimmered through the drops.

It did not seem like there could be a place more different from that graveyard at Al-Boreij where she had bid her grandmother a last farewell, yet it was the first place in a long time where she felt safe enough to go inside herself and feel her emotions, though she couldn't quite pinpoint why.

Was it the eyes of her partner in the listening partnership looking at her, really wanting to understand? Or Ann, the leader's, words – that all feelings are welcome in this room, no matter what they look like and how terrible they feel? Or was it the 22 Jewish, Christian, Muslim, Israeli, Palestinian and American women in the room who seemed to care so much? She did not know, but after two days of revealing more and more of herself and feeling so accepted, Aya was ready to bring her anger to the group.

Holding a tennis racket in her gloved hands, she began hitting the four-by-four-foot foam cube that Ann had placed at the center of the room. At first no words came. Not even a sound. But as the energy coursed through her body and she heard the encouraging words around her, sounds began emerging from deep within. Soon the sounds became words. "How dare you!?" Aya screamed, looking directly at the Jewish women in the group. The loud blow of the tennis racket hitting the cube echoed in the spacious room, causing some women to raise their hands to protect their ears. Not caring what they or anyone else thought, Aya hit it again and again, shouting, "How dare you deny me this right? It is my right! MY RIGHT! Do you hear me?" And then the tears began flowing as she whispered: "All I wanted was to see her one last time, just to touch her hand..."

As she began sobbing, she seemed to collapse inward, and had no strength to move her arms. A woman standing next to her implored Aya not to retreat into helplessness: "You have to continue hitting," she whispered in her ear, "continue feeling your power because you don't want to be a slave anymore, not to your own feelings of helplessness, not to anyone else. This is your opportunity to set yourself free. You can do it..."

The woman's powerful words seemed to flow through Aya and she raised her hands once more to hit the cube. "I hate you... I HATE YOU!" she shouted, voicing her anger towards the soldier who denied her such a basic right. Tears flowing down her face, she remembered that moment when she had faced him alone and begged. "My people would never do this to you!" she cried forcefully, looking around the room at all the women before leaning back into the woman's arms, sobbing.

Hearing Aya 's words, some of the Jewish women in the room began fidgeting. Ann sensed it. She looked at Liry, who seemed restless, and said, "Liry, there seems to be a truth that wants to come out through you... Please speak it."

Slowly Liry stood up and faced Aya. Then she began to speak. "I am just tired of feeling fear. For almost 50 years I have been breathing, drinking, eating and feeling fear. Fear coming through my mother who is a Holocaust survivor and lost both parents when she was six, fear of living with my children next to the border, fear of being bombed in my home or in public places where suicide bombers explode... I am so sorry about what happened to Aya and how she was not able to see her grandmother... But I don't think you can isolate this incident from the reason why all this is happening. Our military is not just there at the checkpoints in order to make the lives of the Palestinians miserable. They are there to defend us from a very real threat."

She stopped for a moment, sighing and looking around as tears rolled down her cheeks. Then she continued. "I wish it was possible to stop only the person who is trying to hurt us instead of punishing everyone. But every time we have taken a step back hoping for change, like when we pulled out of Lebanon or Gaza, the other side has used it against us..."

"Well, you should be afraid!" retorted Mona, a young Muslim Palestinian woman, as she jumped up and faced Liry. "Because we are growing and becoming stronger from within, and we can no longer agree to being oppressed!" She looked angry and frustrated.

Looking around the group, Liry said: "You see?"

Aya, still held by a friend from behind, seemed relieved that Mona had joined her side, that she was not facing the group alone.

Ann invited Mona to share more of her frustration with the group.

For a while Mona spoke and then hit and screamed, remembering the things she and her family had lost during years of living in Israel. Her mother's family had become refugees in 1948, fleeing to Lebanon. Mona's grandfather had returned to Israel a couple of years later, but only part of the family was given permission to return with him. Every morning Mona's mother, Mariam, would wake up to see her own mother crying by the kitchen table as she gazed at the photos of her son who had stayed behind in Lebanon and whom she was no longer able to see.

Mona continued hitting and shouting until something shifted and tears began flowing down her cheeks. Underneath her anger was so much pain... She lowered her arms and just stood there, facing the group, allowing us to see for a moment the intense sadness in her eyes.

Deeply touched, the women moved closer, encircling her, gently stroking and holding one another. A moment later I saw Liry and Mona, sobbing in each other's arms. A few other women moved over to hug Aya, who was still crying.

It seemed that, despite all the words that had been said and the pain that was still present in the room, the women felt closer to one another than before.

Perhaps it is true that when our pain is heard and acknowledged in a safe, supportive space – when we are able to finally show our tears, express our anger and speak our truth – then we can go back home, home into our hearts where we can once again feel love and connection to one another.

Chapter 29

Finding Our Voices
2010-2011, Yafiyeh, Kissufim

You ask me to speak. How shall I speak when I have been taught
silence since birth? I have been taught silence in my parents' house, in
my own house; I have taught silence to my daughter. I have forgotten
the sound of my voice. I have forgotten I have a voice.

Silvia Margia

Vulnerability is not winning or losing; it's having the courage
to show up and be seen when we have no control over the outcome.
Vulnerability is not weakness; it's our greatest measure of courage.

Brene Brown

"He's been killed, Nitsan, he's been killed..." Silvia cried as soon as she
saw me. I looked at her red eyes filled with tears, her swollen face and felt
overwhelmed by the onslaught of pain that was coming towards me. But
when I opened my arms and hugged her, stroking her curly brown hair
while she wept, somehow my body adjusted and I could be there with her,
tears rolling down my cheeks.

When we'd heard the news, Liry and I drove to see her in Yafiyeh, an
Arab town bordering with Nazareth. Silvia, our co-leader, our friend,
had just returned two days ago from a trip alone to Thailand. It is rare for
an Arab Palestinian woman, a divorced mother of two children, to go to
Thailand on her own to celebrate her 40th birthday, but Silvia is this rare
woman. A beautiful dark-skinned Christian Arab, she had grown up in
the Jewish town of Dimona near her father's workplace and was connected
to both Jewish and Arab cultures.

On her way back from the airport, Silvia heard the news: Tamer Margiyeh, her only brother, had been killed while trying to save his friends from a gas leak in the oil refineries where he worked. The screaming and crying that began at the hospital when the family first heard the news was all around us now in a room full of weeping women, of mourning and loss. We held Silvia for a long time while she wept in our arms.

After eighteen years of being around emotional discharge, crying, shouting and screaming, I had become more comfortable in these situations but my heart was breaking. Why did this awful thing happen? And why on the day of her return from such a wonderfully nourishing vacation?

What helped in those moments was Silvia's openness to sharing her grief. Her feelings were never hidden, they moved through her body and they moved me. On that day and on the days that followed, her ability to cry when she needed to and release another wave of pain, anger and grief enabled her to support her father, mother, sisters and her brother's widow, who had given birth to their fourth child just a few days before the accident.

Five months after that painful day, Ann came to Israel once again to work with our groups. Silvia joined Ann, Liry and myself in co-leading a group of Bedouin women from Southern Israel.

It was a Thursday in April 2011 and we drove from Jerusalem, arriving in Kibbutz Kissufim – located less than two kilometers from the border with Gaza – in the early evening so we could begin, the following morning, a two-day workshop with 20 Bedouin women from towns located about an hour away.

On Friday morning, the women arrived by bus and filed into the large room with a linoleum floor that the kibbutz guest house allotted for the workshop. Most of them were wearing the traditional abaya and hijab. They sat on thick mats we had arranged in a circle and looked with curiosity at us and at the large cube sitting in the corner of the room. We began by introducing ourselves, following with a relaxing opening exercise. Then, we asked the women to share what they would like to receive from our time together. Some spoke of wanting more courage, some mentioned relaxation and time for themselves and then the last woman received the talking piece and began to speak:

"I want my dreams," she said loudly. "Where are my dreams? Please give me back my dreams… I want my dreams!"

All at once the room erupted and everyone seemed involved. Some were crying, while others just joined the chorus saying over and over: "Where are our dreams?... We want our dreams."

I looked over at Silvia, whose eyes were bright, and wondered what happened to her dreams after her brother died.

Then Kaukab, a beautiful dark-skinned 38-year-old mother of eleven children began to speak. She told the story of standing up courageously against her entire tribe: "I loved school and studying so much. One day when I was sixteen my family burned my books and school pack because I refused to marry my cousin. Although they did not let me go back to school, I never changed my mind. Then, when I was eighteen, I chose a husband and fought for permission to marry him because I recognized in his eyes a pain similar to my own – his first wife had died from cancer and he was left with three young children.

"Years later, while I was in my early twenties, I left my husband, taking my own three young children with me. He'd decided to take a second wife and I felt so betrayed. I only agreed to return to him a few months later when he divorced his second wife. Yet even now, after many years have passed, I still feel the pain of that and of other betrayals..."

Silvia, who was sitting nearby, gently put an arm around Kaukab who leaned over placing her head on Silvia's shoulder. Her eyes were closed and tears flowed down her cheeks. Silvia stroked Kaukab's hair, looked around the room and began speaking in Arabic and then in Hebrew: "I am not sure where your dreams are or mine for that matter, but I so clearly see your courage..."

Women were nodding their heads, some crying.

Another woman shared how she loved nature and had a special tree that was precious to her (there is a scarcity of trees in the desert area where she lives). This beautiful tree grew in front of her house and she cared for it every day, watering, caressing it and sitting underneath it. One day when she was sixteen, she returned home from school and noticed the house looked different. Something was missing, there was too much light. Then it dawned on her. Her tree was gone. It had been chopped down.

Later she found out that her mother was angry because she had refused to marry the man intended for her and so she asked her son to destroy the one thing her daughter loved so much – the beautiful tree. This woman never married.

"Oh my God," Ann said, "I am so sorry..."

Then she invited women to beat the foam cube with the bataca bat, giving a voice to their pain, their anguish. While hitting and screaming they seemed to recover their strength, voices became louder, clearer.

As she brought down the racket unto the cube in a huge thump, one woman cried: "Mother, mother, I need you mother!!!! Why have you abandoned me? Why have you betrayed me? Why are you allowing them to do these things to me? – Mamma, I need you... Mamma..." A new wave of pain washed over the room as we all called out to our mamas...

Laila, a large woman, seemed despondent. She sat on the mat, her eyes on the floor, not communicating with others. The other women whispered in our ears that she had been beaten by her husband. When she finally shared her story in a very soft voice, she told us that her husband beat her for years until finally she reported him to the police and he was no longer able to live in the house with her and their five children. Two years later she took him back. Now he sometimes beat their children and she did not have the strength to stop him.

Ann asked if she would like to do some work. Laila said yes. Supported by others, she stood up. With our encouragement she started hitting the foam cube with the bat, despite Ann's encouragement, no voice came through. I felt frustration in the room, as if each one of us was remembering the moments in our lives when there was so much to say, yet we could not speak. Addressing Laila in Arabic, Silvia encouraged her to hit, to bring her voice, reminding her again and again how strong she actually is.

Silvia's powerful words lifted us from the mats and we sprang up to encourage Laila and shout with her. Gradually Laila's voice became clearer and stronger. It was not quite a shout or a scream but it was much louder than before: "NO!!! Stop it!!! You will not hit them again!!..." she cried while the group echoed her words.

At that moment it seemed like the pain being released in the room belonged not only to those present; it was the pain of generations, of whole communities.

When two of the Bedouin group facilitators also joined the crying, adding their own pain to the rest, some of the participants grew nervous. *What is wrong?* they wondered. *Are our leaders falling apart? What will happen now?*

Ann explained that we are witnessing a new type of leadership, a leadership that exists within each of us. It is a leadership whose time has come and whose power is based not on physical strength, manipulation and the oppression of others, but rather on the courage and willingness to feel everything, to be vulnerable and authentic.

"Just like you are all doing now!" Silvia added, gazing around the room.

That evening when the workshop ended, I left the kibbutz to return home to my children. The Bedouin women also returned to their towns and villages because sleeping away from home is often frowned upon in their society. Silvia, Ann and Liry stayed in the kibbutz guest rooms so they could continue facilitating the workshop the following day.

Early Saturday morning they woke up and were getting ready for breakfast. Silvia sat outside in the sun, gazing at the green grass and trees surrounding the guest house and enjoying her coffee with a cigarette. Liry and Ann were busy with their morning routines. Everything was peaceful and serene.

Then out of nowhere loud booming sounds interrupted the idyllic moment.

Liry ran out of her room, looked at Silvia calmly sipping her coffee and said, "What was that?"

"I don't know," Silvia replied, "Maybe Israel is bombing Gaza this morning for some reason."

"It sounds more like the Hamas is bombing us," Liry responded, her voice rising with apprehension. "Maybe we should go to the bomb shelter."

"Let's wait," Silvia answered, feeling so comfortable in the warm spring sun and having no desire to go anywhere.

Suddenly there was a huge explosion that sounded like it was next door. Silvia jumped up, her cup of coffee falling and spilling all over the grass, Liry screamed and Ann ran out of her room, shouting; "Did you hear that?"

"Yes! Let's RUN!!" Liry yelled, following others who were running towards the bomb shelter. Once there, they shook and laughed hysterically, huddling together trying to figure out what to do next. Still feeling exhausted from the emotional volcano that had erupted the previous day, they now found themselves caught under a different kind of volcanic eruption.

Sitting in the bomb shelter, confused and shaky, not knowing what to do, they looked up when the door was flung open. Three of the Bedouin women who had participated in the workshop the day before appeared at the entrance, smiling widely and seeming full of energy. Taking in the leaders huddled together on a bench, they ran over with open arms.

One hugged Liry, who was trembling with fear. Later this woman shared how much she loved Liry and wanted to comfort her and yet at the same time how sad and angry she felt about the pain of the Palestinians suffering in Gaza.

Another woman who came in was Laila, the woman who had difficulty finding her voice the day before. When she saw how scared Liry, Silvia and Ann were, she laughed and said: "Look at me, all of you, after what happened yesterday, I have begun facing my fears!" They looked up at her and smiled. She did seem different today. Her eyes were shining, shoulders back and chest open. She seemed taller, so unlike the woman from the day before.

Then Laila added: "What's the matter with you? If this is your day to die, you will die... Now let's get out of here, we want to continue the workshop!"

Encouraged by Laila and the other Bedouin women, Silvia, Liry and Ann stood up and joined them. During a break in the shelling, they ran quickly to their rooms gathered their belongings and the cube and drove away from the kibbutz. Later that morning they held the workshop in Lod, at the home of Eyad, one of the Arab Palestinian women leaders who participated in the Esalen retreat. When Eyad heard what transpired she invited them to her house where the rocket fire could not reach them.

In the closing circle that evening, women shared how meaningful these past two days had been for them. And the woman who had lost her dreams said she now found one... She wanted to learn how to do this healing work so she could help other women find their voices.

Chapter 30

Sharing Our Fears

Peace Leadership Workshop, 2018, Nes Ammim

Now is the time to understand more so that we may fear less.
Marie Curie

Maya, a dark-haired 45-year-old Jewish woman with a beautiful smile, speaks about her fear of Arabs: "I was born and raised in Ariel, a settlement in the Occupied Territories. When I was very young, I began hearing about incidents of rock throwing and shooting at people in my community, my neighbors. I became terrified of what the Palestinians who lived all around us might one day do to me or my family. This fear has always been in the background even when nothing happened for days or months."

Adam, a dark-haired and bearded Christian Palestinian from Bethlehem who is sitting next to her, listens to Maya, tension growing in his shoulders.

Ann, who sees his tension and the fidgeting of the group of Israelis and Palestinians seated on floor pillows around Maya, turns to Adam and asks: "I wonder if there is a truth that wants to come out through you?"

Adam looks at Ann for a moment and then turns his intense gaze towards Maya, swallows hard and begins speaking:

"Maya, have you given any thought to what was on that land before your family moved there? Who did the land belong to? Do you think there might be people who still feel pain because of the loss of this land, that maybe it was not just an empty space before your parents settled there?" His gaze never leaves her face while he awaits her response.

Maya closes her eyes for a moment as if trying to escape something that is too hard to feel. A lonely tear makes its way down her cheek.

"Please acknowledge our pain, too," Adam presses on. "Please do not ignore it..."

Finally, Maya opens her eyes and looks at him. "Truthfully, I have never really considered your pain..." she says.

Her honesty hurts. I feel a growing constriction in my throat.

As if to explain her words, Maya shares that a few years ago she was at a bank during a terrorist attack: "I saw the man with the rifle run down the street shooting everywhere and was terrified he might enter the bank where I was hiding. He shot and badly wounded a woman before he was caught. Since then, I feel stress every time I leave my house. I am always on edge when deciding where to sit on a bus or in a restaurant. I try to find the spot where I would have the best chances to survive a terrorist attack. I would love to be able to just sit outside in a coffee shop on a sunny morning, my back against a comfortable chair, enjoying a cup of coffee while the sun warms my face... but I can't, my fears haunt me."

Adam looks at her as though he understands something and then he shares: "When I was seven, I played hide-and-go-seek with some friends. Suddenly I ran into a tall and scary looking soldier holding a big, black rifle. I guess he suspected that I wanted to throw a rock and began chasing me. I ran and ran. For God's sake, I was only seven years old!" He stops and looks at us, wiping sweat from his forehead with the sleeve of his white t-shirt. "I managed to reach my home, shaking with fear, and hid under my bed for what seemed like hours."

Maya nods, tearing up. She looks at Adam and then reaches over and places her hand on his.

I look around the room, and see some people are crying. I too, feel my heart aching. I also feel a sense of relief that right now, in this moment, we created a space where both narratives can be held compassionately without one overshadowing the other.

Chapter 31

The Whistle

2012, Nazareth

*Here's to strong women. May we know them.
May we be them. May we raise them.*

Rose Tory Anne

*Behind every successful woman is a tribe of
other successful women, who have her back.*

Jackson Bart

"I heard this story from two African women who came to the *Womenspeak* event in Mobile, Alabama, in March 2010," began Paula D'Arcy, looking around the circle at the expectant eyes of Israeli and Palestinian women on a beautiful clear morning at the Esalen Institute in January 2011.

"They told me that in their small village in Africa, many men were behaving badly towards the women. Finally, the women met and decided to do something about it. They resolved to buy a whistle for each woman that she could blow to call for help whenever she was mistreated. The whistles were bought and each woman received her own.

"One evening, a couple of days later, the women all heard the telling sound coming out of a small hut in the village. No matter what they were doing – preparing a meal, eating, hanging the laundry – they stood up and walked towards the hut from where the whistle sound emerged. Soon there were 50 women standing on or around the porch of the hut of the woman who blew the whistle. They did not go in. They simply stood and waited with silent determination. Before long the husband felt their presence and stopped whatever he was doing to his wife, because now there were one hundred eyes watching him.

"When everything seemed quiet, the women left to go home to their own huts. The following morning, another woman blew the whistle and the same thing happened. After this scenario recurred a few times, the mistreatment stopped, perhaps because no man wanted 50 women on his porch looking at everything he was doing."

Because I too had a moment in my life when I was thrown to the floor, strangled and screamed at, a moment when I wished I had a whistle and a community of women who would come running, the story made a huge impression on me, especially when Paula proceeded to give each one of us a whistle.

A year later I recounted this tale to a group of Bedouin women in a workshop led by Liry and Silvia. They loved it. One said "Let's do it too" while another responded: "It would never work for me because the women in my village don't trust each other."

Then Liry said: "Let's divide into small groups and share stories about a time in your life when you could have used a whistle... and the women in your group will support you in the Beyond Words way with whatever feelings come up."

I sat in one of the groups and heard a story of a woman whose husband would marry another wife every few years because he had the money and then would leave that second, third or fourth wife when he tired of her. She, as the first wife, had to stick around for all that.

Another woman recounted how her uncle forced her to marry a crazy man instead of the man she loved because he received money from the crazy man's family. Nobody in her family stood by her and she didn't have a whistle. She was able to get a divorce a month after the wedding because the man's emotional state became obvious. But now she was "tainted" and could no longer marry the man she loved. Eventually he married someone else.

Finally, I learned something about the Arabic name Kifayah (there was a woman in our group with this name) – which means Enough. It is given to a baby girl who is born after a number of births of daughters in the hope that the next birth would be a son. *But what if it isn't, what if a son is not born next?* I thought. *What would the daughter who came after "Enough" be called? And why should a woman go through life with the name "Enough" unless it's ENOUGH of this oppression and ENOUGH of the abuse and of treating us like we are **not enough** because we are born female. If this was the meaning of the name then let's all take on the name Enough, at least* *as our middle name.*

Days later I still heard and saw the tears and angry words shared that day while women held and supported each other. I hoped that maybe now when one of us blows the whistle the rest would come to support her...

Chapter 32

"We are not Occupied"
2013, Beit Jala

It took me a long time and most of the world to learn what I know about love and fate and the choices we make, but the heart of it came to me in an instant, while I was chained to a wall being tortured. I realized somehow, through the screaming in my mind, that even in that shackled bloody helplessness, I was still free; free to hate the men who were torturing me or to forgive them. It doesn't sound like much, I know. But in the flinch and bite of the chain, when it's all you've got, that freedom is a universe of possibility. And the choices you make, between hating and forgiving, become the story of your life.

From *Shantaram* by Gregory David Roberts

We met in the train station in Jerusalem to begin our journey to the West Bank. One woman who brought her car was afraid to drive into the Occupied Territories, so she and a few other Jewish women attending the workshop took a cab.

Itaf, my Palestinian co-facilitator, was not afraid. She picked three of us up at the train station and we began the ten-minute drive through the hills to Beit Jalah. A moment before we reached the checkpoint she parked her car on the side of the road and tied her headscarf behind her head so she would look like a religious Jewish settler rather than a religious Muslim woman. Randa and Hala, two Arab Druze women from the Galilee, who were sitting in the back looking worried, smiled at her resourcefulness. The cab ahead of us, with the Jewish women, was stopped and their IDs were checked, but our car, driven by Itaf, the new "Jewish settler" was waved right through.

The Together Beyond Words Organization's first couple of workshops in the Occupied Territories had been in collaboration with AJEEC-

NISPED[55], and they generated the desire to create our own group. But gathering this group of Israeli and Palestinian women from four religions – Muslim, Christian, Jewish and Druze – still took a year and a half and was a challenging undertaking mainly because of the distance and the fear of traveling to meetings in the Occupied Territories[56].

Since most of the news we hear in the Israeli media about the territories involves violence and terror attacks, during the first meeting, the Israeli participants who joined the group felt they were risking their lives (more than usual) to attend the workshop.

I, too, was nervous; I felt responsible for the participants' well-being and wondered, *what am I leading them into?*

Yet as soon as we entered the beautiful, serene school grounds of Talitha Kumi in Beit Jalah where the workshop would be held, my breathing became deeper and I stopped imagining everything that could go wrong. As we stepped out of the car and walked towards the stone building, Randa, who now also seemed more relaxed, said to me:

"Did you know the school is named after Jairus' young daughter who died and then Jesus held her hand and said to her "Talitha Kumi" which means "little girl arise" and she did?"

"I didn't know that." I responded with a smile.

I looked at other women from our group who were walking towards the door of the building that holds a kindergarten and school, as well as the guesthouse where rooms were rented for meetings like ours, and knew that one of our challenges would be communication. Some of us spoke all three languages – Arabic, Hebrew, and English – and others two or only one. There was not one language common to everyone, so every sentence spoken would need to be translated by group members.

In the opening circle Itaf picked up a rose quartz heart stone talking piece from the center of the circle, held it in her hands for a moment as she gazed at the sixteen Israeli and Palestinian women sitting next to one another. Then she began speaking: "I am wondering if you could share a bit about yourself and what made you want to join us today?"

She passed the talking piece to Hala, a Druze woman sitting next to her.

---

55. AJEEC-NISPED is a non-profit organization dedicated to social change and Arab-Jewish partnership, based in Beer Sheva. https://ajeec-nisped.org.il/

56. Some of the Palestinian women could not get permits to enter Israel so our meetings were held in the Occupied Territories.

"Actually I was scared to go into the Occupied Territories," Hala began, "I have never been here and the news makes it look so terrible. But I wanted to join the group because I was curious and it felt important so I asked my father what to do and he encouraged me to go."

"I am here because I want the Israeli women to hear about the suffering Israel is inflicting on the Palestinian people which is not described enough in the Israeli media," Samia, a Palestinian woman, explained. "For example, we have a holiday coming up when we are supposed to go into Jerusalem and pray at the Al-Aqsa Mosque and we are not permitted."

"I understand what Hala and Samia are saying," Randa, a Druze woman, interjected, "and we have only just begun but for me it already feels so good to be here. I know that we come from different places and have four different religions but I feel there is a fifth religion here in the room – my religion – Love."

I smiled and saw others smiling too.

Nira, a Jewish woman shared: "I came because I want to meet the Palestinian women. I am so tired of hearing about suffering, the conflict and the violence that I hardly ever listen to the news anymore. I also stopped being socially active as I had been in the past. But this group attracted me because it not only offered dialogue but also healing and an opportunity to revive my tired spirit."

Edna, another Jewish woman said, "I am not so optimistic about the situation but I came because I thought these meetings are important. At home my husband and son who is in the army, see things differently from me and there has been so much anger and discord between us on these issues, almost to the point of violence. Now we never talk about politics anymore. Being part of this group will hopefully give me an opportunity to feel less alone."

Other women spoke about all of us being mothers and the power of women to change things. "When we give birth something in our heart is also born," one of them said.

Finally, Aisha, a young and pretty Muslim Palestinian woman with a green dress and a white headscarf received the heart stone talking piece.

"Whenever I think of Israeli women I see the severe, harsh women I met while visiting my brother in an Israeli prison," she began. "Also, when I was very young, I would go to help my father in the olive grove situated next to an army camp surrounded by a fence. Many times, I saw soldiers – both women and men – on the other side of the fence and I waved to them.

I learned to say: 'Shalom, ma nishma?' (Hello, how are you?) in Hebrew and I would say it quite loudly hoping they would wave back and greet me too. But their response was always the same 'Yala zuzi mipo'– 'Go away... get out of here already!' This is the first time I ever met Israeli women who seem different."

I looked at Itaf. She met my gaze and nodded, perhaps also moved by the possibility to support a new kind of connection.

We invited them to stand up and began by sharing our inner weather in movement, then danced, played games, listened to stories that broke and warmed our hearts, ate a delicious pot luck lunch together and massaged each other's hands. Four hours after we began, we met for the closing circle.

I was feeling drained from waking up at 4 AM, from the long, emotionally taxing journey to get there and the painful stories we heard. Yet even in my exhausted state, the sharing in the closing circle touched me deeply.

Nira said with tears running down her cheeks: "I can now look at the news and hear about the conflict because I know there is also this possibility."

A few of the women shared a feeling that they had known each other for years even though today was the first time they ever met.

"I am so sorry for my words in the beginning about how harsh Israeli women are," Aisha said. "When I received a massage today, it was the first time I ever felt the hands of a Jewish woman on my skin and it felt so good! I am embarrassed by what I said before because the women I just met are so different. I have a friend who spent time in the Israeli prison and never wants to see or meet Israelis again. I want to bring her to this group."

The women sitting on both her sides touched her hands with gentle gratitude.

"It is really good you shared your pain in the beginning," Samia said, looking at Aisha, "because Israelis need to know, since they never hear about it in the media."

I agreed with Samia and yet for me the fact that Aisha shared her story was more than a reminder of the Palestinian suffering; it was also the beginning of healing. Aisha had been authentic and courageous and trusted us enough to share her pain.

Turning to Aisha I said: "Thank you for leading the way in our circle today and sharing what you truly feel. Hopefully, this circle will expand and hold many more of our feelings and stories."

After the group ended, I walked over to speak to Naseem, the Palestinian program director of Talitha Kumi. He asked me what the *Together Beyond Words* Organization did, and I explained about our groups in the Galilee.

"But this is the first time we've had our own group in the Occupied Territories," I added.

Naseem looked at me. "We are not Occupied," he said quietly.

I was taken aback. "What do you mean? How are you not Occupied?" I inquired.

"The land is occupied," he responded, "but our hearts and minds don't have to be. We have a choice in every moment how to relate to this Occupation and how to struggle against it."

Surprised by his words I looked at Naseem and thought of Gregory Davis Roberts' opening paragraph in his book *Shantaram*. Does Naseem also believe the choices we make, between hating and forgiving, become the story of our lives? I almost asked him but he seemed busy and I had a train to catch. On the way home I prayed that the safe haven we had created that day would affect the choices we would make once we returned home.

Chapter 33

The Self that Heals

Esalen, 2009

The wound is the place where the Light enters you.
Rumi

What happens when people open their hearts? They get better.
Haruki Murakami, *Norwegian Wood*

I am coughing again and I hate myself. During the group meetings I am that person in the circle with the annoying cough whom everyone looks at wishing she would leave the room. At least that's what I imagine. Luckily I have my own room at night, so my annoying cough is not keeping anyone else awake.

Because of a change in diet, my cough had stopped for five years, but now at Esalen in the middle of our Internal Family Systems (IFS) Peace Leadership Training with Dr Richard (Dick) Schwartz, it has returned with a vengeance. At one point a friend, seeing my distress, tries to help and asks if I would like a session, a time to share what I am feeling while she listens.

"Yes, I would," I respond immediately. "I'm willing to try anything!"

During the break we move towards a corner of the large room and sit on pillows facing each other while she listens and I cry and cough and then cry and cough some more.

Feeling hopeless, I watch as Toni, an assistant in the workshop, makes her way over. She bends down and touches my shoulder. I look up, eyes full of tears.

"Nitsan," she begins, "I see you are not doing so well... Would you like to try and see if an IFS session might help in this situation?"

I see the compassion in her gentle smile and beautiful blue eyes and wonder if there might be a way out of my current state of misery. Maybe IFS **can** actually help.

"Yes", I nod.

She holds out her hand and I take it. I stand up and Toni leads me to the center of the circle, where I lie on a pillow next to Dick. My hand is on my chest, trying to control the incessant cough. I close my eyes to avoid the curious, concerned eyes of the other women in the circle.

"Let's focus on the part of you that is coughing," Dick begins. "Please check, where in your body it is located?"

"My chest," I reply quickly.

"What does it look like – color, shape or any image you have?"

I breathe and look inside until an image appears.

"I see a small cartoon-like character, totally orange except for the white of the teeth and the blue eyes. He is jumping up and down inside my chest, coughing and laughing."

"How do you feel towards this orange cartoon character?" Dick inquires.

"I hate it and wish it would just vanish from my life."

"All right, now tell the part of you that hates the coughing orange cartoon character that you get the hate it feels, but if it is willing to step to the side for a moment and let you get to know the coughing part, maybe something will shift and then maybe you will not cough so much."

I do as he asks, and the hating part is willing to move to the side. I am left with curiosity about my coughing part; I want to get to know it better.

"Ask the coughing cartoon character why it is there. What role does it play?"

I ask and the answer I receive surprises me.

"It says it is here to protect me," I reply.

"Yes," Dick says encouragingly. "Protect you from what? What does it think would happen to you if it wasn't there?"

"I would be feeling so lonely and helpless that I might even die."

"How many years has this coughing part been protecting you from feeling lonely and helpless?"

"For a very long time."

"Can it show you a moment when it first came into your life?"

I breathe, focus in and then I see her/me, a small baby girl with lots of dark hair, crying in a white crib. She looks about three or four months old.

I tell Dick about her.

"Would you like to go visit and find out what actually happened to her?"

"Yes, I would."

I go to visit my crying baby. Standing a couple of yards away from her, I feel so much compassion for that little one. Then I walk up to the crib, look at her more closely and sense that she sees me and wants me to pick her up. Lifting her gently, I hold her close to my heart and get a sense of how painfully alone she is in the kibbutz nursery and that there is nothing she can do to change the situation.

I cry, feeling her pain.

After holding her close for a while, I hear Dick's voice asking me if there might be a belief, feeling, thought or sensation that this young baby had at four months old that she is ready to release now.

I check inside.

"No. Nothing is coming to me. Wait... maybe that she has to be alone with her pain and that if she cries no one will come."

"Would she like to let go of that?"

Checking in, I respond, "No, she is not ready yet, she just wants to stay close to me. Maybe I'm imagining it, but she seems so content that I finally came to be with her after so many years."

"Good," Dick says. "Just be with her."

I continue holding her, feeling her warmth on my chest.

A few minutes later, I hear Dick speaking in a quiet, faraway voice that seems to be coming from another world or lifetime, "Now let her know that very soon you will need to come back here and check with her: where would she like to be when you return to this room?"

"She wants to stay with me."

"Great, so the two of you can make your way back here now and as you do that, check in with the part that hated the coughing part and see how it is doing. Also see what is happening with the orange cartoon character in your chest."

The little orange man I had seen in my chest is no longer jumping up and down and laughing. He is sitting quietly and seems smaller. The part that hated it looks relaxed and is gazing with empathy at the calm baby girl in my arms.

Slowly opening my eyes, I re-enter our meeting space and glance up at Dick. He is looking at me with so much compassion that I cry again. Then, hesitantly, I peek at the women surrounding me. When I meet their eyes, they smile reassuringly. Relaxed, as if awakened from a deep slumber, I notice that my hands are still on my chest and I don't want to move them because the warm energy from her tiny body is now filtering into my heart. It is as if she is healing me. I notice that in this moment, I am not coughing.

The following day my cough disappeared. It did not gradually lessen, as it used to in the past; it simply disappeared. When I told the group and they witnessed my miracle, all of us were curious about what had transpired in my session with Dick. What had he done that made the cough go away?

While we sat in a circle on pillows, Dick explained, "In the eighties I discovered that we all have parts or 'conflicted subpersonalities that reside within us.' I divided them into **exiles** and **protectors**. **Exiles** are the young parts that carry the feelings that were too painful for us to feel when we were very young, and **protectors** are those parts that help us push down and hide the painful emotions carried by the exiles so we do not have to feel them again. Examples of emotions carried by exiles are hopelessness, shame, helplessness, fear of death and/or abandonment, feeling unworthy of love. Examples of protectors are over-niceness, control, criticism, anger.

"Then there is the **Self**, our core essence, that can heal the entire system and includes our courage, curiosity, compassion, connectedness, confidence, calm and much more."

Dick paused for a moment and looked around the room. He must have noticed our confusion.

"Let's take the session with Nitsan as an example," he continued. "All of you noticed her cough, I'm sure. When I heard it I wondered whether there might be emotions involved that her cough was somehow trying to suppress. The cough would be the protector and the feelings this part was trying to keep at bay are the loneliness and helplessness that the baby girl was feeling... Now you are probably wondering what made it possible for the healing process to begin?" he said, gazing around the room.

Many of us nodded, myself included.

"It was Nitsan's Self, her core essence. As soon as she was able to step back and look at the part of her that was coughing with curiosity and then with compassion, the healing process could begin. The Self can get to know all the parts and develop a trusting relationship with them. Once the parts realize there is an adult in the system they can trust, then they relax, let go of their extreme roles that were needed in childhood, take on more mature roles and work together with the leadership of the Self to bring harmony to our inner system and bring forth Self qualities to the world."

I looked at Dick in amazement, still not quite sure what had transpired yet so happy to be without my cough and aching chest.

Dick also explained that in the IFS process, we do not try to get rid of any of our parts; we realize all of them have good intentions for us and that they have been forced to behave in extreme ways in order to protect us from emotions that were too painful to feel when we were young children.

The miraculous transformation I experienced drove me to search for a way to create the first IFS Level I course for Arab Palestinians and Jews in Nazareth. With Dick's support the IFS community raised the funds for this course, which was taught by two wonderful teachers, Einat Bronstein and Osnat Arbel[57].

In this course and in further workshops at Esalen (where Dick again volunteered his time), we learned about legacy burdens: those emotional burdens that are not picked up through direct experience in life, but rather inherited through family or cultural legacy.

After thousands of years of pogroms, the Holocaust, the Nakba, the Occupation, the 100 years of conflict, I assumed most of us here were carrying layers upon layers of such burdens. These burdens were constantly triggered by events in our region, causing us to behave in ways, no longer useful, intensifying the cycle of violence and suffering, rather than breaking it.

I began to wonder what effect unburdening our legacy burdens would have. How would releasing those emotional patterns change the way we see and behave towards one another? Was it even possible to let go of our burdens, our beliefs, after decades of bloody conflict and trauma?

57 . http://www.ifs-israel.org/

Chapter 34

A Museum of Humanity's Suffering and Healing
2015, Big Sur

It happened; therefore it can happen again:
this is the core of what we have to say.
Primo Levi

The most valuable possession you can own is an open heart.
The most powerful weapon you can be is an instrument of peace
Carlos Santana

Out of the five years of IFS workshops at Esalen, one session remains engraved in my mind, not only because it was filmed but mostly due to its far-reaching effect on our work in the realm of legacy burdens.

It was a session where Dick worked first with Jamal, a Muslim man, and then with Noa, a Jewish woman, both from Israel. The goal was to give them the tools to speak to one another from an openhearted place even about the most difficult things, and rather than speaking *from* a part – as in, "How could you do this to me? I am so angry with you!" — they would be able to speak *for* a part, as in, "There is a part of me that feels angry and I would like to speak for it right now. Are you open to hearing it?"

When we speak *for* a part, the person listening to us senses there is less of a need to defend themselves because it is not an attack, they are not facing an onslaught of anger. Rather, they are being told about the anger through the mediation of a third entity, the Self. This makes a huge difference in their ability to hear and take in what is being said.

Dick opens the session by asking what they would like to work on. Jamal, a dark-skinned, powerfully built man in his early forties, responds almost immediately. "I would like to talk about the situation in Israel between Arabs and Jews, Israelis and Palestinians. I constantly feel I need to defend my family and that I have to be so vigilant."

"Tell us more," Dick urges.

Jamal takes a deep breath. I can tell it is not easy for him to speak in front of people. Usually, he only shares a few words about how he is doing, yet his eyes constantly speak; when I look into their depths, there is sadness I can hardly begin to fathom.

"During the last war (2014) I was driving and a car hit me from behind. I stopped immediately, not sure what happened. The other car parked behind me, and an elderly Jewish couple stepped out. They looked at my dark skin and the prayer beads I was holding in my hands to try and calm myself and began screaming at me as though I was responsible for what had happened, as though I was the guilty one. I did not say anything because in my culture we are taught to respect our elders, so I just stood there staring at my beads, stunned by their response. Other cars stopped nearby, people came out and began moving towards us to see what all the screaming was about. I began to worry they might attack me and looked around for an escape route. Luckily, a Jewish man who knows me was there also and he intervened, arguing that the accident had not been my fault.

"The elderly couple became upset with him for intervening, angry that a Jew would defend an Arab rather than another Jew but his words grounded me. I realized he was right; it was not my fault and I began taking photos of the accident that I could show my insurance agent. This incident reminded me of the fear always lurking inside me: that I, my wife, or my children will be targeted simply because we are Arabs."

Dick begins working with Jamal, asking similar questions to the one he asked me several years earlier. Noa and I and the rest of the group witness the path towards healing that leads Jamal to see himself at eight years old when something happened in his village that terrified him.

"One day when we were sitting in class there was a loud noise and then screaming in the village. Later I found out that my classmate's house was demolished by the police and his father was killed. His mother had died when he was born so he was now an orphan. I will never forget that day,"

With Dick's guidance, Jamal was able to go back to himself as a young boy, hear more of the story and comfort the eight-year-old. Afterwards, he said, "I feel my heart is now open, softer." The shift was clearly visible, his face seemed more relaxed, unguarded.

Then it was Noa's turn. Noa shared that while listening to Jamal, parts of her that were afraid of fully sharing Israel with the Arabs who live here came up. Her father was a Holocaust survivor, who died when she was seven, yet the memory of the number etched on his forearm was still so clear. She sat facing Jamal, her fingers brushing through her dark curls as if seeking to soothe the emotions coursing through her body.

"I am debating this year whether to finally vote for Hadash in the national elections, because it is the only Arab and Jewish party," she begins, "but there is a part deep inside me that is very scared and needs my country, Israel, to be mostly Jewish." She looks into Jamal's eyes and asks: " Do you still like me when I say this?"

"I understand you, but put yourself for a moment in our shoes and try to understand what it feels like for us," Jamal replies.

"As soon as you ask me to put myself in your shoes my fear of losing control as a Jew is coming back." Noa's foot taps on the floor nervously.

Dick looks at her and inquires, "Noa, would you be open to working with that fearful part?"

"Yes, sure... The idea Jamal mentioned earlier of living all together in a sort of a commune happily ever after with no government, feels utopian, unreal. It's great but it's imaginary. I don't see it ever happening because we are always going to be forced to choose, right or left, Arab or Jewish, Black or White because that's the way it's been set up, so I don't feel we can really change that."

"OK. But are you open to working with the part of you that is feeling fear?" Dick insists gently.

"Yes," she takes a deep breath and closes her eyes.

"Find it in or around your body."

"It's on my whole left side," Noa says, moving her left arm and shoulder.

"When you notice it there, how do you feel towards it?"

"I don't feel anything towards it, it is all of me. I feel flooded," Noa responds with some irritation, shaking her left shoulder as if to rid herself of an insect that had settled there.

"OK, so maybe ask the part to separate a little bit so we can help it? It's hard to help when it floods you."

Noa exhales. "OK." Her shoulders relax slightly.

"Great. How do you feel towards it now?"

"It's like... it's like a helpless child, like a little puppy. I want to help it." Noa sounds surprised by the revelation.

"So let it know that and see how it reacts."

"It doesn't believe me because it sees I don't have any answers that can help."

"Yeah, that's OK, but do you still care about it?"

"Yes," Noa says, gently nodding her head.

"OK, so check if you can keep showing it you care about it even though you don't have the answers."

"OK." Her eyes are shut, turned inwards, and something is happening in her body.

"How does it feel now?"

"Even though this process in only in my imagination, it somehow feels real. I am telling the part that I don't have the solution, but let's be with this together. It's like I changed my tone of voice and I am speaking with him as I would to a child. He is no longer lying on the floor but sitting up."

"Good."

Noa is quietly crying. I look around the room and see the compassion in people's faces. Dick's voice is gentle but firm. "How close are you to him, to this child?'

"About one meter, but he is on the floor and I am above."

"So maybe we'll just be with him in this comforting way until he really trusts us," Dick suggests. Noa nods and takes a deep breath.

"He is smarter than I thought." I asked him if he wants to play and he said: "let's make a puzzle." I asked why a puzzle and he said: "because even though it looks chaotic, fragmented and with lots of pieces, there is still a logic to it and you can piece it together."

"Good, Noa. Now see if there is anything the part wants you to know about its fear."

"Actually," he says, "this fear is an inheritance, a family legacy I received from my father and uncles who asked that I keep it, guard it, take care of it and pass it on to the next generation. There are many stories that I was expected to listen to, write down and pass forward."

"So, he carries all that?"

"He has to, he has to stay there so all those stories and everything he carries will never be lost or disappear."

"Ask him if he likes carrying all that," Dick prompts.

He immediately says: "of course, that is why I exist."

"Well... do you want to say something else?"

"Yes, there is a story about the horrific way my aunt was murdered in the Holocaust which I cannot even bear to utter and it is absolutely crucial that this story is passed on. It is mandatory that it will never be forgotten!"

Noa exclaims passionately.

"So, your exile really does not want to let go of these stories?"

Noa is quiet for a moment. Then she continues.

"I am trying to see if he understands what holding on to these stories and passing them to the next generation is doing to me."

"OK."

"He says there is a plan. He has some plan but he does feel bad about the trauma I am having to carry because these are such painful stories."

"Yeah. I get it."

"So what he suggests or I suggested, I am not sure who is doing the suggesting, is that we take all the stories and give them to Yad Vashem" – Yad Vashem is the Holocaust Remembrance Museum in Jerusalem where they collect stories, memories and artifacts of Holocaust survivors – "and then my family and I will no longer need to continue carrying them.

"However, this part also needs a commitment that the Holocaust Museum will continue to exist and that it would be possible for people to come and hear the stories... I feel we can be relieved of the intense pressure of these stories only if someone else holds, not just the stories, but all the emotions that go with them."

"Or else what? What does this part think will happen if someone does not hold the emotions connected to your stories?" Dick asks.

"Then this part will demand that I continue to hold on to the family legacy stories and pass them to my personal future generations."

"I see, so it's not enough for the stories to go into the museum, someone has to hold the emotions?"

"It's not enough that these words are just written because words can be cold and distant. All the emotions need to be passed to the readers along with the words."

"What is this part afraid would happen if someone did not carry the emotions?"

"Is it not clear to every Jew?"

My heart clenches at her words. I know what she is referring to and looking around I see others in the room wiping tears or sighing. They get it, too.

"I think I know the answer, but please speak it out loud," Dick requests quietly.

"The answer is that it could happen to us again. That if we don't remember and pass the memory with all the emotions to the next generation, a Holocaust will happen again."

"But that is based on the idea that you cannot trust your Self to make sure it does not happen again. Does the fearful part not trust the Self that it could prevent a Holocaust from happening again?"

"When I use the word Self, I see my little child holding on to the stories for dear life and saying 'I am not going to let go until you reassure me that there is enough Self in you and in all the peoples and all the countries in the world. Because if they don't have enough Self and they still have destructive, hateful and terrorizing parts then it is not safe for me and I will not let go of this bundle of horror.'"

"Is this what the part is saying?"

"Yes."

"So, let him know we understand how dangerous the surrounding world feels to him." Dick pauses for a moment, then continues. "But let me ask you, Noa, if he were to give over the stories to the museum and no one held those emotions, would you stop being careful and would you as your Self stop making sure the Holocaust does not happen again?"

"I don't feel I can let go of what is holding this part at the moment maybe because I don't have enough Self. It feels like these emotions fuel my drive to work for peace. I can't imagine doing my work without these emotions."

"Just take a moment and try to imagine..." Dick suggests.

"No, I have a very deep commitment to knowing the emotional impact of these stories still resonates, I don't want them to make another movie like *Life Is Beautiful* where people laugh about the horrors of the Holocaust. No, the horrors and the impact have to be maintained. I am very connected to this little child who is holding this commitment," Noa replies passionately, wiping tears from her eyes.

"I am fine if the part wants to hold on to these stories or give them to a museum, but the fear it carries is not good for you and is not good for peace."

Noa reflects for a moment. "Yes... You are right. It's not good to keep the fear because if we do end up in this government-less commune of peace and equality, that fear is not going to allow me to trust you," she says, turning to Jamal for the first time since the beginning of her session.

"That's what I'm saying." Dick nods. "So, ask the part if it is willing to let go, just of the fear?"

Noa turns inward, eyes closed again. After a while, she responds, "OK.

It is willing but first I have to make an agreement with you, Jamal, and all of you that the museum where all my stories go to will not only be a museum for the Jewish Holocaust but also a museum for the Nakba, and the Ethnic Cleansing and Genocide suffered by different peoples in the world. If we have this kind of institution that documents the suffering of all the peoples and all the nations, that reminds all of us about the horrors that we endured, then it will help make sure we don't do it again to each other and that we maintain our humanity. If that happens then my part is on board with letting go of the fear he is holding."

"I love that idea," Dick says with a smile. There is a sense of excitement in the room and others are nodding their heads.

Noa smiles back and says: "I am now checking with the part how he likes it... Yeah he's excited about it... He feels very happy about saying something important."

There is laughter in the room.

"Great. Is it willing to let go of the fear?"

"Yes, but only after we sign the contract for the museum. It still needs to hold on to it for a bit until then."

"So how about if the part puts the fear in a box so it does not have to carry it any longer and puts the box in a place for safekeeping until that day comes?"

"But the part is the fear – how can I put a part of me in a box?" Noa protests.

"No, I promise you, the part is not the fear, the part is carrying the fear. The part itself is an exile, a very young child that took upon himself to hold all this fear."

Noa is quiet for a moment and then: "Wow! Yes, if he puts the fear somewhere than maybe he can actually grow up... He is wondering where he can put the fear?"

"What would he like to give it up to?"

"Some kind of temporary museum until the joint Museum for Humanity's Suffering is built."

"Can you tell him how to do that?"

"He wants to do it in his own way," Noa replies.

"Great... And how does he feel now?"

"He is growing, he is no longer a small child." Noa puts her left hand up and behind her patting the air above her left shoulder as if there was a real entity standing behind her. He is turning into my son Zeevik."

"Tell me more."

"When Zeevik was three years old, he found out that he is named after my father, who survived the Holocaust and died when I was seven. I told him about it and then for a whole week he walked around the house saying to me 'Ima, Mommy, look, I'm eating, I'm healthy!!' It took me another week to understand that he was so terrified that he would die because he thought all people named Zeevik die. He had to deal with a tremendous amount of fear in his life. He grew up to be a big husky man, an amazing human being – and I am not just saying that as his mother. I felt connected to him when I saw the child part growing inside me."

"Good. So how is the part feeling now?"

"It's hard for him to find a place within me because he is so big now. I put him behind me so he can give me strength."

"How is he doing now?"

"He feels that he will always have some trepidation or cautiousness but also feels much more grounded."

"Good. Let's go back to the question of voting. What do you think you will do now?"

Noa smiles and looks at Jamal. "It is very clear to me now that you are okay and I will vote for the Arab/Jewish Party. My inner conflict has subsided. It's amazing how this works."

"Great." Dick turns back to Jamal, who is watching intently, his eyes on Noa. "Jamal, what was it like for you to watch that?"

"I felt we have such similar stories, that her pain is also my pain. It felt good that I could trust her when I looked into her eyes."

"Great. I am now wondering, Jamal, if you have a part that carries such stories and would like to put in the world's museum too?"

"Yes, that is a very good idea. I would like to forget my stories. I don't want to see them anymore. Let other people hear and see them."

Dick nods encouragingly. "Sounds good."

Sitting and listening to this exchange, I could see in my mind a large museum with a room dedicated to each country, each people, where they could show not only the horrors they have suffered but also the pain they inflicted upon others and, very importantly, what they have been doing to transform and heal since then. Such a museum would have the potential both to connect us as human beings who have suffered and caused suffering, and also to transform our legacies from a load that burdens us to an experience that redeems us.

Almost seven years later when I spoke with both Noa and Jamal, they said the session had been transformative for them. Jamal said he became more centered and relaxed. When he returned to Israel, friends and clients asked him what happened to him and why he is so different. He tried to explain that he is no longer burdened by the fears of the eight-year-old Jamal. And since that session, in every election, Noa has voted for the Arab/Jewish Party.

Chapter 35

Acknowledging the Pain of Others
May 15, 2012, Lod

Love ye therefore the stranger: for
ye were strangers in the land of Egypt
Deuteronomy 10:19

It is a Jewish custom during Passover, as we drink the wine
and celebrate our liberation from bondage, to take out drops of
wine from our glass and unto our plate when we remember the
ten plagues. We do this to symbolize that our joy is not complete
because these plagues that ultimately led to our liberation were
also the source of immense pain to the Egyptian people. While
we rejoice in our freedom, we also acknowledge their pain.

Anonymous

"We just want to be able to feel our feelings and tell our stories," Kayid, a young, dark-haired Muslim teacher explains.

His large brown eyes seemed sad as he looks at the circle of teachers sitting around the light of a single candle in the basement library of an Arab junior high school in the city of Lod.

Many of the other teachers nod in agreement.

According to historians, Lod was first constructed more than 6000 years ago and is mentioned in the Hebrew Bible as a place where ancient Hebrews once resided[58]. Since then, it has changed hands many times. Today, about 70,000 people live in the city, a quarter of whom are Arabs. Even though there has been some improvement in recent years, Lod is still known as a drug capital and a city of crime and violence. Prejudice is rampant and the cause of some of the violence both in the separate and mixed Jewish and Arab neighborhoods. The kindergartens and schools

---

58. **Chronicles 8:12 ; Ezra 2:33** ; Nehemiah 7:37; 11:35.

are also mostly separate, and this particular junior high school, where 900 Arab children between ages 12 and 15, study, is located in one of the poorest neighborhoods of the city.

Today, May 15th, is the day when Palestinians throughout the world commemorate the Nakba, the Palestinian Catastrophe, that included the permanent displacement of a majority of the Palestinian people during the 1948 war when 700,000 of them fled or were expelled from their homes and land and became refugees.

For two years between 2007 and 2009, the teachers in Israel were permitted to talk about the Nakba with their students as long as they stated that it began because the surrounding Arab countries refused to agree to the partition plan and instead declared war against Israel. But in 2009 the new Minister of Education once again forbade the mention of the Nakba in the schools.

In addition, the Israeli Ministry of Education requires everyone to attend school on this day, as it does during the Jewish memorial days. However, because the Arab Committee[59] called for a strike, many of the students decided to stay home. The teachers, on the other hand, had to go to school, otherwise they would be reprimanded by their supervisor.

Kayid, who had been teaching math at the school for eight years, continues: "I would like to be able to explain to my students about the Nakba. I am an Israeli citizen living in Israel and I am also a Palestinian. Just as we talk with the students about Independence Day and the Holocaust, we would like to be able to talk about our own history without feeling fear."

Fatma, an Arab math teacher who has been in the school for 17 years, speaks up: "A few years ago, I went to Auschwitz with a group of teachers. I saw all the horror, and took pictures to show my students. I came back and told them about it and they were really saddened by the suffering of the Jewish people. Today, I don't understand why I cannot talk with them about our own suffering. I don't understand why I am being told I should not be feeling these feelings, that I should be feeling thankful I do not live in one of the surrounding Arab countries where my situation would be much worse. How can anyone tell me what to feel or not feel? My feelings are my own!"

Hearing them one after the other share their pain on this day, I don't

59. An extra-parliamentary umbrella organization that represents Arab citizens of Israel (https://en.wikipedia.org/wiki/Arab_citizens_of_Israel) at the national level.

know what to say so I just listen. It seems that sharing their stories with me, the only Jew in the room, is somehow helping.

Years later, while writing this book, I remembered how difficult it was for Noa to let go of the stories passed down by her family and of the emotions attached to them. In her mind, she had to hold on to these legacy burdens because if she forgot them, the horror of the Holocaust might recur. She was only willing to give them over to a place where they would be **acknowledged and cherished**, a museum that would include space for people from every country to share their suffering.

I wondered why it is so hard for us, the Jewish people, to acknowledge the pain we have inflicted on the Palestinians. Why is it so difficult to hold both realities, both narratives? Yes, we were struggling for our survival and yes, it was right after the horrific genocide of the Holocaust and yes, all the surrounding Arab countries fought against us and we had to create our homeland to survive and yes, we are still under threat from Hamas, Hezbollah, Iran and even ISIS. It is all true, and it is also true that while we were creating our own homeland we caused great suffering to others.

Acknowledging our complicity, giving the Palestinians space in the museum of the world to share their pain, will not detract from our own suffering. Rather, it might enable the Palestinians to release some of the emotional burdens they have been carrying for generations and open their hearts to genuine dialogue.

Our ancestors were very wise when they insisted that every Passover, when we celebrate our own freedom from bondage, we must also remember and acknowledge the suffering inflicted on the Egyptians through the ten plagues. Those who came before us were able to make space for the two narratives. We can and must do the same.

Chapter 36

Intertwined
2010, Nes Ammim – 2015, Othona

...There is no fear that this human being has that I cannot
understand, no suffering that I cannot care about, because I too
am human... Whatever their story, they no longer need to be
alone with it. This is what will allow healing to begin.

Carl Rogers

It is July of 2010 and we are holding a two-day weekend workshop at Nes Ammim, a small community in Northern Israel. This community was started by Swiss, Dutch and German immigrants after WWII and is dedicated to improving relationships between people of different religions who live in Israel.

There are twenty of us sitting on mats in a circle, an odd mixture of four religions – Muslims, Christians, Druze and Jews – all women, from different communities, who have participated in our groups in the past. For some, it is the first time they have ever met.

After the opening circle we begin moving and dancing together, learning about listening partnerships, sharing life stories – crying, laughing, playing and touching. There seems to be a heartstring connecting us together, and by the end of the day it becomes palpable to everyone. After dinner the whole group lingers together, sharing stories, telling jokes. I can still hear their loud voices and laughter when I walk over to my room to rest for the night.

The following day we sit in small groups to share stories from our past. Listening to the women in my group I wonder if these stories have ever been shared before and if the pain they reveal has ever been acknowledged.

Ahlam, a Muslim Arab woman from a well-known family with 10 brothers and sisters, speaks first: "My father was the mayor of our town until he lost in one election campaign because some of his own clan did not support him," she begins. "He was very angry and in order to punish them he decided to give me, his eldest daughter, as a wife to a member of the opposing clan. I was only 17 at the time. When I heard about it, I was horrified, I did not love my intended husband, heard bad things about him and did not want to become a part of his family. Why should I go and live with people who hated us? I begged my father to change his mind. Kissing his feet, I cried for mercy. But his heart was closed and no amount of pleading made a difference."

Swallowing hard, Ahlam looks at us, her eyes filled with tears.

"I was married off and began a 25-year journey of suffering. I gave birth to a baby daughter at age 18 and soon after began to bleed so profusely that my uterus had to be removed. I was never going to be able to give birth again. There would be no sons from me. My spirit was not crushed even when my husband beat me again and again; fighting for my daughter's life gave me the strength. A few times I escaped with my little girl to my parents' house and begged my father to agree to a divorce. But he always forced me to go back to my husband. Still, I worked and studied to become a kindergarten teacher and was able to support my daughter and myself.

"When my father was on his deathbed a few years ago I sat next to him and held his hand. He looked at me and said: 'Ahlam, my daughter, I know what I did. I sacrificed you like a lamb... I am asking for your forgiveness. Please forgive me...' All I could do was cry."

There is a moment of silence while tears roll down her cheeks. I feel choked and look around the circle at other eyes brimming with tears.

After a while, Ahlam adds, "Last week my daughter married a good man. Before she left the house, she told me – now I want you to get a divorce. I spoke with my husband after her wedding and so far, he has agreed."

A hopeful smile spreads through the group and we all hug her.

Then I look at Suhad, one of the Muslim women leaders in the group. This beautiful woman in her early forties, with light hair and green eyes, had been so happy the previous day, laughing and dancing joyfully. She stayed up with the others gossiping and giggling until almost two in the morning. Yet this morning when the group began, she seems different; something has changed. *Perhaps she is just tired*, I ponder when I watch how she interacts with others, speaking softly, eyes down.

Before dividing into the small groups, I asked the participants to draw what they were feeling. Walking around the room, I observed their drawings – blue skies, sun, green grass, children playing or families holding hands were present in most pictures except for Suhad's. On one side of the paper, she drew in red and black what appeared to be a terrible fire or storm and on the other side a dark fence, surrounding a building that looked like a prison. In contrast to all the other drawings, there was no sun or grass or flowers or blue sky in her picture, only darkness.

In our small group, she is the last to share. After some hesitation she tells us the story weighing on her heart. "Eight years ago, in August 2002, a young Muslim man, a suicide bomber, exploded on bus #361 near Meiron Mountain, killing nine and injuring forty people," she begins.

"Over breakfast this morning, Rozet, one of the women from the Arab Druze village Maghar who is in the workshop and whom I have never met, told me that her cousin had been on that bus and was killed. She talked about her enormous pain and I froze and could not utter one word. How could I tell Rozet that it was my two cousins who had helped the suicide bomber? That they were the ones who had purchased the battery for the bomb, gave the man food and a place to sleep, drove him to the bus station and picked out the bus that he would board and explode himself on 15 minutes later? How could I tell her about the sleepless nights, the psychiatric medication I have been on for the past eight years? How could I explain about the destruction of our family name, the inability to feel joy at family celebrations? How could I share the shame and pain of being called "murderer" by my Jewish neighbors or the anger I feel towards the boys' mothers for raising them that way? How can I scream about the unfairness of suffering for someone else's sins and the thousand small and large ways in which my life has changed forever since this horrible event? Or about the pain I saw in my grandma's eyes when she realized she will never see her grandchildren, who are serving a life sentence, ever again?" When she begins to cry, we move closer, folding her in our arms.

As I listen to her sobs, gently caressing her hand, tears are rolling down my cheeks and there seems to be nothing to say, no words that could heal or make better, just a wave of pain and sadness at the horror of it all.

After a while, enfolded in our arms Suhad takes a deep breath and looks at us. For the first time today, a tiny smile appears in the corners of her mouth.

In 2015, almost five years to the day after the Nes Ammim workshop, this story comes up again. I am with a different group, Arabs and Jews, women and men, at a retreat center called Othona in Southern England. Somewhere towards the middle of the five-day workshop Amiram, a powerfully built 65-year-old Jewish man, works on painful memories from the day in August 2002 when the bus exploded.

"Look at what you've done... Look at what you've done!" he cries, tears rolling down his cheeks. He is gazing beyond all of us as though he can actually see the two young Arab men, Suhad's cousins, who had helped the suicide bomber, the man who exploded on bus #361 and killed his son. I can hear the grief and rage underneath his cry and my throat tightens.

Aimee, one of the workshop leaders, takes his hand and looks into his eyes.

"Amiram," she begins, "I want to help you express your pain and move the energy that has been stuck inside you for so long. Look at me... Please look at me for a moment..." she entreats.

Amiram turns towards Aimee, his brown eyes coming into focus on her face.

"Would you like to hit the foam cube with the bataca bat and finally have your feelings fully?" she asks. "We are all here to support you."

"I want to," he says in a choked voice, "but I can't... it's too much... I don't have the strength..."

Standing behind Aimee, I look into his eyes, filled with tears, his shoulders stooped with the weight of it all and I know he is right. He can't do it. Not now.

But what if someone else could do it for him? I wonder. Someone who understands this pain... Someone who has not yet been so beaten down by life. Someone who still has the strength to lift up a fist (or, in this case, a bataca bat) and scream... Scream against the injustice, the endless violence, the death of a beloved son, a young Jewish man, at the hands of somebody else's son, a young Muslim man.

So we ask for volunteers. Would anyone be willing to step into the center of the room, pick up the bataca bat and hit the cube, supporting Amiram by giving his inner scream a voice?

Yusra, a young Muslim Bedouin woman, volunteers. Already a lawyer at 23, only slightly older than Amiram's son was when he was murdered, she knows about pain and anger from years living with a violent father who sometimes beat her and her siblings. But she fought against this injustice; even when she knew he might hurt her, she did not keep quiet.

Now, deeply touched by Amiram's story, she steps forward and picks up the bat. Her intense brown eyes focused on Amiram and the group let us know that she can no longer stand the pain and injustice of it all. Taking a deep breath, she holds the bat high above her head. Then the dam breaks and she hits and screams and hits and screams again and again and again.

"Look at what you've done! LOOK AT WHAT YOU'VE DONE!"

And the more she hits, the more he cries: remembering, releasing, supported by the loving arms of group members. And in her screams, and in his tears, their pain intertwines.

Looking at them both I too am sobbing. Then I remember Suhad's story and pray that wherever she is now, she is sensing this moment, and is somehow, comforted.

Chapter 37

Feeling What is Yours to Feel
2012-2014, Meilya

Emotional pain cannot kill you but running from it can.
Allow. Embrace it. Let yourself feel. Let yourself heal.
Vironika Tugaleva

Grief can be the garden of compassion. If you keep your
heart open through everything, your pain can become your
greatest ally in your life's search for love and wisdom.

Rumi

"They said in the news that an American killed an Israeli. That is not true. It was a Jew killing an Arab!" blurts Nivin, a dark haired Christian Arab woman in her late thirties, looking directly into my eyes, her face puffy from a recent tooth operation.

"Tell me more," I ask, noticing the mixture of sadness and anger in her green eyes.

In our workshops we encourage participants to share their stories, their truth. "If your tears could speak, what would they say?" we ask them. We have seen that rather than having unspoken pain fester in hearts and minds, sharing the story and experiencing the connected emotions is crucial to healing and deep connection.

"It was last week," she continues. "William, a young American Jew who came to Israel on a work-study program, killed Armando, an Arab man who lived in our town and worked as a chef at a hotel in Eilat. I guess William was angry because Armando fired him for not doing his job well. So he came to the hotel with an axe and then fought the hotel guard and took his gun. Armed with an axe and a gun, he stormed into the kitchen and threatened everyone there. The other staff ran away and William shot Armando four times at close range. The newspapers called it a work dispute crime. I and all the others in my village call it a racist hate crime. Yes, Jews also commit such crimes!" she cried passionately.

Tears are running down her cheeks while women sitting nearby move closer, reach over and hold her hands.

"What hurt the most was the funeral. Thousands of people came. Abed Armando was 33 and not yet married. During the funeral, his mother, who struggled all her life to support her family, asked his cousin to sing a song and others to play music that is usually played at weddings. Then she started dancing around the gravesite, crying 'this is your wedding dance, my son...' All the women were weeping and I ran away, I couldn't stand looking at her dance on top of his grave. It was too awful."

Nivin wiped her tears and continues: "I don't feel safe here anymore. I'm afraid to send my daughter on a trip, afraid to send her to school. I'm just afraid all the time."

Listening to her, I also felt fear. Fear for my son, my daughter, all those I love, fear for myself.

Then she speaks again: "You know that during the shooting guests at the hotel were told to stay in their rooms. When it was over, they came out clapping, feeling relieved and one woman said: "We will not let this ruin our vacation."

"Yes," I said, "I can see people doing that, forging ahead, moving on to the next thing instead of stopping to feel. Until we learn the huge benefit of feeling the pain, most of us try to avoid it. But you, Nivin, you are not avoiding. You are courageously feeling what is yours to feel. Thank you."

Between 2012 and 2014, there were 44 kidnapping attempts of Jews in Israel and the West Bank/Occupied Territories. In 2014, three young men were kidnapped on their way home from their Yeshiva School and murdered. Their murder ignited the Tzuk Eitan (Protective Edge) Operation/War.

As the war dragged on and on, I kept wondering.

Why are we fighting again? Is it the Palestinians who are fighting to end the oppression? Or are we fighting those who want to return to their homes in Israel and throw all the Jews into the sea? Is this a religious war of the Muslim people who want to take over the world? Is this a war to divert attention from the building of more settlements in the West Bank by the Jewish religious right and the confiscating of more land from the Palestinians? Who are we actually fighting against and who is fighting us? And why?

I was not sure. Hearing the news every day, my tension mounted. In one workshop I shared:

"Last week my daughter Shir had a performance with a theater group she has been part of during the past two years. It was at night and about an hour away from my house in Northern Israel. As I prepared to drive over, fears flooded me. I tried to think of which road would be the safest to drive on and where would there be the least chance of being kidnapped. I never had these thoughts before here in the Galilee."

"Me too," Noa said. "Last night I dreamed I was kidnapped on the way to work in Nazareth."

A Jewish woman shared: "The other day my son was hitchhiking and called me from his ride. My first question was: 'Is the person driving the car a Jew...?' Or, in other words, 'Are you safe?'"

Others in the room were nodding.

Laila, a Muslim who lives in the Southern Bedouin town of Rahat, shared: "I am not going to Beer Sheva these days because I am religious and afraid Jews in Beer Sheva will curse me, and pull off my head covering, as they did to a woman I know, and call out: 'Death to the Arabs.' I am also terrified of the constant bombing over my house and have trouble sleeping at night. I scream whenever there's a siren, scaring my children. They sit and wait outside the bathroom when I shower because they are afraid to be alone. My heart aches when I see on TV the death and suffering in Gaza. I just want it all to end..."

"Me too," a Jewish woman says. "Last night bombs fell near my home in the Galilee from Lebanon and that means that from North to South there is no longer any safe area in Israel."

It was not easy to arrange a meeting during the war, yet all the participants in our Peace Leadership group made a special effort to participate. We met, shared stories, held hands, expressed our anger and cried. For me those meetings were the sanest place to be.

A few days after one of our meetings I read a conversation in our WhatsApp group between two of our participants, both men: Ahmad, a Muslim dentist from Beer Sheva in the South, and Gal, a Jewish engineer from Northern Israel.

Ahmad: Despite all my anger about the murder of my people in Gaza, I am now thinking about the bomb that fell near the house of my Jewish assistant and damaged her home. I looked inside and found space in my heart where I could reach out to her and invite her to my own home to stay with us... With all this pain and anger, I am trying to hold on to my humanity...

Gal: It is very hard for me to express what's inside me now because I feel so shaky, scared, angry and confused. You, the people in our group, are very dear to me and I am doing my best to keep my heart open and not become an extremist. Even though sometimes what is written here is so hard for me to read, I am mostly able to stay open to the pain of others in the group because I know it is very real and I thank you for sharing it. Please know our home is open to all those who would like to come and be in a reality that is a bit saner than what is going on in the South. There is even a Mosque nearby for those who want to pray during Ramadan.

Ahmad: Thank you Gal. I guess the work we have been doing over the past year is helping us now so that even in these difficult moments we are staying connected to our ability to love. Perhaps we can give some of our light to the blind majority in Israel and Gaza...

Gal: You know Ahmad, I am in a supermarket shopping for food so I feel uncomfortable to cry here but I really want to...

While reading their words written in the midst of the war, I visualize a Jewish man, standing in the middle of a supermarket feeling so moved by the message of an Arab man that he wants to cry, and I too want to cry... and I feel hope...

Chapter 38

The Courage to Be a Woman with a Voice
June, 2015, Hurfeish

Feminism isn't about making women stronger.
Women are already strong; it's about changing the
way the world perceives that strength.

G.D. Anderson

I raise up my voice — not so that I can shout, but so
that those without a voice can be heard. ... We cannot
all succeed when half of us are held back.

Malala Yousafzai

"Please come and help me gather the women. We have to do something about the situation..." my Druze friend Samira called to urge me one day in June 2015.

Samira lives in the picturesque Druze village of Hurfeish nestled amongst the slopes of the Zvul mountain in the Upper Galilee. Almost 6000 people, mostly Druze, whose ancestors came in the 16th century from what is now Lebanon, reside in the village today.

Just last week at 2 a.m. an Israeli military ambulance passed through Hurfeish. It was carrying Syrians wounded in the fighting near the Israeli-Syrian border who sought medical help from Israel and were being transported to the hospital in Nahariya, a Jewish town. They were ambushed in the village because the local Druze wanted to check if the wounded Syrians were the ones who had been fighting against their Druze brethren in Syria. The ambulance was stoned and barely managed to escape. Luckily, no one was hurt.

Fear and anger have been growing in the village because of the news about ISIS victories and their horrible deeds towards the Druze and other religious communities in Syria and Iraq. This fear has led many to turn to their religion for protection, which means the women in the village are pressured to go back to wearing the traditional Druze garb, to cover their faces, stop driving and stay in their homes within the village.

But some of the women, who are educated and have worked outside their homes and driven for several years, are trying to change the situation. This is a challenging task because the village is a tight-knit community with a great deal of family involvement in each other's lives in order to ensure tradition is upheld and no one steps too far outside the social norms. If a woman rebels, quite often the weapon of shunning is used to pressure her to "behave".

On a sunny morning in late June, we drive up the winding road to Samira's house, located in the midst of an olive grove and a fruit orchard on the edge of the village. Samira smiles widely when she opens the door for Noa and I, her face crinkling kindly in welcome, round cheeks rosy. She ushers us to one of the three living rooms of her large house. Already present are four other women Samira has invited, all of them professional women who had studied for their degrees years ago, when the atmosphere had been more open. They hold Bachelor's and even Master's Degrees in a variety of professions including Art and Drama Therapy, Law and Education.

When Noa and I ask them to share a bit about themselves, we are not prepared for the torrent of painful stories that flows into the room as though from some hidden inner river whose dam had burst. They speak of waking up each day to see that another woman had become ultra-religious and covered her face, of the constant pressure on girls, especially from other women, to conform and return to their religion by the time they reach adolescence, of the pressure not to drive outside the village or not to drive at all.

Samira shares that when she was four years old, she tried to pee while standing up like her five-year-old brother because she also wanted to be a boy. Her mother chastised her, repeating the statement she would hear over and over throughout her childhood: "Boys are blessed while girls should be eradicated."

Deeply empathizing with their sense of injustice, my first instinct is to tell them what I think they should do, to offer solutions, but almost immediately I realize I don't really know what they could do. I have never lived in that society and while I had passed through the village hundreds of times on my way to the Upper Galilee, in all those years I hardly ever stopped to have a heart-to-heart dialogue with anyone. I was clueless.

But this doesn't bother Samira and her friends. They sense they can talk to us about things they never share anywhere else and soon I realize that this is the key, just as it had always been. Our role as facilitators is not to offer quick solutions, to try and save people from whatever they are going through. No, our task was and is to support the creation of Safe Havens: places of safety, support and caring where nothing has to be hidden, where everything can be felt and shared. Our shame, anger, disappointment, mistrust and our longing for justice, peace and love would all be welcome. Once we no longer had to suppress these feelings, no longer needed to expend our psychic energy hiding them, we could use that energy to speak out and change the situation.

On our way out, Samira hugged me and I felt she was thinking the same thing, especially when she said: "I feel so relieved, empowered. When can we do it again?"

Chapter 39

A Moment in Each Other's Shoes

2009-2017, Kfar Vradim

Walking a mile in someone else's shoes isn't as much
about the walk or the shoes; it's to be able to think like they
think, feel what they feel, and understand why they are
who and where they are. Every step is about empathy.

Toni Sorenson

In the winter of 2009, Jerry and I decided to separate. I returned to Israel feeling a light had been turned off in my soul and I would never love another man. Once in a while there was feeling of relief – our marriage had never been easy – but the deep sadness almost always won.

After I had cried and shared my feelings with Liry, she told me about a Playback Theater class with Efrat Ashiri that she was attending and encouraged me to join.

I called Efrat, and a few days later she paid me a visit to get to know me and see if I would be a good fit for her class.

I was not sure what to make of the petite, blonde woman who entered my tiny one-bedroom apartment. Once we began chatting, her compassionate eyes and beautiful smile put me at ease. I felt comfortable, appreciated, seen.

She asked about me and then explained Playback Theater, that it was first developed by Jonathan Fox and Jo Salas, that it is now very popular in many places around the world and that it is an original form of improvisational theater in which audience or group members tell stories from their lives and watch them enacted on the stage. According to Makeshift Theatre, "Playback Theater is created through a unique collaboration between performers and audience. It provides a space where any story – however ordinary, extraordinary, hidden or difficult – might

265

be told, and immediately made into theater. And where each person's uniqueness is honored and affirmed while at the same time building and strengthening our connections to each other as a community of people." [60]

"Why do you think I should join your Playback Theater class?" I inquired, feeling doubtful.

Looking into my eyes, she replied: "How are you feeling?"

"So sad," I admitted, tears rolling down my cheeks.

"Playback Theater will bring you joy," she replied with a sense of certainty. And in that moment, I believed it might actually be true, so I joined.

During our weekly three-hour class, I met women who later became dear friends. Being with them and sharing what I was going through, hearing their stories and challenges and then watching or participating in the playback of the stories made me feel less alone, less sad.

A few months later, on the morning of Memorial Day for all the Jewish soldiers and citizens who died in our wars, we had a class. During the class, Efrat, or Effie as I began calling her, shared a story that touched me deeply.

"I grew up in Kiryat Shmona[61]," she began, "and throughout my childhood there was always fear of Katyusha bombs falling on us. We never knew when they would come. Our only warning would be a loud siren which meant we had thirty seconds to run to the nearest underground shelter. During the 1973 Yom Kippur War, I was seven years old and every evening we would look up towards the Golan Heights and see the sky orange with fires that were burning because of the fighting with the Syrians. It felt so close and scary.

"Our underground shelter was very crowded, never enough beds for everyone, so when we had to run to the shelter at night, there were often angry words about who would sleep where. But my neighborhood was also a community where people helped each other.

"My father was away fighting in the war so we did not see him for several weeks. One day, during the hour allotted to leave the shelter in order to buy food, my mother, who was pregnant, sent me to the tiny grocery store in our neighborhood to buy milk.

"I ran quickly and very soon saw Amram, our tall, dark-haired Moroccan grocer, standing at the entrance to his store. In his right hand

---

60. https://www.makeshifttheatre.co.uk/about-playback-theatre/

61. A Northern town very close to Lebanon.

he was holding up a plastic milk bag and shouting at all the people waiting in line: 'It's the last one I have...'

"People pushed one another, trying to be the first in line so they could buy it. Because I was only seven and smaller than everyone else, I sneaked through the line and reached the front, holding my hands out and hoping that by some miracle, he would have pity and give it to me.

"Amram was holding the milk tightly, as if not sure what to do, when a young woman ran to the front of the line crying: 'Please, I need the milk'.

"Amram immediately handed it to her, saying to the crowd: 'She needs it for the baby.'

"Nobody said anything. We lived in the same neighborhood and knew she had just given birth. As she took the milk and paid, my heart contracted. I was only seven and wanted the milk so badly but understood, like everyone else, that she needed it more."

Effie stops for a moment to take a sip of water. Looking around the room, I see everyone watching and waiting for her next words.

"My teacher in the second grade was 22 when she received news that her brother had been killed in the Yom Kippur war. She was heartbroken. Then on April 11th, 1974, a few months after the war ended, during the Passover holiday I was away with my family when a horrific event happened in my neighborhood.

"Three terrorists infiltrated from Lebanon with weapons. Walking all night through the valley, hidden by the trees, they entered Kiryat Shmona early in the morning and immediately went to the first elementary school they saw, Yanush Korchak, my school.

"The school was empty because of the Passover break so they ran into a nearby apartment house, knocked on the door of an apartment on the first floor and when the door was opened, began shooting, killing everyone inside. Then they moved to another apartment house where they shot everyone they saw. Some people managed to escape through the windows but others were shot and killed while trying to escape. Reaching the 4th floor, they broke into an apartment and began shooting.

"The father was at work but the mother, Fanny Shitrit, and her four children were in the apartment. The terrorists shot and killed her and two of her children; Yocheved who was 11 and Aaron who was 8. One daughter, nine-year-old Iris, managed to escape by running into the bedroom and hiding in a closet. She tried to pull her five-year-old brother Moti with her, but he freed himself from her hold and ran towards their mother, where he was shot and killed. Iris hid until they left the apartment and then she ran to the window screaming for help. It took more than an hour before the military stormed the apartment building. Later she said that, had the military arrived sooner, her mother and siblings might have been saved. In other apartments more children from my school were murdered."

Imagining Iris and her brothers and sisters, I feel choked. Other women are crying. Effie continues:

"Afterwards, I remember everyone walking around dazed. Every loud noise we heard scared us. I could not understand how Aaron, who sat next to me in class, was suddenly dead. I felt so much fear but never spoke about it, probably because the adults around us were also shaken and had no idea what to do and how to support us through such trauma. Neither did the teachers. Our own teacher was young and still devastated by the loss of her brother in the war. The fear never left me and every time I hear a siren, even if it's just an ambulance, something contracts inside me and I want to hide.

"When all of us who studied at the school during those years met again 40 years later, we sat for hours talking about the terrorist attack, the war, the bombs, as if trying to get some relief for our angst from those who had been there and understood us best. Almost all my childhood friends and classmates had become right wing, believing we had to stay strong, and that there is no way to make peace with the Arabs, because they could never be trusted.

"I feel that one of the things that made me different, a pursuer of peace, was the Playback Theater. Because of Playback, my heart stayed open to possibilities of connecting with those that most of my other classmates consider "the enemy". In some way I feel that Playback Theater saved me."

Days later, still thinking about Effie's story, Playback Theater and the work we had been doing with Together Beyond Words, I realized it would be amazing if we found a way to collaborate. I felt that Together Beyond Words' safe havens to feel and heal, which had until now been mostly workshops with a limited number of participants, needed to reach a larger audience and a collaboration with Playback Theater would provide an amazing opportunity to reach so many more people.

I envisioned how stories about the conflict and women's issues could be shared by the audience and played back to them by an ensemble of Arab and Jewish actresses who would be "walking the talk", both as women bringing their voice to the public sphere in communities where women's voices are often missing and as Arab and Jewish women providing an example of the possibility of working together for healing and peace.

A year later I was able to raise the funds and we began a program together called "From Stage to Change". We recruited Lamis, a Christian Arab Palestinian actress who had been working with Effie for several years, to be our co-facilitator.

I had first seen Lamis in a Playback Theater performance a few months earlier. I could not take my eyes off her. An attractive woman in her early thirties, Lamis seemed so openhearted, sometimes light and funny and at other times deep and wise. She and the rest of the ensemble under Effie's profound and at times hilarious leadership heard the painful, challenging stories from the audience and turned them into a miraculous act of healing.

Later, Lamis told me that it hadn't always been this way for her.

"I have loved acting and theater since I was very young," she said. "When I grew up and longed to pursue acting as a career, my father told me that being on the stage is like being a whore and he would never permit me to do it. And the more I entreated the more adamant he became."

"So, what did you do?" I asked.

"I decided to study drama therapy. He could not say no to that because being a therapist is considered to be a respectable profession for a woman in our village."

"Smart," I quipped.

"And as part of my studies, I had to take theater classes. My father did not know about it but the man who was then my fiancé and is now my husband did and he asked me to stop attending those classes because it was a mixed group of men and women and we were busy with rehearsals until late at night. He felt threatened by it so I stopped going to rehearsals.

"Luckily at around that time Effie came to the college to teach my class Playback Theater. I finally felt I had found my niche and Yusuf, who was my husband by then, did not try to stop me, both because our group was only women and because he saw how happy I was when I came home after a rehearsal or performance."

"Wow! What a journey..." I said with awe.

When we began *From Stage to Change* with Noa, Effie and Lamis, it was the only Playback Theater Ensemble of Arab and Jewish women in Israel and possibly in the world.

We were also unique in that our events had two parts: a performance followed by a storytelling circle. During the performance, volunteers from the audience were invited to share personal stories related to oppression/ empowerment of women, to life in Israel and to Arab-Jewish relations and the conflict. The stories were then re-enacted by the actresses of the ensemble. Following the performance, the audience was divided into storytelling circles led by the actresses/facilitators, enabling those who had not shared their stories to have an opportunity to share and listen to the stories of several other women.

Why stories?

Because stories, whether they come in words, songs, a play or films, can very quickly awaken our ability to understand and empathize with 'the other.' Stories create experience, create empathy and encourage action. This is because stories, unlike PowerPoints or explanations, can put our whole brain to work. When we tell stories that have helped us shape our thinking and way of life to others, we can have the same effect on them[62].

Three years after our project was launched and we had performed and led circles for hundreds of Arabs and Jews, we began teaching our combined approach of Playback Theater and Storytelling Circles to young Arab and Jewish women at Tel Hai College.

During the second semester, our class met towards the end of April, the time of year when the Holocaust Memorial Day is followed by the Memorial Day for all the soldiers and citizens killed during wars or terrorist attacks, followed immediately by Independence Day. The day of the Nakba on May 15th comes right after. During both the Jewish Memorial Days, air raid sirens are sounded throughout the country to commemorate all those who were killed or murdered. When those sirens are sounded, everyone is expected to stand silently in respect for the victims. As Jews these are difficult days, reminding us yet again of our pain, loss and anguish and, without a break in between, also of our joy for having a country of our own. For the Palestinians these days are more complex.

Following the warm-up, Lamis invites the young women in the class to share stories related to these loaded days. The classroom is quiet for a moment until Nura, a beautiful Arab woman in her early twenties with long curly brown hair, speaks.

"I work as a waitress in a coffee shop called Aroma and my colleagues are mostly Arabs and Russian immigrants. My Arab colleagues and I sometimes speak with one another in Arabic, our mother tongue, and

---

62. https://buffer.com/resources/science-of-storytelling-why-telling-a-story-is-the-most-powerful-way-to-activate-our-brains/

the Russian immigrants speak with one another in Russian, their mother tongue. The Arabs are constantly reprimanded and shushed, told to speak only in Hebrew, but the Russians are never criticized."

"I also feel uncomfortable and nervous when I hear Arabic around me," Tal, a young Jewish woman with a dark ponytail, says quietly. "And now I realize it is because I don't understand what they are saying and, in my mind, Arabic is the language of the enemy."

"Thank you, Tal, for sharing, and please continue Nura," Lamis says encouragingly.

"Every year my friends and I face a dilemma whether to stand up when the sirens are sounded or not. We want to respect the pain of the Jewish people but don't feel like we are being seen and respected for our suffering. Not standing up has become for us a form of nonviolent rebellion, protesting the lack of acknowledgement we feel from the Jewish side. Some of my friends at Aroma are scared to lose their jobs, so they stand up with a heavy heart but this year I decided to sit in a quiet corner while others were standing. I felt good about following my heart and not doing something just because it was expected."

There is silence for a moment. I look at Nura and think about Independence Day, another issue altogether, a day when most of us Jews celebrate having our own country with fireworks and picnics like the 4th of July in the USA, while many Arabs sit at home and feel they don't belong. "I am not sure what to do during Independence Day," Nura continues, as though her mind had been on a similar path. "I usually feel agitated and can't wait for it to be over."

Jewish actresses play back her story and Nura is visibly moved. After feeling so unseen and misunderstood, not only is her story being acknowledged on stage, but playing her in the story is a Jewish woman, Tamar.

Afterwards Tami seems shaken: "This is the first time I understand that the day of my joy is also the day of your sorrow... The chasm is so large between us... How can we ever bridge it?"

We sit with her question for a moment, feeling into it. Then Shani, a Jewish woman, asks to share her story.

"My grandmother survived the Holocaust and yet I feel uncomfortable with having to stand for the siren and being asked to feel at a specific moment the pain that is constantly present in my life... I also really don't like having Memorial Day so close to Independence Day. It's like one moment we are supposed to mourn our losses and the following moment feel joy for having our own country. Every year I felt shaken by this ritual and did not participate until one year a young Jewish man I met in an Arab-Jewish coexistence group, and whom I loved, was killed in the military while flying into Lebanon with his army unit during the war. Now I feel that I don't have a choice. Every Memorial Day I spend with his family. I don't know what to feel anymore..."

Arab and Jewish actresses play back her story with great sensitivity. I look at Shani and see the tears running down her cheeks.

In the closing circle, when the talking piece reaches Nura she says, "I'm feeling a sense of relief. I have shared something that has been in my heart for a long time and instead of being silenced and criticized I was supported and accepted..."

Tami turns to Nura and responds: "You know that I was raised in the Golan Heights and now live in a settlement in the West Bank surrounded by people who don't like Arabs. Recently, while I was driving home, a rock was thrown at my car by young Palestinians. It flew through the window and landed in the back seat. I could have been killed. We are on different sides of the conflict and earlier I felt only the immense distance separating us, but now after what you have shared, I feel so close to you."

Nura reaches over and squeezes her hand.

Another young woman, Amit, also seems touched: "I feel the open sharing was possible because we created a space where we don't judge one another. Like most of the Jewish women here, I spent all my school years from kindergarten to high school in Jewish education. Here in Tel Hai is the first time where I have Arabs in my classes and after what I just heard I am sorry that I never considered approaching them and asking how they feel during these special memorial days. I am happy that now I know a little more... And in this moment, I feel very fortunate that we, the women in this group, might have a chance to raise our children differently..."

Lamis seems deeply moved by their words.

"You know," she tells the Jewish women in the group, "I still remember the day when I began understanding your pain. The pain of the Holocaust, wars, terrorist acts. It was the day a Jewish friend of mine said that now she sees how much the Palestinians have suffered and are still suffering. At that moment I felt a wall in my heart begin to melt and suddenly I could see your pain. In that moment, I could see myself in your shoes."

Chapter 40

A Place to Belong
2014, The Galilee

To heal is to touch with love that which we previously touched with fear.
Stephen Levine

"This week I went to protest against the war in Gaza as a Palestinian because I am an Israeli Palestinian. This is my identity" says Elham, a tall beautiful woman with curly light brown hair reaching the middle of her back "And the police stood there and took photos and I felt threatened. I felt that when we protest, we need to worry about our job and life in this country. So, I feel there is no place for me, that I can be persecuted if I express my opinion. So where is the democracy everyone is talking about? And where is my place?" she demands looking angrily at the actresses on stage and the audience of about 150 women.

"We did not receive this auditorium for a political event!" Dalia, a Jewish woman in the audience, loudly voices her disapproval.

"OK, stop!" Effie, the playback theater leader, moves quickly towards the center of the stage. "I would like to tell you all something about a Playback Theater performance." She gazes around the room; everyone's attention is on her.

"First of all, thank you Elham. I invited you to speak and gave you a microphone. The contract in a Playback performance is that we create a safe space for people to express a feeling, a story, a thought or an opinion and see it reflected back to them from the stage. Playback supports Peace because there is an agreement between actresses and audience that we listen to and play back not only our own narratives but the narrative of the 'other', of those who are different from us. And yes, there will be room for different narratives later in the performance."

Everyone is quiet but I can tell by the way some women are moving restlessly in their seats that there is tension in the room.

We are in the midst of Operation/War Tzuk Eitan (Protective Edge) of the summer of 2014 and so many of us are worried, scared and upset not knowing when this current war will end and the painful price each side will have to pay.

In the midst of the fighting, rather than letting the tension and fear drive us apart, women from TBW in collaboration with Women Wage Peace[63] decided to hold a gathering with a Playback Theater performance and workshop for Arab and Jewish women from the Galilee. We expected 20 -25 women to show up and were surprised by over 150 women wearing the colors of Women Wage Peace – white with a turquoise scarf – who flowed into the auditorium this morning. We were hoping this gathering of women might help us feel less divided, more connected to one another.

After hearing the exchange between Effie, Hunaida and Dalia, I am just hoping this meeting will not add to the discord.

Effie looks at Elham and then at the eyes of the women of all ages sitting in the room and continues. "So here in this room, even though there is a Jewish majority, there is room for Elham and there is room for her experience and there is room for her story to be played back from this stage... Elham, I would like to invite you to watch the playing back of your story."

The actresses stand up and form a diamond-like shape behind Lamis, who begins to speak and move her arms and hands while the other actresses move behind her, mirroring her movements wordlessly like a silent chorus.

"Once upon a time in a faraway place, there was a land with a lot of people – children and adults, trees and flowers. People worked, ate and rested," Lamis says, her hands moving to symbolize the activities. "Once upon a time in a certain place there was a mouth that was closed, a heart that was broken, but it was not possible to protest because if someone protested or demonstrated, they would be distanced. They would be told: 'You have gone too far – don't talk, the price is heavy.' So where is my place? Where is it?"

Extending their hands forward with this question on their faces all the actresses freeze. The audience claps and Elham wipes her eyes.

"How are you doing, Elham?" Effie inquires gently.

Elham is quiet for a moment and then she says, "I feel more seen."

---

63. https://womenwagepeace.org.il/en/

Effie asks if there is anyone else who would like to share a story and a woman raises her hand.

"Please come up to the stage," Effie says, tapping the empty seat next to her, inviting the woman to join her there.

The woman is in her thirties, thin, with light hair. Her flowing white dress with tiny purple flowers flutters around her knees as she makes her way up the steps and unto the stage. As soon as she sits down and receives the microphone, she turns to Effie and looks at her silently. Then she begins to speak.

"Hi, my name is Naomi, and in this moment I am finding it difficult to begin talking, perhaps I am taking someone else's place?"

"We are gathered here today to make room for issues like having or not having a place to be, a space to share. Please notice that what is happening within you is also happening on the outside," Effie reminds her.

"Thank you... I felt a need to share a story and when I heard Elham's story I understood it is my mission to tell my story today. Right now I feel flooded and I cried earlier. My story is about an experience I had this past year.

"My grandmother was in the Holocaust and a few months ago I was shown a vision of Jews who were murdered in the Holocaust. I cried a lot and thought about how, in the context of my life here in Israel, I could possibly help those who were murdered. I said to the Jews in my vision: 'I can feel your pain and am crying your agony. Is this how I can help you?'

"'No, we do not need for you to cry about what happened to us,' they told me, 'We need for you to understand that our deepest pain is not that we died. We died and it's over. Our deepest pain is that many people looked at us as though we did not deserve to be, as though there was no place for us. And now we feel some of you are looking that way at the Palestinians and it really hurts.'

"Listening to them I realized that the part that shuts others out also exists within me. That everything exists within us and that we have a choice."

Hearing her share, I feel stunned by how the two stories, Naomi's and Hunaida's, connect, especially given the context of the war, the struggle for a place to exist, to be part of.

Naomi chooses Yoli, one of our Jewish actresses, to be herself in the playing back of her story.

Soon the story comes to life and we can see the agony of having no place to belong felt by Yoli and the Jewish ghosts of the past. Then Yoli says, "And then I understood that everything is inside me, even the shutting out of others..." She looks at the three other actresses who have now become Arab Palestinians living in Israel. "So if everything is inside me, then I can make room. Yes, there is lots of room... Come, come here." She gestures towards the other women. "In my heart there is space for everything and everyone and we need to make sure that everyone who lives here feels that they belong, that there is space for them in our hearts and in this country." The actresses slowly move closer to Yoli as if not quite sure if to trust her. But the warmth in her voice and her beautiful smile pulls them in until their arms wrap around each other. They gaze towards the audience, suspended in a moment of hope.

Chapter 41

Bringing a Bit of Light...
2016, Kisrah

There are two ways of spreading light;
to be the candle or the mirror that reflects it.
Edith Wharton

"Thank you for coming," the Druze women tell us. "Her mother has been waiting for days. She wants to go to the place in the park where the body was found... Now we can do it together..."

Twelve days ago, Wijdan, a sixteen-year-old Arab Druze girl, was stabbed to death by a young Druze man in a village less than ten minutes from the town where I live. The body was found in the scenic Stone Park located across the street from her home.

I was shocked when I saw her beautiful face on my computer screen and heard the terrible details of the murder. *I will never go to that park again,* I thought, *because if I do I will constantly see images in my mind of that horrible act.*

A few days later on a cold, dark, rainy evening I decided to go for a jog, hoping it will help me feel better. While running a memory flooded me. I remembered the spring semester of 2004 when I was teaching in the Peace Studies Department of Goucher College. One day my students told me that a student committed suicide two nights ago by hanging himself from a tree. They shared that afterwards some people wanted to cut down the tree.

Shocked by this painful loss, I went to visit my friend Kelly, who was the pastor of the school's house of worship. I asked her about it and she shared:

"Yes, some people did suggest cutting down the tree as if that would erase the memory and make it all disappear but I decided to hold a prayer vigil last night for the community of students. Afterwards all of us walked towards the tree, holding candles and singing "We Shall Overcome" and "May the Circle Be Unbroken" and other songs. When we reached the tree, we formed a circle of candles around its perimeter while continuing our singing." Kelly looked into my eyes and paused for a moment. I took a deep breath and gently touched her arm. "My heart was beating fast but I knew what I had to do" she continued, "I slowly approached the tree and placed a hand on the trunk, stroking it gently. I prayed and sent love to the young man who spent the final minutes of his life hung from it and to the tree itself for having witnessed such despair. Then I invited students to come closer so they too could touch the tree. Some of them did, standing alongside with me, caressing the bark, others stood around the tree crying and singing. There was something so comforting, so connecting about being there together."

As I jogged in the dark remembering Kelly's words spoken twelve years earlier, I realized what I was called to do. I say *called* because for so many years I have worked with Arabs and Jews to create places to transform pain related to life here and the conflict so it will not be transmitted from generation to generation. And now at the moment of need I wanted to run away? To avoid?

No, this was not a time to run away from the darkness and the pain. It was a time to go there and bring a bit of light and healing just as Kelly had.

I spoke with a friend about my idea and she shared it with the women from the village, reporting back how touched they were that others in the surrounding communities cared about their pain.

So, on December 31, 2016, the last evening of Hanukah, and another cold and rainy day, we gathered at the entrance of the Stone Park.

Arriving a bit early with a friend, I was nervous. The young man who killed her was from a nearby village and there had been talk about a vendetta, an eye for an eye. A couple of days ago someone had thrown a hand grenade in the murderer's village.

A few women met us at the entrance to the park and explained that we would all go now to the family home of the young woman who was murdered to meet her mother, who felt she needed to see the place where her daughter's body was found, but until now nobody had been willing to go with her. Perhaps they did not feel strong enough to face the pain of standing with her next to the place of the murder and needed the support of people who cared but were not part of their community to help witness something so painful.

We climbed up the steps and walked into the living room of the family home. More than twenty women were sitting on floor pillows, speaking softly to one another, some crying.

Feeling overwhelmed and not quite sure what to do, I stood for a moment gazing into the eyes of the women around me. The friends that came with me were also silent. *What does one say to a mother whose daughter was brutally murdered 200 yards from her home?*

"Welcome, welcome," one of the Druze women said, inviting us in and pointing towards the mother.

The mother, Ghadir, was surrounded by other women, many wearing the white head scarf, an indication that they are religious Druze. She looked up, her beautiful green eyes red and bright from tears.

Seeing her, I felt my throat contract and said, "All of us here are mothers or have mothers and can understand the love for a child and the fear of loss. Please tell us how we can help, how can we support you?"

"Pray with us," one woman said. "This is what we need now."

Then another woman added: "We would like you to walk with us to the place in the park where Wijdan's body was found."

"Yes," I nodded. "This is why we came."

A few minutes later, holding our umbrellas, we gathered for a procession towards the park. Leading the way was Ghadir, the mother, held in the arms of Salman, her husband, the father.

I breathed deeply, feeling tears rolling down my cheeks, and began to pray.

When they reached the steps going down to the park Ghadir began sobbing. "My daughter, my daughter," she cried.

"Are you sure you want to go?" Salman asked, turning towards her and gazing into her eyes.

All around us it was drizzling and behind me I could see a line of women and men, holding black umbrellas, enveloped in the mist, quietly waiting for her response.

"Yes," she said in a choked voice "I do."

I could feel the collective sigh as she began making her way down the wet steps towards the Stone Park. We followed, many of us crying with her, staying close to one another.

When we arrived at the place where the body was found, we stopped and stood, glancing at one another, not quite sure what to do. The mother looked at the tree and the wet ground covered with leaves and cried: "Where are you now my daughter, my love, where are you?"

Feeling almost unbearable pain and calling upon the courage of Kelly, the pastor from long ago, I walked towards Ghadir with a candle and some matches. I touched her shoulder gently and brought the candle close to her hands, asking wordlessly if she would like to light it.

"Please," Salman said gently, leaning towards his wife, "light it for our daughter. She was our light..."

And she did. Then she walked with the candle and placed it in a nook amongst the stones protected from the rain. We all joined her with our own candles.

Standing there amongst the Druze, Muslim, Jewish and Christian women and men, I knew that one day in the future we might meet there and hold circles for the two divided communities: of the victim and the perpetrator. But today we stood together moved by a desire to bring healing to the family, the community and the beautiful Stone Park...

May it be so...

Chapter 42

Then Oren Approached
2019, Tuval

> *Then Judah approached him and said: "Pardon your servant, my lord, let me speak a word to my lord... Now then, please let your servant remain here as my lord's slave in place of the boy, and let the boy return with his brothers. How can I go back to my father if the boy is not with me? No! Do not let me see the misery that would come on my father.*
>
> **Genesis 44 ; 18.33,34**

I received his message one afternoon in October:

Dear Nitsan,
I had an experience today that was very hard for me. Then I thought about you. Can we talk?
Oren

I had not seen Oren for almost a year and this was his first message, aside from the usual "have a happy holiday" on Passover and Rosh Hashanah.

Sure, I wrote back, wondering what could have happened to him. Although I knew Oren was serving in a combat unit in the IDF, I could not picture him as a soldier. So young and connected to his heart... I didn't want to see him hardened, traumatized or disillusioned.

Oren first came to visit me with his friend Natan when he was 18, as part of the "Face-to-Face" program initiated by their Rabbi in the Maalot Yeshiva School. The goal was that Natan, Oren and the other young men at the Yeshiva School would step out of their bubble and get to know their neighbors. In our conversations we spoke about the current Torah portion, Kabbalah, handling feelings of anger or frustration, and my peace-building work with Arabs and Jews, Israelis and Palestinians.

When my secular brother came to Israel for his son Ari's bar mitzvah, I asked both Natan and Oren to join us for an evening and read the Torah portion connected with Ari's birth date, Genesis 44. I always loved that portion, with its themes of transformation, responsibility and the desire to stop inflicting pain.

"Judah and the other brothers had changed," Oren explained. "They were no longer willing to abandon their brother, Benjamin, to a terrible fate and lie to their father about what had befallen him, as they had done to Joseph 22 years earlier. 'Let my brother Benjamin go,' Judah says to Joseph, 'I will stay here as your slave and experience the pain. I don't want to see my father suffer any more. This cycle must end.'"

"Wow," I said as I looked at my family and especially at my nephew Ari, who seemed touched. "Such a powerful moment of transformation that happened so long ago," I continued, "And right afterwards Joseph was so moved by Judah's gesture he began crying and revealed himself to his brothers."

"Yes," Oren said and smiled.

When we finally speak that evening, there is not a hint of a smile in Oren's voice.

"What happened?" I ask.

After a moment of silence, I hear him take a deep breath. Then he begins to speak. "This morning on my way home from Jenin in the West Bank where I serve, I was dropped off at the Afula bus station and stood in line waiting for the bus. Suddenly I heard screaming behind me: 'He has a knife.' I turned around quickly, trigger finger on my rifle.

"Nearby I saw two Israeli Jewish men, a soldier and a citizen, pointing a rifle and a gun at an Arab man who stood in the middle of the busy station, eyes wide open, his body shaking. On his face I saw terror. As I watched, everything around me seemed to freeze. I could feel his horror and shame grow when they shouted at him, 'Get on the floor!' in front of everyone and all I could think about was: 'This could have been my uncle, my father...' I was not sure what to do or how to intervene so I just stood there, frozen. Out of nowhere an Israeli Jew walked up to them and said, 'I know this Arab man; he is not a terrorist. Let him go!'"

Oren pauses for a moment and I sit up, phone glued to my ear. When he speaks again it sounds as though his throat is constricted.

"The two men slowly lowered their weapons towards the ground while the Arab man cautiously rose from the floor and walked away, shoulders stooped, eyes down, not looking back. I could still see him making his way through the crowd when I got on the bus and squeezed into a window seat.

"For the next two hours on my way home every time I closed my eyes, I saw the fear and shame on his face and kept thinking about what I could have done or said but didn't. Now, hours later, I can't get rid of these thoughts and don't know what to do. Maybe I should try to find him and explain... but how? I know nothing about him. Finally, I decided to call you, maybe you can help..."

I take a deep breath. My heart aches, yet I am so proud of him for asking for help, for not staying alone with his pain.

"What is most difficult for you right now?" I ask.

"Seeing his face and thinking of all I could have said or done, but didn't..."

"OK, so let's say he was standing at this moment right there in front of you – do you see him?"

"Yes," Oren says.

"What would you like to say to him?"

The phone is quiet for a moment, and then: "I would say: I wish we could both live without fearing each other, I want to ask for your forgiveness. I am so sorry about what you went through today... Can you understand that the people who were doing this to you did not want to make your life miserable? That they are not bad people? They are also afraid and I hope you don't hate them or me and our people because of what happened today."

"Perhaps you can look at him now and see if he responds?"

There is a moment of silence.

"I would like to think that he says OK, I understand, but he doesn't...

"He says, 'Look at what you are doing to me and my family. I can't even get on a bus without having a gun pointed at me by you people. I just want to be treated like a normal person. To have a job, provide food for my family, a home..."

"And what do you say to him when you hear this?"

Oren's response comes quickly, passionately:

"You are right, I can't expect you to see things differently just because of what I said to you. These incidents probably happen to you so often... But you must understand how hard it is for us after so many years of living in fear of our Arab neighbors from terror attacks, bombs. We are not doing it because we hate you. We have to do it to protect ourselves..."

He is quiet for a moment. I wait and then I say:

"So, you are hearing his anger with the situation, his desire to be treated equally, fairly, like everyone else, and you are expressing your own longing to be understood, that even though you and others sometimes point guns at people you are doing it for a good reason, to protect your people who feel, and are, threatened. Is this right?"

"Yes," Oren says.

"And how is he reacting?"

"I don't know, but I feel a little better because I was able to say these things and listen to him. But I don't know if this is enough. Is it enough?"

"I don't know either. Go inside and ask."

"No," he responds after a moment, "it's not enough. Something is on fire inside me telling me there is more I can do, but I don't know what. What should I do?"

"Go inside again and ask."

I wait for his response. Finally, it comes.

"I need to befriend an Arab person. To get to know him or her more deeply. But how do I find this person? I am a religious Jewish soldier and there are no opportunities for me to meet Arabs on a deep level and yet I feel it's what I would like to do. How can I do it?"

"Maybe you can come to one of our workshops this November," I offered.

Usually, I don't like to tell people what to do. I feel that it's best they figure it out on their own, which they usually do when there is someone who really listens to their feelings and asks questions that take them deeper. Yet in this moment Oren is asking me and I know how hard it has become for Jews and Arabs, Israelis and Palestinians, to meet and connect on a deeper level. And so, I offer this suggestion, pretty sure he won't take it seriously.

But he does.

And this is why on Friday morning, November 15th, 2019, he joins us for a workshop with a group of Israeli Arab Palestinians and Jews led by Ann Bradney.

We introduce him and the other new people who just joined. I put some music on and we warm up, move and play. People around me seem to be connecting to their bodies, to their feelings, to one another; there is a comfortable atmosphere in the room.

Then Soheila walks in.

Soheila is a beautiful, auburn-haired 64-year-old Christian Arab Palestinian woman who is the CEO of a Center for the Elderly in a nearby Arab town. This morning she is not looking happy.

We invite everyone to stand in a circle. Ann Bradney, the leader, looks around and asks, "How are you all doing this morning? What is present for you?"

I am expecting a long, drawn-out sharing and then some work with a few or all of them on the issues they bring, so I'm taken aback when Soheila, suddenly begins speaking – or rather, shouting.

"I am so tired of all of you and your words that I just want to throw up!" She looks around the room angrily.

Where did this come from? I have no time to wonder because it feels like a fire has just erupted in the middle of the room. Soheila is burning with rage.

"How is this helping, I am asking you? How is it helping? We talk and talk and feel good about ourselves for a moment but nothing ever changes. In fact, things just get worse. The nationality law, the violence in the Arab cities that nobody cares about because it's Arabs killing Arabs... I don't need these meetings. Do you hear me? I don't need all of you!!!"

She moves quickly around the room, staring at us directly, willing us to look at her without flinching, to meet her anger without running away.

A part of me wants to run away.

Adi, a Jewish woman, moves to face her; standing tall and placing a hand on her heart, she says, "I hear your pain, Soheila. I understand you. I want to cry with you."

Soheila doesn't buy it. She gets angrier, if that is even possible. "I don't need you to feel my pain!" she shouts, beyond herself. "I don't need you to pity me, I don't need your compassion. I am so tired, in fact, we *all* are, of being "understood" by you. You oppress us and treat us badly and then you add insult to injury by "understanding" us. Just leave us alone, leave us alone already! Go do your own work on your own fears and paranoias; they don't belong to us, so stop putting them on us. We are so tired of being the victims of old fears, so tired of meetings where we share our pain, feel your compassion, begin to hope and believe that something will change and then things only get worse. Go do your work, maybe that will actually change something!"

The room is silent. In a cloud of confusion, I am trying to think of something to say but nothing comes. Usually I trust the process, but this is really uncomfortable...

Suddenly Oren, all of 20 years old, lanky, six feet tall, with a small skullcap covering his military haircut and his tzitzit (ritual fringes) sticking out from under his white shirt, the youngest person in the group, takes a step forward and says:

"I want to say something... I am sorry."

"I don't want to hear you or your apologies," Soheila shouts, unwilling to let him finish. I see him flinch and my heart contracts. I hope he is okay.

But the group wants to hear his voice, that seems so out of place amongst us veteran activists and group leaders, so Ann tells Soheila, "Wait a minute, let him talk."

Soheila is quiet for a moment, her expression wary.

Oren looks at her and says, "I have a business proposition for you."

A business proposition? What does that have to do with anything? I wonder.

Then I realize that when we are doing business with another it can be an exchange between two equals. *Maybe this is what he means?*

He levels his gaze, standing strong though his voice is shaky. "I am a religious man and a soldier," he says. "I am the one who enters homes in the middle of the night in the Occupied Territories, waking families up, scaring children and looking for suspects, and I want to tell you why I'm here."

Oren shares the story of his encounter at the bus station, repeating the words: "He could have been my father, my uncle..."

My throat tightens.

"So, you want to know why I'm here?" he continues. "I am not here for you. Yes, I care about your pain, but I am not here for you. I am here because of my pain, the moral outrage, the emotional pain, the injustice... I can't stand it anymore. I am here to do something so I don't feel the pain inside me all the time. I am here for me."

The room is quiet. I'm not the only one crying. Something just shifted and the ground feels shaky. I breathe deeply to regain my balance.

Over the past twenty years, I had seen so many meetings where people shared their stories, expressed anger and pain on issues related to the conflict, their personal and collective traumas, the Holocaust, the Nakba and everything in between. But I had never experienced a moment like this.

Soheila, the Arab, the oppressed minority, is no longer in the role of the victim. She is telling us 'We the Palestinians are strong enough now to do our own healing work, to feel what is ours to feel. Stop oppressing us, and go work on your fears, your paranoias your privilege or whatever you need to work through so this situation can actually change, so we can get on with the business of peace-making.'

And the response of the Jewish religious soldier as he steps forward is: "Yes... this is what I am here to do."

Epilogue

*The only power that has any real meaning
is the power to better the world.*

Gregory David Roberts

In the years following the workshop with Oren and Soheila our programs continued. Like so many others, with the onset of COVID-19, we faced challenges because we were unable to meet in person.

For almost two years there was no healing touch, no holding hands while listening to a friend, no hugging or leaning back-to-back, no moving and dancing together in pairs, groups or a circle, no pushing and shouting against someone's hands, no physical human contact.

While Zoom made it easier to meet because we did not need to travel, the depth of communication, our ability to create safety and foster change decreased tremendously. Still, we met with several groups and provided support and healing to Arab and Jewish women who were facing myriad challenges with their children at home, their relationship with their partner and/or their career. Both Ann Bradney and Richard Schwartz held zoom workshops with our participants during this time.

In February 2022, Ann returned to Israel and together we ran six groups for over 130 participants. We are currently working on a two-and and-a-half-year Radical Aliveness Peace Leadership Practitioner Training, due to begin in January 2023.

In November 2021, our Playback Theater actresses began meeting and practicing in person and in April 2022 they began performing. In October 2021 we started a collaboration with a nonprofit called Roots-Shorashim-Judur[64] who runs programs for Israelis and Palestinians living in the West Bank.

Then, in August 2022, our new collaborator, Roots, and another group called Galilee Dreamers[65], invited our Playback Theater Ensemble, The Heart of Our Stories, to perform for a group of their youth (16-20 years old) in a kibbutz in the upper Galilee.

---

64. https://www.friendsofroots.net/

65. https://www.galileedreamers.com/

Before the performance began, the group's facilitators shared that on the way across the Green Line they were held at a checkpoint for six hours. Something had gone amiss with the permits for the Palestinians and they waited together in the July heat, Jews and Arabs, Israelis and Palestinians, almost giving up altogether on the plan to enter Israel for a retreat. Finally, after great hassle, they were waved through.

When our performance began, Lamis, the Playback Theater leader, asked the 40 young women and men in the audience a question about this experience:

"Please tell me **lies** about what happened to you yesterday at the checkpoint?" She inquired with a smile.

Her smile spread throughout the room and several hands were raised.

"We were met with flowers and chocolate."

"It took only one minute to get across the checkpoint."

"The Jews had to wait but the Palestinians were waved right through."

"When we arrived, there was a big party for us with singing and dancing."

"The soldiers were holding brooms, not rifles."

"They were so happy to see us and we all hugged and laughed."

Through their fabrications we could sense what had actually transpired at the checkpoint and how challenging it had been. And when the actresses played back those lies amidst hoots of laughter from the audience, we could also imagine a different future. A future that would include hugging and partying at checkpoints or borders which seems so absurd and unreal right now but could perhaps, one day, through all our efforts, become a reality.

How can we move towards this reality?

By each doing our part to better the world and by creating more and more safe havens where Israelis and Palestinians can meet, get to know one another and feel what is theirs to feel. Havens where people from both sides share and work through their anger, frustration, despair and grief together so their pain and legacy burdens can transform into understanding, empathy towards "the other" and a desire to work together for change.

When this transformation occurs, and it shall one day, we will truly be a holy spot on earth where an ancient hatred has become a present love.

May it be so.
Nitsan Joy
October 2022

Afterword

Healing, Transforming, Peacebuilding and Never Stopping

By Leymah R. Gbowee

Nobel Peace Laureate, peace activist,
social worker and women's rights advocate.
Founder and President of the
Gbowee Peace Foundation Africa[66], based in Monrovia.

*Be bold. Step out. And never walk on tiptoes,
because anyone who walks on tiptoes can never
leave footprints for people to walk in.*

Leymah R. Gbowee

Throughout my years of working for healing, reconciliation and peace I have seen in intimate ways, both large and small, how women and children bear the brunt of wars and mass atrocities. In my country, I have met and worked with women who were raped and tortured, vulnerable children who became soldiers, and even children who, while on drugs, raped and killed innocent victims. I have seen homes that were burned, destroyed and looted. I have experienced the physical and emotional tolls of war firsthand. I have held children in my arms who were hungry, and cradled women who lost their children to violence. Amidst the despair around me and even stretches of intimate violence in my own home, I struggled to

---

66. https://gboweepeaceusa.org

Women bear the brunt of wars and armed conflicts. Today, 90 per cent of the casualties in conflicts and wars are non-combatants, of whom 70 per cent are women and children. Moreover, women are left out of peacemaking, stabilization and reconstruction processes.

Women's international League for Peace

survive and raise a family and knew I wanted to do something to change structures and systems of violence. I often wondered why women who bore the brunt of war were expected to remain quiet while men debated how to make peace. From firsthand experience I realized that peacebuilding isn't just ending a fight by standing between two opposing forces. As Nitsan Joy Gordon so effectively demonstrates in her book, it is also those moments of holding and healing those victimized by war. It is supporting them in becoming strong again, and bringing them back to the people they once were, where glimpses of peace shine through. It is helping the perpetrator rediscover their humanity and dignity so they once again become productive members of their communities.

Women have such an important role in healing and in creating a culture of peace, a culture where people learn to see beyond the walls of stereotypes, those walls that obstruct our ability to get to know one another and see each other's humanity.

When I visited Israel in 2016, at the invitation of Women Wage Peace, I wondered why the conflict between Israelis and Palestinians has lasted for so many years, why it can feel intractable. Through my conversations there, it was clear that a majority on both sides want to live in peace and security. It was also clear how both sides experience pain and worry for their families, how they see themselves as victims. I wondered why some of the parties try to convince people on both sides that there is no partner for peace. I realized that like in Liberia and other parts of the world the answer lies in both individual and collective traumas. Our experiences of violence and war program us to view the reality around us from a place of fear, suspicion and hostility.

When I read *Together Beyond Words: Women on a Quest for Peace in the Middle East*, I learned about similar and different strategies towards peace as compared to the ones we used in the Women in Peacebuilding Network (WIPNET). But a common thread across both is the desire to work through traumas and towards collective healing.

The approaches I read in Nitsan's book can be used as great tools in conflict areas to help survivors work through their individual and collective traumas and strengthen their role as peace builders. Women can become peacemakers when they have safe places to release the pain that keeps them from feeling their own strength.

We are now in unprecedented times, our communities, countries and Earth are in grave danger. The world is calling for us to listen, and to change. We are each being asked to do our part to heal and resolve our conflicts.

I call on all who read this book to join the courageous women and men who continue working for peace, in the collective making of a better world. And I want to express my gratitude to all peacemakers in Palestine, Israel, South Sudan, Congo DRC, Central Africa Republic, Ukraine, Russia, Belarus and around the world. May God continue to guide and sustain you.

October 2022

Appendix I

The Together Beyond Words Approach[67]

*We can always perceive ourselves and others as either
extending love or giving a call for help.*
Ababio-Clottey and Clottey (1999, p. 193)

*Like life, peace begins with women. We are the first to forge
lines of alliance and collaboration across conflict divides.*
Zainab Salbi

Our multidisciplinary approach, Beyond Words, uses both verbal and nonverbal interventions. This combination seems to work extremely well in quickly breaking down barriers and creating an atmosphere of trust and acceptance. Within this safe space old wounds can be healed, hidden strength recovered and emotional understanding and empathy enhanced.

Our groups consist of Palestinian Arab and Jewish women who meet on a regular basis and work with the *Beyond Words'* unique interventions together, hence *Together Beyond Words*. This experience provides an opportunity for the participants to see that beyond all the differences in culture, tradition and religion—there is so much more that they share as women, mothers, and wives. Once they become aware of their similarities and learn to understand and respect their differences, they can work together to create a change. In a society where the struggles between Arabs and Jews have lasted for so many years, there is an incredible potency when women from the two sides of the conflict are able to work together rebuilding trust, encouraging diversity and promoting reconciliation and peace.

We use dance/movement therapy because complex emotional wounds and traumas require complex healing – involving the body

---

67 . Taken from the article: Gordon-Giles, Nitsan, and Wafa Zidan. "Assessing the Beyond Words educational model for empowering women, decreasing prejudice and enhancing empathy." American Journal of Dance Therapy 31, no. 1 (2009): 20-52.

level, emotional and aesthetic expression, social interaction, symbol and metaphor (Lumsden, 2006, p. 29). Dance/movement therapy often involves or initiates a cathartic process and as Bernstein (1995) notes: "catharsis through dance releases unexpressed feelings and memory and is an important part of trauma resolution" (p. 54).

Dance/movement therapy also involves the ability to practice taking action and broadening or expanding our movement style and patterns. Taking action helps to remedy patterns of helplessness, ambivalence and inactivity, while broadening movement patterns is another way of introducing new behaviors directly linked to changes in self-concept and interpersonal dynamics (Chang & Leventhal, 1995, p. 62).

Our meetings start with an opening circle followed by a movement experiential set to music, movement games, theory and practice of listening partnerships, healing touch and finally, a closing circle.

CIRCLES

We begin and close each meeting sitting in a circle. These two circles usually encompass the more cognitive component of our meetings. In conducting these circles, we often use techniques borrowed from the *Way of the Council* developed at the Ojai Foundation (Zimmerman & Coyle, 1996) which include: speaking and listening from the heart, speaking only when holding the talking piece and being spontaneous, nonjudgmental and aware of the time.

OPENING CIRCLE

The opening circle is designed to welcome participants to the group while enabling the facilitators to verbally and kinesthetically gauge the mood of the group and become aware of relevant issues group members are dealing with. In the opening circle each participant shares of herself–how she feels that day and perhaps some of her experiences during the week. She may also talk about something 'good and new" that recently happened in her life. Because we later deal with traumas and painful emotional wounds, it is important that we remind ourselves that the positive in our lives also exists. Usually after a couple of meetings participants start looking for good and new events that they could share with the group and are surprised that each week these events seem to increase possibly because whatever we focus on, grows.

Dance and Movement

The dance and movement section is designed to reawaken a sense of childlike wonder and joyfulness, of being in our bodies, a feeling that many of us had as children. It helps to increase body awareness, encourage the use of weight and other efforts, uncover old wounds stored within the body and begin releasing them. When a woman can find her strength through bodywork within the group, it can encourage her to interact more assertively with the important figures in her life and begin to perceive herself more positively (Chang & Leventhal, 1995, p. 62).

Following the opening circle, we begin to move and dance, using skills learned and techniques borrowed from dance/movement therapy. Movement is a form of expression we begin to use even before we are born. We react to the world through movements and sounds much earlier than through language and speech. After sitting in a circle and sharing verbally with each other, we return to the world of the nonverbal. We may begin laying down, sitting or standing, sometimes staying on the same level and other times moving from one level to another. Usually, we begin by moving on our own, sensing our bodies, listening inward. Later we shift to working in pairs or in small groups and sometimes with the entire circle.

Like a dance, the facilitation of this part of the meeting flows. The leader begins by listening to the needs of the group during the opening circle, being aware of those needs and aware of her own goals, she then suggests movements, borrows ideas from group members and creates a dance where it is not always clear who is leading and who is following. What does become clear by the end of the session is that some form of healing transformation has transpired.

Dance/movement therapy is the psychotherapeutic use of movement as a process which furthers the emotional, cognitive, social and physical integration of the individual (ADTA, 1966, par. 2). In our model we use dance/movement therapy towards integration by accomplishing three objectives:

1. Helping the participants explore new ways of moving in space that can affect how they think, feel and behave;

2. Accessing and bringing out into the open the emotional pain stored within the body;

3. Enabling and supporting the beginning of a cathartic process.

Exploring new ways of moving in space

Very early in our lives we develop movement patterns also known as muscle memory that are ways of moving and standing in the world. These movement patterns gradually evolve as a response to events in the outside world and become a part of the way we express our emotions. Because our external circumstances change as we grow older these movement patterns and muscle memory are sometimes out of tune with our present life situation (Berger, 1972; Feder & Feder, 1981).

Prejudiced attitudes can also be seen through certain movement patterns. Gordon (1986) found that the range of movement of adults who tested as having higher prejudice was more rigid and restricted than those who were less prejudiced. In other words, our feelings and attitudes can be reflected in our movements.

During the dance/movement therapy part of the meetings participants are encouraged to explore new ways of moving in space or experience again movements they used as young children and have since forgotten. These movements increase awareness of their bodies, what feels good and what hurts, what is comfortable and what is uncomfortable.

As they become more aware and try on new movements their ability to express emotions, moods, attitudes and ideas also expands. Sometimes they may even realize that when they change the way they move and stand they can also change the way they feel about themselves and relate to others.

In other words, there has been more and more evidence showing that the ways in which we move not only reflect our thoughts but actually our movements often precede and create our thought processes (Feder & Feder, 1981; Gallese, 2005; Rizzolatti, Fogassi & Gallese, 2001).

Accessing and bringing out emotional pain

Moving in new ways through the space gives rise to emotions and memories that apparently reside not only in our heads but are also held deep within our bodies: a central principle underlying the practice of dance/movement therapy is that all of our thoughts and emotions are inextricably interwoven with physical movement (Feder & Feder, 1981, p.159). The connection between our minds, bodies and emotions has now been proven at the neuropsychological and bio neurological levels (Winters, 2008).

Our innermost thoughts are often betrayed by our unconscious movements or gestures (Feder & Feder, 1981), while manipulation and movement of specific muscles as well as pressure or touch on particular body parts can often stimulate memories, sensations and emotions (Berger, 1972; Damasio, 1994; Feder & Feder, 1981; Rubenfeld, 2000; Van der Kolk, 1994). It is very hard to hide our emotions in our bodies. When we are silent and guarded, they are communicated through our movements and stance, when we are touched in certain ways memories and feelings begin to emerge. Even if we don't tell anyone, our body is still talking. Perhaps through the chattering of fingertips or the raising of an eyebrow our secrets are being revealed to the keen observer (Freud, 1959). It is therefore plausible to presume that these feelings are far more accessible when we invite their expression in movements rather than in words.

ENABLING AND SUPPORTING THE BEGINNING OF CATHARTIC RELEASE

Catharsis is the release or discharge of emotions that facilitates the healing of traumas and wounds from the past. Sometimes this process is assisted by certain movements and exercises used in dance/movement therapy such as pulling on a stretch band, stomping on the ground, playing hug or snake tag, or hitting pillows with a tennis racket. In many cases individuals who are inhibited in their verbal expression of anger, fear or anxiety may feel safer acting out their emotions in this manner. The emotions that surface during these activities find further release in the next part of the healing process which we refer to as Listening Partnerships.

LISTENING PARTNERSHIPS

Listening partnerships include emotional release and listening techniques, we gleaned from Jackins (1982) and Wipfler (1990). During the dance/movement therapy session as participants become more aware of emotions stored within their bodies, a cathartic process may begin. We then move to creating a space for the release and integration of the emotions that have surfaced. Listening partnerships introduce a new level of listening helpful in transforming our own and others' emotional pain related to past and present hurts and traumas. The emotional release that occurs in this section enables participants to re-evaluate old issues in a new light.

Heider (1974) explains that a cathartic process, such as crying while talking about a painful memory, is often followed by a sense of relief and wellbeing. After experiencing catharsis, the possibility for growth, healing and transformation increases tremendously, some of the psychosomatic symptoms disappear and new insights about the way we conduct ourselves in the world flow simply and naturally. A sense of oneness and interconnectedness with nature and other human beings also occurs. Many dance therapists agree that physical release can lead to a condition of receptivity to therapy, growth or self-awareness but also stress the importance of a complimentary cognitive component (Feder & Feder, 1981).

Listening partnerships provide both the place to continue with the cathartic process and the possibility for a cognitive integration as we become able to re-evaluate our present distress.

The first stage of this process includes learning to listen to one another in pairs. Time is divided and each one gets a turn to be on the receiving end of a type of listening we do not normally encounter in our everyday lives. This means listening without judgment, without telling our own stories, interrupting with our reactions or asking questions to satisfy our curiosity. As one partner's hurt feelings begin to surface, we help her release the pain related to that hurt by keeping her focused on the painful event and by using a technique called "contradiction". Wipfler (1990) describes the benefits of the emotional release that occurs within the *Listening partnerships* context:

"Like children, when adults laugh, cry, tremble and perspire, have a tantrum, or yawn while they talk about their troubles, emotional tension lifts. Their ability to think and act more flexibly is restored. They become more reasonable, more fun loving, more sure that they are good people, inside and out" (p. 19).

The release of the emotional tension which previously controlled our behavior allows us to think more flexibly and find new solutions to problems that seemed insoluble. In the beginning, while listening to each other and moving together, both Jewish and Arab women usually realize there is much more they have in common as women, mothers and wives than that which tears them apart. As their ability to listen to and acknowledge each other's pain increases a sense of empathy and trust develop and they become allies in supporting each other's empowerment. Thus, when divisive issues arise later in the process, they do not pull the participants apart but rather strengthen their connection and enhance their ability to be even more honest with one another.

After the first few months, once their listening skills have improved and a strong bond between the women based on their common experiences has begun to form, we explore the hardships of being a Jewish or an Arab woman in Israel.

Issues begin to arise: *This is the only place in the world that we as Jews have as a home, you have so many other Arab countries why don't you move there and leave us alone* or, *We were living on this land for hundreds of years and then you came, took it from us and turned many of us into refugees. It is not our fault that so many Jews were killed in the Holocaust, why do we have to suffer because you suffered?* Or: *Most of your leaders supported the Nazis and then did not agree to a partition and attacked us, also many of your people left their homes voluntarily, sure that the Jews would lose in the War of Independence so you brought this upon yourselves.* And: *You who talk so much about justice why don't you walk your talk and treat us justly as equals in this country?*

Because they know their own stories will also be heard and acknowledged, they are able to listen to one another and hear the pain, anger, sadness, hopelessness and longing beyond the words without becoming defensive or hostile. Those who are sharing their pain feel, perhaps for the first time in their lives, that they have been truly heard and seen by the "other side". This acknowledgement enables them to begin letting go and release some of the emotions that have been controlling their attitudes and behaviors and open up to new possibilities of thinking and being.

One way to encourage further honesty and release of pain related to our past and present as Jews and Arabs is to work in separate groups some of the time so we can first gain a sense of safety to talk about the most painful issues with those who have suffered from similar life circumstances. Then we return together and are able to share with one another more easily the pain caused by existing side by side with the other group.

Listening partnership can be called an emotional first aid kit. In Israel as in many trouble spots around the world something happens almost every day that triggers feelings of fear, anger, hopelessness, despair, etc. *Because pain that is not transformed is transmitted*, it has proved very helpful to provide women with a simple tool they can use on a daily basis to discharge/release emotions that cloud their vision and overwhelm them. All they have to do is call a friend and ask: "Do you have five or ten minutes to listen to me?" And then by applying the tools they learned, they can avoid acting out their pain and thereby transform their whole day.

HOLISTIC TOUCH

As our painful emotions surface and resurface, we introduce touch because it seems to help us feel more connected to ourselves and one another and because it is another way to reach and transform some of the pain related to the emotional hurts. Montague (1986) explains that touch is a basic need shared by all human beings and recounts the suffering caused to babies and children who were not held and touched. Rubenfeld (2000) who has helped people heal through the use of touch for almost fifty years writes that: "touch is crucial to life itself, not only in infancy, but through all your years [...] the combination of touch and words represents the highest form of communication." (p. 18).

We ask the women to divide to pairs, and while one of them lies on the mat, the other is guided to gently massage her back, shoulders. hands, feet or forehead. Then they switch. We find that this type of touch helps us relax and feel good. The relaxation of our bodies affects our minds and afterwards we tend to be more open to seeing our problems in new ways. In addition, touching another person helps develop nonverbal listening skills. As we touch, we become more aware of the other and what feels good for her and what does not, as well as where tensions are held. We also become more aware of what feels good to us and where our own tensions are held. Thirdly, because touch is such a basic need and most of us are rarely touched enough, touching one another helps foster a sense of wellbeing and intimacy. Receiving this type of touch is a nurturing experience for women who have little or no time to nurture themselves. It reminds them of the importance of taking the time to care of their own needs, which is a key component of empowerment.

As Borysenko (2000) notes: "touch is one of the best ways of facilitating the alchemical transmutation of wounds into wisdom" Thus, healing touch assists in the integration of the emotional work and enhances our listening capacities while encouraging a sense of intimacy and connectedness."

CLOSING CIRCLE

Finally, the closing circle is a time of cognitive assimilation of the insights acquired during the meeting as participants are asked to talk about which parts of the meeting were meaningful for them or what insight/gift they are taking with them back into their lives.

Appendix II

The Creation of a Nonverbal Prejudice Scale

From the findings of my Master's Thesis Research, Goucher College, 1986

The purpose of this study was to find the nonverbal cues which distinguish between high and low prejudiced individuals. These cues were used in the creation of a nonverbal prejudice scale which could detect prejudiced individuals. Twelve subjects were chosen out of a pool of 150 students, according to their score on the MMPI scale for prejudice (Pr). They were seven high prejudice individuals and five low prejudice individuals. All subjects were filmed in both structured and unstructured situations. The films were shown to two CMAs (movement analysts) who were asked to describe each subject separately on the dimensions of space, shape, effort and body. The CMAs were blind to the existence or lack of prejudice in each of the subjects. Their descriptions were analyzed for significance using the F-test and the Chi-Square test. There was a significant difference between high and low prejudiced individuals on a number of dimensions. On all these dimensions the low prejudiced individuals exhibited better use than the high prejudiced individuals. Ability to shape and mold around others was significant according to both raters (interrater reliability was $r = .85$). In addition there were significant differences in awareness of space, body connectedness and use of flow and weight efforts.

Specifically I found that high prejudiced individuals exhibit:

1. Very little or almost no shaping or molding of their body to the body of others;
2. Unclear awareness of space;
3. Their body is not well connected and they use more bound flow and passive weight.

Other cues approaching significance were:

1. Most high prejudiced individuals have a one-unit torso;
2. They initiate most of their movements distally;
3. They have a restricted use of their kinesphere and make almost no eye contact.

I hypothesized that the **difficulty in molding or shaping to the body of others** may arise from issues with trusting others. When a person does not trust others and is convinced that the world is hostile to him or her (Hirsh, 1955), he or she is more likely to lean away from others and/or to make very little or no attempts to get involved while moving together. In the analysis the CMAs saw very little "interactional synchrony" (Condon, 1980) which connotes "being with" the other in their movements. It is clear that in order to shape and mold one's body to the body of another one must trust the other and feel secure and open with him/her which is not the case with prejudiced individuals.

The **unclear awareness of space** has to do with an ill-defined sense of boundaries regarding where one's space is, where it ends and where does the space of others begin and end. This may be the result of caregivers not respecting boundaries of the HP individuals as young children. In order to have fulfilling interactions with others we must have an awareness of space. This includes an awareness of one's own personal space and the space of others so that one does not invade their space.

Their body is not well connected (one unit torso) and they use a great deal of bound flow and passive weight. When emotions such as fear, insecurity and loneliness are hidden they might manifest in the body. Bound flow and a one-unit torso may be the bodily expressions of these emotions, or more precisely they may be the bodily defenses to prevent the expression of these emotions. The seat of emotions is usually in the chest and abdomen and if these parts of the body are bound up, they allow the person to lock the emotions inside him or herself. By locking them inside, the person can temporarily not feel those anxiety provoking emotions. This may be the reason why high prejudiced individuals exhibited more bound flow and mostly a one-unit torso in comparison with low prejudiced individuals. The lack of flexibility in the torso may also be the bodily manifestation of the lack of flexibility in the way of thinking. The prejudiced personality is often described as being rigid.

Mehrabian and Wiener (1967) add that a tense posture relative to a relaxed posture indicates a more negative attitude. A tense posture has to do with bound flow and a negative attitude may be the propensity to find faults in others in order to feel better about ourselves, which is the basis of prejudice.

HP individuals had less active weight than LP individuals. They tended towards passive weight in their movements. The use of weight actively indicates a strong sense of self and an ability to assert one's self and make an impact on the environment. (Bartenieff, 1983) The literature talks about the prejudiced individuals as creating their sense of self through cataloguing who they are not. In other words, their sense of self comes from the outside and not from within and for this reason is less active.

Distal initiation found in most of the HP research participants has to do perhaps with their external locus of control. Prejudiced individuals are mostly described as being fatalistic and believing that they do not have much power over the outer world. Things happen in the world through the control of some stronger powers, just as they did when they were children. They do not assume responsibility for their actions or exercise their freedom since they do not believe they have freedom. All this is reflected in their movements and especially in the initiation of the movement.

When movements are initiated mostly from the core it suggests that the individual feels that he/she has some control over the outside world as she or he does over their movements. The control is within. On the other hand, when a person initiates mostly distally, the control seems to be from the outside both movement wise and feeling wise. Distal initiation also points to the fact that HP participants are not truly involved in what is happening around them. If one is really involved in what is happening around him/her, one assumes responsibility for whatever it is that is happening, and exercises one's freedom by making decisions. This type of living involves moving from one's core, or feeling from the "gut". The prejudice person who locks his or her feelings within in the attempt not to feel them, will have trouble feeling from the "gut" or moving from the core.

Based on these results I created a nonverbal prejudice scale.

Appendix III

Increasing Emotional Intelligence

De Martino and colleagues (2006) described a breakthrough which seems to indicate that our emotional system processing (localized in the amygdala) plays a critical role in biasing rational decisions. Damasio (1994) suggests that the brain stores memories of past decisions, (like those we made when we were very young) and the memories of those decisions are what drive people's choices in life. In order to stop behaving based only on our past experience or decisions, and using rationality based on present situations, something needs to change in the way we relate to our emotions. He explains that what makes us rational people is not that we repress and hold back what we feel, but that we know how to deal with our emotions, whichever they might be, in a constructive manner. He also mentions that our schools and educational system overlook the role that our feelings play in how we learn and the choices we make in our lives. Damasio (1994) also notes that people who lack emotions because of brain injuries have difficulties making decisions at all. If emotions play such an important role in the decisions and choices we make in our lives, it seems especially important to transform our most painful emotions, so they do not continue to guide our choices and behavior and create havoc and destruction in our lives and the lives of those around us. Transforming the emotional pain is similar to increasing emotional intelligence. Part of Goleman's (1995) definition of emotional intelligence has to do with the ability to control our impulses and read emotions in ourselves and others which leads to the ability to empathize with them. According to Goleman (1995), courses that have attempted to increase emotional intelligence have shown several benefits. Participants become more aware of their own emotions and are better able to identify what causes these emotions. By learning to differentiate between "feeling something" and "acting based on a feeling", their ability to control their emotions increases and they are better able to just feel anger or emotional pain, for instance, without immediately doing something about it, or acting it out. Once students become aware of their own emotions they are also better able to empathize with others, better listen to them and see their differing perspectives. They also improve their capacity to be in relationship, resolving conflicts and communicating their needs better. Ability to share, being cooperative and dealing more democratically with others also increase.

Our workshops and courses take into account these processes, hone the participants' emotional intelligence and ultimately aids them in improving their communication skills, their cooperation and their understanding of democratic values.

Appendix IV

Other approaches that we apply in our work

Because I met Nancy Lunney and Gordon Wheeler and through their support brought groups to the Esalen Institute, I was blessed to study two healing approaches from the best: Radical Aliveness from Ann Bradney and IFS from Dr Richard Schwartz and later from Einat Bronstein and Osnat Arbel.

Below is further information about the two approaches.

Radical Aliveness

Since childhood I had always been uncomfortable and even scared around anger and other messy emotions. Learning Listening Partnerships helped me feel comfortable with crying. Radical Aliveness helped me stay present and in my leadership with an ability to intervene around anger. This ability has been immensely valuable in my peacebuilding work.

Nitsan Joy Gordon

Says Ann Bradley: "The goal of Radical Aliveness is to help create a reality where human beings can move past the polarization within and without – and walk through the world in ways that bring connection, understanding and healing.

Radical Aliveness focuses on the intersection of systemic reality and emotional process, creating a dynamic space where participants are supported to engage with heartfelt awareness of world and social realities as well as family-of-origin issues. The container we create is one where people from all walks of life, all positions, perspectives, and roles can coexist. In this space they have the opportunity to learn from their relationships and differences and to cultivate understanding, identify their own deep values as well as feel, heal and transform on all levels of their being.

Radical Aliveness is not easy work. It is sometimes scary but also very transformative to face deeply held assumptions and biases along with the powerful feelings that accompany them. In this work there is room for difficult feelings, memories and experiences to be seen, heard and validated. It happens in a group setting where conflict is welcomed and emotional expression, in all the ways it manifests in different cultures, becomes a foundational part of the process. Participants grow in awareness and are supported to see their own and others' deep goodness and essence, often for the first time — especially in settings where race, tribe, class, religion and other systemic realities have created perceived barriers to understanding.

We work with all levels of the human experience: the body, emotions, expression, movement, sensations, thoughts, beliefs and spirit and specifically focus on supporting human beings in effecting positive change in the community and world.

Our work with individuals, groups and organizations is based on a foundation of six principles:

1. Cultivating a non-shaming heart and attitude.
2. Knowing I don't know.
3. Welcoming multiple perspectives.
4. Being willing to be changed.
5. Saying YES to all feelings that arise within with an intention toward consciousness.
6. Doing our part.

Our starting point is the understanding that human beings are powerful and have innate wisdom and therefore we respect individuals as the authority on themselves. We are also aware that all of us have been socialized and have learned to make sense of the world through a myriad of systemic influences: family of origin, culture, language, ethnicity, class, religion, etc. Through recognizing this, we hold an expansive space that allows transformation to come not from a fixed theory and techniques, but through a fluid process that invites the complexity of each human to be known and integrated.

When people have an opportunity to feel everything, all the way – their fear, their rage, their pain, their hate, their joy, whatever it is – in a safe, non-shaming environment, and when they have an opportunity to see their socialized thoughts and beliefs, they become more able to navigate life from choice rather than reaction.

When we are unafraid to know anything about ourselves because we know that everything in us is human, we also become more able to see and feel parts of ourselves that would otherwise be hard to see and accept. We are then able to make choices about ways we might want to change so we can live from our brilliance, our creativity, and all that makes up our life force. When we are no longer afraid to let ourselves flow or be seen, we are also able to truly to see and receive others with empathy and understanding" [68]

INTERNAL FAMILY SYSTEMS (IFS)

Realizing that what people are saying or doing is just a part of who they are and that we all also have a Self has helped me tremendously in feeling compassion towards myself, towards clients, in my relationships and towards participants in our peacebuilding groups. Below is one of my favorite explanations of IFS and how it connects with Attachment Theory by Dr Richard Schwartz.

"How many of you have been influenced by attachment theory in your work?

In fact, this theory had a huge influence on the field and that's great. People are now more hip to the fact that it is not enough to just correct irrational beliefs. Young avoidant or insecurely attached parts of us need to find a trusting relationship with someone trustworthy. If this person is the therapist, the process can be very healing. It can also take a long time, involve a very intense therapeutic relationship, include dependence, transference, and countertransference.

What if it was possible for the clients themselves to become that person? A good attachment figure rather than the therapist and rather than their spouse. What if clients could become the primary care takers of these exiles and free up their partner and/or their therapist to be the secondary caretaker of these parts?

If that were the case, the therapist or the partner's role would shift considerably, and they might feel relieved and the client would feel less dependent and would feel instead empowered, like she healed herself and would know how to regulate herself better in the future and the therapy could be briefer.

For that to be possible we need a model that says a couple of things – first, it says that people have parts, some of whom are quite adult like and confidant, other are needy, lonely and ashamed. Second it needs to be a model that says that in addition to those parts there is an essence that has the qualities of a good attachment figure and could become the good internal parent to these parts. In IFS we call this essence the Self.

---

68. From the writings of Ann Bradney.

In contrast to mindfulness where you stand on the side and witness your thoughts and feelings parade by, in IFS we look at those thoughts and feelings as emanating from suffering beings/parts and we use curiosity and compassion from Self to help them.

Getting back to the Self I found that as clients began embracing their exiles not only did these young parts feel better, they also calmed down and could actually unload the extreme beliefs and emotions that they got from traumas and attachment injuries. And when they do unburden/unload, they can transform into their valuable natural states. And they return to becoming innocent, creative, or joyful just like they were before they were hurt.

Another piece of good news is that secure inner attachment can happen much more quickly than secure external attachment, which can take months. Before we get hurt, these exiles were the most playful, sensitive, innocent, creative parts of us, but because they are so sensitive they are the ones who got hurt most in the family, through the trauma, and as I mentioned before they got stuck carrying this burden. These young parts are frozen in scenes from the past. Because we don't want to feel these emotions we lock them up not even knowing we are locking up our most valuable resources. Adding insult to injury these young parts are hurt by the world and then abandoned by us.

What do the exile need in order to heal? They need a new inner attachment relationship. They need the client to really get what happened in the past where the part is stuck and become witnesses to their own pain and then there is a possibility to take those parts out of those scenes where they have been stuck to safe places.

Over 30 years ago, I discovered that right beneath our parts lies an essence that cannot be damaged and once accessed it can become that good attachment figure. All that needs to happen is for the client's parts to open space for it. It is not a state where there is no self but rather a state where there are no parts where the parts have relaxed and moved back. The emptiness that is so full is what I called the Self. When parts are trusting enough to open the space, Self will emerge spontaneously with qualities like curiosity and compassion. In addition once accessed the client's self will begin relating to the parts in a healing loving way spontaneously without any directive from the therapist.

Appendix V

Peacebuilding Organizations

There is only one radical means of sanctifying
human lives. Not armored plating, or tanks, or planes,
or concrete fortifications. The one radical solution is peace.

Yitzhak Rabin
Nobel Peace Prize lecture, December 10, 1994

Peacebuilding organizations with whom we have collaborated over the years.

- **ALLMEP** is the largest and fastest-growing network of Palestinian and Israeli peacebuilders. https://www.allmep.org

- **A New Dawn in the Negev** is an organization founded in 2009 whose goal is to elevate educational standards in the Negev with a strong emphasis on the Bedouin community.
http://www.anewdawninthenegev.org

- **Bat Shalom** is a feminist grassroots organization of Jewish and Palestinian Israeli women working together towards peace, a just resolution to the Israeli-Palestinian conflict, respect for human rights, and an equal voice for Jewish and Arab women within Israeli society.
https://batshalom.org

- **EcoME** was an intercultural living experiment, devoted to gathering and sharing peace knowledge, exploring sustainable ways of living environmentally, socially and spiritually.

- **Hand in Hand: Center for Jewish-Arab Education** is a growing network of bilingual and multicultural accredited public schools for Arab and Jewish citizens of Israel, educating the next generation, from kindergarten through high school, who will create a more democratic, secure, and peaceful future.
https://www.handinhandk12.org

- **Givat Haviva** Educational Foundation is the American arm of Givat Haviva, an NGO established in 1949 whose mission is to bridge the gap between Israel's Jewish and Arab citizens and to put forth the building blocks of an Israeli Shared Society.
  https://www.givathaviva.org

- **Holy Land Trust** exists to lead in creating an environment that fosters understanding, healing, transformation, and empowerment of individuals and communities, locally and globally, to address core challenges that are preventing the achievement of a true and just peace in the Holy Land.
  https://www.holylandtrust.org

- **Magical Children of Light Initiative**. We are Palestinian and Israeli women and mothers who see it as our maternal responsibility to speak out and act for our children. We believe that Peace is possible when women of courage and faith stand up for the future of their children.
  https://www.themagicalchildrenoflight.com

- **Nes Ammim Dialogue** is dedicated to hosting and facilitating dialogue groups.
  http://nesammim.org/dialogue/

- **Neve Shalom.** Wahat al-Salam, located in the center of Israel, is the "Oasis of Peace", the only community where Jewish and Palestinian families, all with Israeli citizenship, have lived, worked and educated their children together for more than 25 years.
  https://wasns.org

- **New Israel Fund** works to strengthen Israel's democracy and to promote freedom, justice and equality for all Israelis.
  https://www.nif.org

- **Parents Circle**. Families Forum is a joint Israeli-Palestinian organization of over 600 families, all of whom have lost an immediate family member to the ongoing conflict. Moreover, the PCFF has concluded that the process of reconciliation between nations is a prerequisite to achieving a sustainable peace and works to further this process.
  https://www.theparentscircle.org/en/pcff-home-page-en/

- **Partners for Progressive Israel** is a progressive American Zionist organization dedicated to the achievement of a durable and just peace between the State of Israel and its neighbors, which includes an end to

Israel's occupation based on a two-state solution.
https://www.progressiveisrael.org

- **Roots-Shorashim-Judur** works within communities at the heart of the conflict; shifting hatred and suspicion towards trust, empathy, and mutual support.
https://embodyingpeace.org/organization/roots-shorashim-judur/

- **Shiluvim B'Galil** is a playback theater ensemble in a creative social spirit, performing in the Galilee and throughout the country for 12 years. The ensemble, consisting of Jewish and Arab actors and actresses, Christians and Muslims, secular and religious in a diverse age range, carries with it a message of true encounter with ourselves and others in the spirit of love and joy, empowerment and growth. The ensemble performs in Hebrew and Arabic and is led by Efrat Ashiri.
https://www.facebook.com/ShiluvimBagalil.PlaybackTheatre/

- **Talitha Kumi** is a safe and peaceful place to study and stay in an environment shaped by the Middle East conflict.
https://www.talithakumi.org/en/home-2/

- **Tomorrow's Women** trains young Palestinian and Israeli women to partner as leaders by transforming anger and prejudice to mutual respect, facilitating an understanding of the other, and inspiring action to promote equality, peace, and justice for all.
https://tomorrowswomen.org

- **Women Wage Peace** is a rapidly growing grassroots movement of tens of thousands of Israeli women, taking action to influence the public and political arena. They are a non-political, broad-based coalition seeking to address politicians and decision-makers in the pursuit of a cooperative peace agreement.
https://womenwagepeace.org.il/en/
https://www.youtube.com/watch?v=YyFM-pWdqrY

Bibliography

1. Ababio-Clottey, A., Clottey K. (1999). *Beyond Fear: Twelve Spiritual Keys to Racial Healing.* HJ Kramer.

2. Akapo, S. (2017). An Overview of Somatics (Body-Mind) Approaches in Dance Therapy. EJOTMAS: *Ekpoma Journal of Theatre and Media Arts* 6, no. 1-2.

3. Barrky, C. (1980). A comparison of the movement profile of battered, ex-battered and non-battered women: A pilot study. Unpublished master's thesis. Hahnemann Medical College, Philadelphia, PA.

4. Bartenieff, I. (1980). Body movement: Coping with the environment. New York: Gorden & Breach.

5. Berger, M.R. (1972). Bodily experiences and expression of emotion. American Dance Therapy Association, Monograph 2, 191–230. Columbia, MD: ADTA.

6. Bernstein, B. (1995) Dancing beyond trauma. *Dance & Other Expressive Arts Therapies: When Words Are Not Enough*, 41-58.

7. Borysenko, J. (2000). Foreword. In I. Rubenfeld, The listening hand (pp. ix-xi). New York: Bantam Books.

8. Burdelski, M. (2020). Teacher compassionate touch in a Japanese preschool. *Social Interaction. Video-Based Studies of Human Sociality* 3, no. 1.

9. Carnelley, K., Boag, E. (2019). Attachment and prejudice. *Current opinion in psychology* 25, 110-114.

10. Chang, M., Leventhal, F. (1995). Mobilizing battered women: A creative step forward. *Dance and other expressive art therapies: When words are not enough*, 59-68.

11. Condon, W. S. (1980). The relation of interactional synchrony to cognitive and emotional processes. *The Relationship of Verbal and Nonverbal Communication*, 49-65.

12. Coyle, V., Zimmerman, J. (1996). *The Way of Council.*

13. Damasio, A. (2005). *Descartes' Error. Emotion, Reason and the Human Brain.* Penguin Books; Illustrated edition.

14. D'Arcy, P. (2020). *Gift of the Red Bird.* Crossroad Publishing.

15. D'Arcy, P. (2009). *Song for Sarah: A Mother's Journey Through Grief and Beyond.* Crossroad; Third Edition.

16. De Martino, B., Kumaran, D., Seymour, B., Dolan, R.J. (2006). Frames, Biases, and Rational Decision-Making in the Human Brain. Science 313, no. 5787: 684-687.

17. De Tord, P., Bräuninger, I. (2015). Grounding: Theoretical application and practice in Dance Movement Therapy. *The Arts in Psychotherapy* 43: 16-22.

18. Egendorf, A. (1985). *Healing from the War: Trauma and Transformation After Vietnam.* Houghton Mifflin.

19. Eshel, D. (2013). Terror related Post-Traumatic Stress: The Israeli experience. *Defense Update: International online defense Magazine.*

20. Feder, E. & Feder, B. (1981). The expressive arts therapies. Englewood Cliffs, NJ: Prentice–Hall.

21. Federman, D. (2011). Kinesthetic ability and the development of empathy in Dance Movement Therapy. *Journal of applied arts & health* 2, no. 2: 137-154.

22. Freud, S. (1905). Fragment of an Analysis of a Case of Hysteria Coll. *Papers 3*: 13-146.

23. Frey, W. H., Langseth, M. (1985). *Crying: The Mystery of Tears.* Harper San Francisco.

24. Gbowee, L. (2011) *Mighty Be Our Powers: How Sisterhood, Prayer, and Sex Changed a Nation at War.* Beast Books.

25. Goleman, D. (1995). *Emotional Intelligence.* New York, NY, England.

26. Gordon, H. (1989). Dance, dialogue, and despair: Existentialist philosophy and education for peace in Israel. *International Journal for Philosophy of Religion*, 26, no. 2.

27. Gordon, H. (1991). *Israel/Palestine: The Quest for Dialogue.* Orbis

Books.

28. Gordon-Cohen, N. (1987). Vietnam and reality – The story of Mr. D. *American Journal of Dance Therapy* 10, no. 1: 95-109.

29. Gordon-Giles, N., Zidan, W. S. (2009). Assessing the Beyond Words Educational Model for Empowering Women, Decreasing Prejudice and Enhancing Empathy. *American Journal of Dance Therapy* 31, no. 1: 20-52.

30. Gordon, N. (1986). Creating a Nonverbal Prejudice Scale. Master's Thesis unpublished.

31. Heider, J. (1974). Catharsis in human potential encounter. *Journal of Humanistic Psychology* 14(4), 27-47.

32. Hirsh, S.G. (1955). *The Fears Men Live by.* Harper.

33. Jackins, H. (1982). *Fundamentals of Co-counseling Manual (elementary Counselors Manual) for Beginning Classes in Re-evaluation Counseling.* Rational Island Publishers.

34. Karnow, S. (1994). *Vietnam: A history.* Vol. 122. Random House.

35. Kaye, F. (2009). *The Divorce Doctor.* Hay House, Inc.

36. Meekums, B. (2012). Kinesthetic empathy and movement metaphor in dance movement psychotherapy. *Kinesthetic empathy in creative and cultural practices*: 51-65.

37. Lumsden, M. (2006). The affective self and affect regulation in dance movement therapy. *Advances in Dance/Movement Therapy: Theoretical Perspectives and Empirical Findings*: 29-39.

38. Melnick, S. (2013). *Success Under Stress: Powerful Tools for Staying Calm, Confident, and Productive When the Pressure's On.* Amacom Books.

39. Mehrabian, A., Wiener, M. (1967). Decoding of inconsistent communications. *Journal of Personality and Social Psychology* 6, no. 1 (1967).

40. Montagu, A. (1986). *Touching: The human Significance of the Skin.* New York: Harper & Row.

41. Nicholson, N. (1998). How hardwired is human behavior?. *Harvard*

Business Review 76: 134-147.

42. Renken, E. (2020). How Stories Connect and Persuade Us.

43. Rubenfeld, I. (2001). *The listening Hand: Self-healing Through The Rubenfeld Synergy Method of Talk and Touch.* Bantam.

44. Schwartz, R.C. (2008). *You Are The One You've Been Waiting For: Bringing Courageous Love to Intimate Relationships.* Center for Self Leadership .

45. Schwartz, R.C. (2021). *No Bad Parts: Healing Trauma and Restoring Wholeness with the Internal Family Systems Model.* Sounds True.

46. Schwartz, R.C., Sweezy, M. (2019). *Internal family Systems Therapy.* The Guilford Press.

47. Szalavitz, M. (2010). How Orphanages Kill Babies--and Why No Child Under 5 Should Be in One. *Huffington Post.*

48. Taylor, S.E. Tend and Befriend Theory. *Handbook of Theories of Social Psychology.* Sage Publications. University of California, Los Angeles.

49. Van der Kolk, B.A. (1994). The Body Keeps the Score: Memory and the Evolving Psychobiology of Posttraumatic Stress." *Harvard review of psychiatry* 1, no. 5: 253-265.

50. Van der Kolk, B.A. (2003). The Neurobiology of Childhood Trauma and Abuse. *Child and Adolescent Psychiatric Clinics* 12, no. 2: 293-317.

51. Wipfler, P. (1990). Listening partnerships for parents." *Palo Alto: Hand in Hand.*

52. Williamson, M. (1996). *A Return to Love: Reflections on the Principles of "A Course in Miracles".* HarperOne.

53. Williamson, M. (2019). *A politics of Love: A Handbook for a New American Revolution.* HarperOne.

54. Yahav, D. (1995). Movement Assessments of Two Groups of Arab Women from Acco. Unpublished manuscript.

Acknowledgements

Peace is its own reward.
Mahatma Gandhi

Some of the incredible people who made this book possible are part of it and you have read about them in the previous pages. Others have supported me and our work behind the scenes and I would like to acknowledge their support, love and faith in me and in our quest for peace.

The Shapiros, who are my second family and have helped expand my mind and heart while supporting our projects for twenty-five years.

Judy from Australia, Karen from Baltimore, Joyce, Phyllis, Felora, Nina and Sammie from Austin, Jon from Boston, Hagit from Los Altos as well as the Krieger Fund, the Sobell Fund and Tikkun Olam Foundation who saw and understood the importance of our work and through their support made what you have read about possible.

Our amazing facilitators and the women from our groups who trusted us and opened their hearts to one another. Our wonderful actresses/facilitators from the Playback Theater Ensembles: *From Stage to Change and The Heart of Our Stories.*

Noa, whose exceptional skills and insight, kept our programs going for several years and Dorit whose open-hearted administrative support makes it possible for us to continue. Danny, Rozit, Wafa, Suheila, Gal, Eyad and Gita for their important work on our board and audit committee.

My beloved group of Zefat's Angels who have been working with me for eight years and have shown me again and again the meaning of deep, heartfelt connection to one another and to God.

Susan, my wonderful editor, who worked with me from the beginning and helped hone and elevate my writing skills. Reuven who assisted in editing chapters and Gail who improved my letters. Ilana, who volunteered her time and did a great job in the final editing of the book.

My amazing publishers/editors/allies Nathalie and Jean-Rémi, who believed in my book from the moment they read it and have been working with me side by side to bring the book to all you peace seekers, joy spreaders, world changers and light bearers around the world who have been affected by conflict.

Hulya Ozedmir, whose beautiful paintings have made the book cover and the spirit exuding from it like no other.

My Rabbi, Nathalie for inspiring me with her spiritual, wise, compassionate activism and the Conservative Community (Family Minyan) of Kfar Vradim who have created a beautiful space where we connect to God, to one another and to the pursuit of justice and peace.

Eyal for years of guidance and support in connecting to my authentic Self.

The people who invited and hosted us at Esalen, Omega and Othona for providing such beautiful safe havens where we could engage in profoundly healing peacebuilding work.

Marianne and Leymah whom I admire greatly and have written so powerfully about the quest for Peace and my book.

My amazing family who have always had my back, I love you all!! Shlomo, who has continued to be an ally for so many years. And Naty for listening, loving, encouraging and cooking great meals. You help me stay centered in a world that often feels scary. Thank you!

Blessings and much love to all of you,

Nitsan Joy Gordon
January 2023

The publication of this book has been made possible
thanks to the work of a whole team.

Editorial and technical coordination
Jean-Rémi Deléage & Nathalie Vandebeulque

Proofreading
Annette Maynard and Beth Lavigne

Les Éditions du Ā

Les Éditions du non-A is the publisher of futuristic literature in the humanities and science fiction. We publish books that allow us to think about the future with a "non-Aristotelian" approach - abbreviated Ā or non-A - meaning open-minded & non-binary.

Our favourite fields: psychology, life stories, futuristic novels, essays, children's stories... any innovative book that helps to sharpen human awareness and better anticipate the transformations of contemporary societies.

To follow us on the Web:
Visit our website and subscribe to our Newsletter
to stay informed of our publications and news.
leseditionsdunona.com

You can also follow us on our social networks:
facebook.com/leseditionsdunona
twitter.com/EditionsdunonA
instagram.com/leseditionsdunona

Printed in February 2023
Legal Deposit 1st publication: February 2023
Printed in the UK & the US

Made in the USA
Middletown, DE
16 May 2023

30294077R00179